AUSTRALIA IN THE TWENTIETH CENTURY

A Political History

AUSTRALIA

in the

Twentieth Century

A Political History

Trevor R. Reese

FREDERICK A. PRAEGER, *Publisher*

New York · London

Frederick A. Praeger, Publisher
111 Fourth Ave., New York 3, N.Y., U.S.A.
77–79 Charlotte Street, London W.1, England

Published in the United States of America in 1964
by Frederick A. Praeger, Inc., Publisher

Printed in the United Kingdom

CONTENTS

PREFACE   9

1 *A FEDERAL COMMONWEALTH* (1901)   11

Australia: the country and colonial settlement. Emergence of an
Australian legend. National consciousness expressed in literature.
Significance of a Labour party. The Federal Constitution. Importance of the states. Problems and traditions carried into the
twentieth century.

2 *THE ABORIGINES* (1788–1940)   24

Origins. Use to the early settlers. Race relations in the nineteenth
century. The European concept of the Aborigines. Government
policy. The Port Phillip protectorate. The missions. Protective
measures. The inadequacy of native policies up to 1940.

3 *THE FEDERATION AT WORK* (1901–1914)   38

Immigration policy. The tariff question. Alfred Deakin. Defence
and the Royal Australian Navy. Andrew Fisher. Social reform.
Industrial arbitration. The Harvester judgement. Difficulties of the
Liberals and the return of Labour, September 1914.

4 *THE FIRST WORLD WAR* (1914–1919)   50

The Australian Imperial Force. Gallipoli. The Somme. The war
effort and domestic controls. W. M. Hughes. The conscription
issue. Labour party split. Offensive in Flanders. Industrial discontent and the second conscription referendum. Final allied
offensive in France. The Australian contribution to the war and
the peace conference.

5 *A COLONIAL POWER* (1888–1940)   66

Early administration in Papua; MacGregor and Le Hunte. Hubert
Murray. The New Guinea Mandate. Difficulties of government.
Local administration. Finances. Native labour. Education. Health.
Land policy. Trade. Australian policy before 1940.

CONTENTS

6 *INTER-WAR PROBLEMS (1919–1932)*   77

Hughes and post-war Australia. Pacific security arrangements.
The problem of imperial consultation. Fall of Hughes. The
Bruce-Page Ministry. The Country party. Industrial difficulties,
1925. Immigration policy. Statute of Westminster and Dominion
status. Foundation of Canberra. The financial arrangements of
1927. Industrial arbitration and economic crisis. The Labour
government divides and falls. The Ottawa agreement, 1932.

7 *THE BREAKDOWN OF INTERNATIONAL*   97
SECURITY (1932–1939)

J. A. Lyons. Economic recovery. Defence and foreign policy.
Relations with Japan. Imperial Conference and general election,
1937. Economic expansion and community advance. Appeasement.
Cabinet differences. The Menzies Ministry. Outbreak of war,
September 1939.

8 *THE SECOND WORLD WAR (1939–1945)*   112

War preparations. The government's weakness. Australian troops
in North Africa, Greece and Crete. Labour in power. Japan enters
the war and Australia looks to America. The Curtin-Churchill argument. Financial rearrangement, 1942. Fighting in New Guinea.
The election of 1943. The Anzac agreement. Creation of the
United Nations Organisation. Australia's contribution to the Allied
war effort.

9 *SOCIALISM AT HOME AND NATIONALISM*   132
ABROAD (1945–1949)

J. B. Chifley. Socialisation and its difficulties. The election of 1946.
Immigration program. Nationalism in Asia. Industrial and
economic problems at home. Bank Nationalisation Act, 1947.
The Indonesian revolution. A republican India in the British
Commonwealth and a Communist government in China. Labour's
defeat, 1949.

10 *THE COMMUNIST BOGY (1949–1955)*   147

The Liberal party. R. G. Menzies. Moves against the Communist
party. H. V. Evatt. Dangers in Asia and the Pacific. Economic
problems and social services reform. The 1954 election. The Petrov
case. National defence and SEATO. Catholic Action and the
Labour party. Economic developments. The election of 1955.

CONTENTS

11 *PROBLEMS IN THE TERRITORIES (1940–1962)*   165

Maintenance of the White Australia policy. Treatment of the Aborigines after 1945. New Guinea in wartime and the Trust Territory after the war. UN criticism of Australian administration. The West New Guinea issue. Australian co-operation with the Dutch. Modifications in Australian policy in the Trust Territory. Improvement in aboriginal conditions.

12 *THE MENZIES HEGEMONY (1955–1962)*   181

Financial restrictions, 1956. Suez Canal crisis. The Labour party's difficulties. Rescuing the universities. The 1958 election. Banking reform. Change in Labour's leadership. Financial measures, 1960. Menzies and foreign affairs. The 1961 election. The European Common Market. The British Commonwealth and Australia's future in 1962.

13 *NEW HORIZONS*   199

Defence and the American alliance. New contacts in Asia. New Guinea the crux. The immigration issue. Economic revival. Menzies stays on. The election of 1963. Problems of the political parties. The nature of Australian politics. The changing federal system. Modern Australia, its people and its prospects.

APPENDIX   223

READING LIST   225

INDEX   233

MAP   36-7

To
Hilary

PREFACE

This book is an historical commentary on the development of Australia since 1901, when the federal commonwealth came into being. In a work of this kind it has not been possible to go as deeply into some topics as their importance might seem to require, and as many Australian scholars, no doubt, would expect, but the reading list indicates where these issues can be studied further.

The book was written at the close of six happy years in Australia, and I hope it will not seem a poor compliment to a people who made me so welcome. The idea of writing it originated with my wife, who left her own country in order to accompany me home, and to her it is dedicated in gratitude for the pleasure its writing gave me.

TRR

I

A Federal Commonwealth (1901)

THE COMMONWEALTH of Australia was born on New Year's Day 1901, when six self-governing British colonies joined together to become one nation. The authority of the newly created federal government extended across a huge island continent nearly as large as Europe or the United States of America and twenty-five times the size of the British Isles. Some 2,400 miles of land lie between the eastern and western extremities of Australia and 2,000 miles between the northern and southern, the whole covering an area of nearly three million square miles. The eastern shores are moistened by south-east trade winds, the northern are monsoon, and the southern recall the climate of the Mediterranean. Two fifths of the continent lie within the tropics; scant rain falls beyond the Great Dividing Range, a mountain system running along the east coast from the north of Queensland through New South Wales and into Victoria, and the vast central areas suffer a hot desert climate all the year round. A third of Australia is arid, and of necessity settlement has been confined largely to the coastal regions, where there is ample rainfall and good pastoral land.

In 1901 European settlement in Australia was little more than a century old, dating back to 1788 when the British colony of New South Wales was started at Sydney for the purpose, mainly, of absorbing transported convicts. It was designed as an economical sluice for the overflow from England's congested gaols. Further settlements followed. Those across Bass Strait to the south in Van Diemen's Land (now Tasmania) were erected into a separate colony in 1825; those in what was known as the Port Phillip District of

New South Wales became the colony of Victoria in 1851; and those on the banks of the Brisbane at Moreton Bay far to the north of Sydney were formed into the colony of Queensland in 1859. The establishment of a colony in Western Australia in 1829 and another in South Australia in 1836 completed the colonial framework into which a federation was built when the century closed.

The basis of economic prosperity in Australia was sheep. Wool production had increased with such momentum during the nineteenth century that it had won a dominant place in the markets of the world; by 1900 the Australian colonies were the largest exporters of merino and the principal source of raw material for British woollen manufactures. The pastoral expansion from the coastal areas into the lands beyond the mountains had also helped to develop among the sheepmen some of the characteristics which Australians now regard as their own. The great distances, the poor communications, and the depressing monotony had produced both the individual self-reliance and the good neighbourliness of the life up-country. The bush, it was felt, was where the real Australia pulsed, and mateship or loyalty to one's fellows became an essential part of the Australian legend. There was also pride in the strong democratic and egalitarian attitudes which had been fostered by the gold rush of the 1850s, when colonial society had been diversified by large numbers of immigrants with varying backgrounds and often with radical political sympathies. By the end of the century there was a distinctive Australian tradition, and three and three-quarter million people in the Australian colonies were beginning to think of themselves as belonging to one independent nation.

This growing national consciousness was discernible in the 'impressionist' school of painters that answered the call of the time for a more nationalist, Australian art, and infused a new authenticity into its portrayal of wide expanses, blue-grey distances, sheep, and gum trees. Appreciation of the individuality of the Australian peoples and their way of life found expression in literature, notably in the writings of Thomas Alexander Browne, who, under the pen-name of Rolf Boldrewood, published in 1888 his successful Robbery under Arms: the story of a bushranger and a useful description of the gold rush days. Boldrewood recaptured the atmosphere of part of the country's history, and his Australian readers perhaps detected in his characters something of the brawny, vainglorious adventurer they were beginning to picture as the typical Australian. His Dick Marston, for example, is a native of Sydney, comes from a family of cattle-stealers, stands six feet high, weighs thirteen stone, and is strong and active. 'It takes a good man to put me on my back', he boasts, 'or stand up to me with the gloves or the naked mauleys. I can ride anything, anything that was ever lapped in horsehide, swim like a musk-duck, and track like a Myall blackfellow. Most things that a man can do I'm up to, and that's all about it.'

The spirit of Australia was copiously expressed in verse. Charles Harpur's *Creek of the Four Graves* was influenced by the bush, and Adam Lindsay Gordon seemed to evoke Australia in the equestrian rhythm of his metres. Henry Kendall's verse was steeped in the beauty and colouring of the scenery in the colonies, but his gentle melancholy shrank from the nationalistic fervour that inspired some of his successors, notably James Brunton Stephens, who in impassioned lines proclaimed his intense confidence in Australia's future. The nationalism trumpeted by Stephens and his kind found a vehicle and audience in the *Bulletin*, a weekly journal founded in 1881, which propounded a robust and patriotic radicalism that suited the mood of the time. Among its contributors were Henry Lawson, who produced prose and verse in which the genuine Australia throbbed, and A. B. ('Banjo') Paterson, whose ballads won a favoured place among bush workers. *Clancy of the Overflow* and *The Man from Snowy River* became the best known and most loved of all Australian verse, exemplifying the veneration felt towards the outback, where, for many people, the real Australia lay and whence Paterson had derived his inspiration:

> I have gathered these stories afar,
>   In the wind and the rain,
> In the land where the cattle camps are,
>   On the edge of the plain.

Neither Paterson, nor Lawson, nor any of the Australian poets of this period, ranks high in poetic craftsmanship: few go beyond ingenuous rhapsody on their country or billy-can yarns in a cantering metre; but in their attachment to the Australian soil and the hard life of the bush, and in their affection for the outback characters, especially the knaves, they gave expression to the pride Australians now felt in themselves, their way of life, and their environment.

In 1901 a majority of the people in Australia had been born there, and no nostalgia for other places detracted from their affection for the setting in which they had grown up. Even among immigrants who remembered homes in Europe were many who loved a land in which they had found the new life denied them in the mother country. Immigrants of good pedigree and education, men with capital and an urge for adventure, were also fascinated by their new country and became reluctant to return to their old.

> It may seem strange to you perhaps [wrote Alfred Joyce, who had left England in 1843 to procure a run in the Port Phillip District] that I should not be looking forward to returning to my native land to enjoy the fruits of my labours, but I have been so long here, have acquired so many ties of kindred and have become so accustomed to this colony that I should not be happy anywhere else. The climate, whatever others may say of it, is to me the finest in the world. I find here a sphere of usefulness which I do not know I should have in England, and my endeavour now will be to make this spot my permanent home for me and mine after me. The prospect of English winters and long gloomy weather would frighten me from going there. I am too used now to sunshine to be satisfied long without it.

Hundreds of thousands of migrant Englishmen have echoed these sentiments since.

This national consciousness was characterised by a social philosophy stemming from the egalitarianism and mateship inherent in the Australian legend. Socialism was propagated in the ardently nationalist pages of the *Bulletin*, but the formation of a Labour party had come only after a humiliating defeat of the trade unions at the hands of government-backed employers in the 'great maritime strike' of 1890. A Labour Electoral League was formed in

Sydney with the aim of securing representation in the New South Wales parliament and of advancing the interests of wage-earners by legislation. In the election of 1891 it returned thirty-six of its endorsed candidates and held to good purpose the balance of power between the parties of protection and free trade. Although weakened for a time by internal dissension on the tariff question, the Labour representatives generally presented a united front. At a conference in 1893 the Labour Electoral League resolved that 'a Parliamentary Labour Party, to be of any weight, must give a solid vote in the House upon all questions affecting the Labour platform, the fate of the Ministry, or calculated to establish a monopoly or confer further privileges on the already privileged classes'. At the 1894 elections, therefore, Labour candidates pledged themselves to act in this sense and to vote 'as the majority of the Labour Party may in caucus decide'. In all the colonies the Labour parties attempted to become a disciplined opposition to the capitalist forces, their policies formulated to some extent upon a philosophical basis of socialism, but pursued in great measure empirically and concerned with particular issues rather than general principles.

/ The formation of the Labour party* was the most important single event in Australian political history. Attention has been focused on the special character of the party's organisation and discipline, on the restraints implied by the candidates' pledge, caucus control in parliament, and determination of policy by a periodic conference of delegates from branches and trade unions. These can be explained in terms of the class nature of the party and the need for working class solidarity against the superior economic power of employers in a capitalist society. Its organisation gave rise to tensions within the party, either between individuals and caucus or between caucus and conference, which have led occasionally to dramatic defections. The trade unions became an industrial wing, usually militant, especially in New South Wales, while the party branches became a political, and moderate,

* The party's formal title, dating from 1916 (see p. 59), is 'Australian Labor Party', but it is customary in Australia to refer to the 'Labour party', the 'Labour movement', etc.; therefore the spelling 'Labor' is used in the text only where the word is part of the formal title of the political party.

wing. The party was influenced by the strong Roman Catholic following it acquired, mainly from the ranks of Irish immigrants, whose working class and radical background drew them naturally into the Labour fold. The Roman Catholic Church had always been powerful in Australia, notably in denominational schooling, and in the Labour party it found a political instrument for its struggle for social justice. The rise of the Labour party was significant chiefly, however, because it compelled its opponents to organise themselves and also to formulate their own political strategy. The idea of Labour as the party of initiative and of its opponents as the parties of resistance to it is now being modified, if not altogether refuted, by historians and political scientists, but it remains true that the appearance of a Labour party at the end of the nineteenth century served to crystallise the parliamentary political structure in Australia.

The non-Labour forces were not homogeneous groups, and it was difficult to differentiate satisfactorily between them. Names such as Liberal, National, and Conservative were used indiscriminately, and it became common to refer to the rival parties simply as 'ministerialist' and 'opposition'. Conservatives favouring a low tariff for revenue purposes and liberals favouring a high protective tariff operated what approximated to a two-party system, but the division was blurred and similar interests were often represented on both sides. The protectionists were particularly strong in Victoria, where they included a reforming section which opposed the authority of the landed oligarchy and sympathised with some of the aims of Labour. The free-traders, those advocating a tariff for revenue only, were strongest in New South Wales, where they included wealthy merchants and graziers who were essentially conservative in outlook. Protectionists and free-traders were agreed on the basic importance of private property and private enterprise in economic activity, and they were eventually to recognise their mutual interest in combating the socialist doctrines they associated with Labour. In the late nineteenth and early twentieth centuries, however, the liberal protectionists and conservative free-traders were the two main contenders for parliamentary power, with the small, but growing, Labour party holding the balance between them.

The young Labour party in New South Wales disliked the federation movement among the colonies because it took up parliamentary time that might have been devoted to social legislation; it also feared a constitution that might transfer power from a local parliament in which Labour was winning some success to a federal legislature which might be dominated by conservatives from other states and become an obstacle to social reform. But the trend of events was unmistakably in the direction of closer colonial co-operation. The people were not divided by racial or national differences, they enjoyed fundamentally a common social and political tradition, and they increasingly possessed common interests, for issues such as tariffs, immigration restrictions, and defence were essentially the concern of all the colonies together and not of each individually.

In 1891 a national convention of representatives chosen from the colonial parliaments met in Sydney to discuss federation. It framed a draft constitution, which, though scotched by opposition in New South Wales, was to form the framework around which successful discussions took place between 1897 and 1899. The constitution bill was passed through the British Parliament with only slight amendment, and on July 9, 1900 received the royal assent. In September a royal proclamation declared that, as from January 1, 1901, the six Australian colonies should become constituent states of the new federal commonwealth of Australia.

The framers of the Australian constitution had been able to use to advantage the successful examples of federation devised in the United States in 1789 and in Canada in 1867, together with the commentaries and judicial decisions since produced on them. In the result the constitution-makers in Australia kept closer to the United States' model than to the Canadian, except in their preferring a parliamentary executive on English lines to the presidential system of the United States. The British sovereign is represented in Australia by a governor-general in the commonwealth and a governor in each state, who occupy in relation to their parliaments a position similar to that occupied by the sovereign in relation to the British Parliament, though, unlike the sovereign, a governor-general or governor is not an hereditary figure; his tenure of office is limited, and he now deals with ministers who have in fact selected him. There is no Privy Council in Australia such as that in Canada or the United Kingdom, but the governor-general acts on the advice of a cabinet formed by the leader of the majority in the lower chamber of Parliament. The commonwealth prime minister's choice of his cabinet is limited by the unwritten requirements of electoral and political strategy; he must give representation to all the states and, in the case of anti-Labour coalitions, to the other party or parties in his administration. Since 1908 Labour prime ministers have been restricted by the parliamentary party's practice of selecting the members of a Labour cabinet by exhaustive ballot, leaving to the leader only the task of allotting portfolios.

The lower chamber in the commonwealth Parliament, the House of Representatives, is elected directly by the people every three years or sooner from constituencies arranged on a population basis, except that no state, however small its population, can have fewer than five members. In accordance with the constitution, the total membership of the House of Representatives must be as nearly as practicable double that of the Senate, the upper chamber, to which each of the six states sends an equal number of members elected by the people of the state functioning as a single electorate. Parliament has the constitutional capacity to alter the numbers in either House, but it did not do so until 1949, when the strength of the House of Representatives was increased from 75 to 123, and that of the Senate from 36 to 60. Although Senators are elected for a term of six years, half the representation from each state retires every three years, thereby bringing elections at intervals similar to those for the House of Representatives. The framers of the constitution envisaged a Senate divided on state lines rather than on party lines and serving to protect the rights of the states; but in practice the division has been between political parties as in the House of Representatives, and as a defender of state interests the Senate has proved less effective than its creators hoped. Moreover, since the Senate is divided on a party basis like the House of Representatives, but, unlike that chamber, has only half its membership elected at the three-year interval, it is possible for an incoming administration with a working majority in the House to be confronted with a hostile Senate. In the event of a deadlock there is constitutional provision for the simultaneous dissolution of both chambers, which must then face the electors: a special procedure used on only two occasions in the first sixty years of the commonwealth (in 1914 and 1951). The two chambers have co-ordinate powers in ordinary legislation, but the Senate is in an inferior position in financial affairs because all proposals for appropriating revenue or imposing taxation can originate only in the House of Representatives.

Under the federal constitution of 1901, the states remained autonomous within their own spheres, their governments were not reorganised, their constitutions were preserved intact by section 106 of the Constitution Act, and they retained all their powers except those assigned exclusively to the federal government, whose legislative authority was extended to thirty-nine matters set out in section 51 of the Act. The matters vested in the commonwealth include defence, external affairs, customs and excise duties, foreign and interstate commerce, and coinage. Both commonwealth and states can legislate on certain matters, such as social services, postal, telegraph and telephone services, marriage and divorce, bankruptcy, banking and insurance; but it is laid down in section 109 that when a law of a state is inconsistent with a law of the commonwealth, the latter prevails and the former is, to the extent of the inconsistency, invalid.

The High Court of Australia, for which the constitution provides, although its establishment was left to the commonwealth Parliament, functions not only as a general court of appeal from state courts but also as a court of original jurisdiction in suits between the commonwealth and the states and in those involving the interpretation of the constitution. In this role the High Court for many years tended to interpret the constitution in a sense restrictive of the authority of the commonwealth and protective of the standing of the component states, but after the first world war the tendency became to increase the authority of the commonwealth at the expense of that of the states. The function of the High Court in judicial review has affected attitudes towards legislation, which may be considered more in the light of its constitutional validity than in the light of its real merits and weaknesses; or, what is worse, if legislation is opposed its critics may find constitutional reasons for condemning what they actually dislike on other grounds. Thus, fundamental political, economic and social questions can be buried by constitutional argument and review.

The procedure for amending the constitution is described in section 128 of the Constitution Act. Any proposed law for altering the constitution must be passed in each House of Parliament by an absolute majority of its total membership and also submitted to a referendum of the electors in each state. The alteration must be approved not only by a majority of the electors voting but also by a majority of electors in each of a majority of the states. The referendum procedure, inspired by the Swiss model, has revealed a reluctance on the part of the Australian electors to agree to constitutional amendments, only four out of twenty-four proposals being accepted in the first sixty years of federation. Several reasons have been advanced for this conservatism, among them the unpopularity of a political party proposing the amendment, suspicion of distant central authority, and cynical disdain for Australian politicians in general. Whatever the reasons, the referendum has proved to be less effective in Australia than in Switzerland as an instrument of constitutional change.

As the federation occupied the fields of government allotted to it, the states were not at once relegated to an inferior position, but continued to operate much as before. Local councils had never been strong or important, and it was the state authorities which provided hospitals, schools, universities, police forces, roads, bridges and railways. The states remained the principal development agencies, and their impact on the daily life of the citizen has been more evident than that of the commonwealth, particularly in rural areas. Education was the largest single charge on the revenues of the states, which maintained the policy of colonial days of making education compulsory, secular, and mostly free, despite objections, especially from the Roman Catholic Church, whose schools, nevertheless, continued to function successfully alongside those of the state systems. The traditions of the educational systems naturally reached back to those of England and Scotland, but educational administration in Australia was more centralised. In a country where population was concentrated in the capital cities and local municipal government was weak compared with that of the United Kingdom, it was perhaps inevitable that education should be administered by a central hierarchy with a somewhat authoritarian efficiency.

Another important responsibility of the states was the railways, which in the nineteenth century had necessarily come under government control when it had proved impossible to attract sufficient private investment, despite the comparatively low capital cost per mile. To complicate matters, New South Wales and Victoria had adopted different rail gauges: a galling and expensive discrepancy which, after the two rail systems were joined at Albury in 1883, necessitated the transfer of freight on the border and prevented direct traffic between Sydney and Melbourne until January 1962, over seventy-eight years later.

When the federation began to tackle national problems in 1901, the states remained the tested, stable centres of government in Australia. New South Wales, with 1,350,000 people, contained more than a third of the nation's total population, but was still recovering from the financial collapse of 1892, and its pastoral industry was to receive another blow in a severe drought of 1902. Victoria, whose capital, Melbourne, was the temporary headquarters of the new federation, was the smallest state in area but second only to New South Wales in population, having nearly 1,200,000 inhabitants; it, too, had been harshly affected by the depression of the early 1890s. Queensland, the second largest state in area, had doubled its population in the twenty years before 1901 to half a million, and though it had not escaped the depression, its sheep, cattle, sugar and gold made it appear a most promising state. South Australia, with about 360,000 people, was chiefly an agricultural and pastoral state, but was benefiting also from the silver and lead mines at Broken Hill, from which a railway had been constructed linking it with Port Pirie. Western Australia, comprising nearly a third of the entire continent, had recently become one of the great gold-producing areas of the world, and since 1886 its population had more than quadrupled to reach 180,000. The island of Tasmania, with 170,000 people, had the smallest population, and suffered from emigration to New Zealand and the mainland; agricultural progress and the discovery of silver, lead, gold and copper mines had helped its economy to recover from a prolonged depression in the 1860s and 1870s, but some of its local industries were to be adversely affected when federation brought about interstate free trade.

The conflict of free-trade and protectionist opinions had been one of the great political issues in the Australian colonies and it was to linger into the early days of the federation. A protectionist movement had appeared in Victoria at the time of the gold rush of the 1850s and 1860s, when a demand had arisen for a tariff to keep out competitive foreign manufactures and for subsidies to foster colonial industrial development in its infancy. The inspiration behind this economic philosophy had come principally from the editor of the Melbourne *Age*, David Syme, who after 1860 had mounted a militant press campaign to secure protection for Victorian industry and safeguard the living standards of its employees. In 1866 the first protective tariff had become law after an impassioned parliamentary struggle that was finally decided in 1877 with the election of an avowedly protectionist government. The other colonies had continued the policy of tariffs for revenue rather than for protection of local industry, but all except New South Wales had gradually inclined to the Victorian example. After federation, the tariff question was to be initially the chief issue dividing members of the new commonwealth Parliament, which met in Melbourne for the first time in May 1901, with the Earl of Hopetoun as governor-general and Edmund Barton, leader of the protectionist group, as prime minister. G. H. Reid was its first leader of the opposition, and J. C. Watson led the Labour group.

Upon the first federal government was laid the task of establishing the new constitutional machinery and setting it in motion. It also had to give effect to a burgeoning nationalism that wished to build in the South Pacific an inviolate European community, undiluted by peoples of different stock, and this necessitated a restrictive immigration policy to prevent the entry of coloured races. The indigenous Aborigines, for whom responsibility remained with the states, were expected to continue to decline and were not regarded as a significant problem. It was in this matter of native policy that the new nation inherited a record of which it had little reason to be proud.

2

The Aborigines (1788-1940)

THE COMMONWEALTH of Australia Constitution Act declares in section 127 that 'in reckoning the numbers of the people of the Commonwealth, or of a State, or other part of the Commonwealth, aboriginal natives shall not be counted'. Any idea of the Aborigines possessing the right to vote or having representation in parliament was not yet a subject for serious discussion. In no sense had they been absorbed into the white men's civilisation; indeed, they had shown a marked reluctance or inability to accommodate themselves to it, with the result that in many areas they had become little more than objects of charity. During the nineteenth century, the colonies had established boards for the protection of the Aborigines, set aside thousands of acres for native reserves, and provided some of the children with education and medical attention, but governmental expenditure had been woefully inadequate, and the native population in every colony had steadily diminished. At federation there was no attempt to integrate the native policies of the several states, governmental disbursements remained low, the decimation of the Aborigines continued, and, as a race, the danger of their eventual extinction increased.

The origins of the Australian Aborigines have been a matter for speculation. It is probable that they have inhabited the continent for a thousand years at least, and possibly for many thousands. The first to arrive in Australia may have been of negroid stock with frizzled hair, and may have been driven southwards by later invaders until they reached Tasmania, perhaps before the subsidence forming Bass Strait made it an island. Their successors in the main part of the continent were a lank-haired people, who, it is conjectured, had come originally from the Mediterranean and were related to the Dravidians of south India. Their skin was not so dark as that of their predecessors, and they were distinguished by slender limbs, hairy face and body, a sloping forehead, a wide, flat nose and a big mouth with a long upper lip, large and healthy teeth and a strong protruding jaw. Their life was necessarily nomadic, for they brought little with them and subsisted only on what the continent itself naturally produced, unassisted by human hand. They ate whatever they could find (such as edible seeds, fruits, yams and witchetty grubs), or could catch (such as kangaroo, birds and fish). The scarcity of food concentrated the life of the Aborigines into a struggle for existence; their inventiveness was directed principally towards easing the daily work of hunting, and their skills were those of the hunter, particularly in the use of traps, nets, spears and boomerangs. Each of the various tribes into which the aboriginal population was divided normally possessed definite territorial boundaries and its own social customs, mythology, and language or dialect. The tribe was subdivided into local groups, the members of each of which were related genealogically by descent through the male line. Notwithstanding the social organisation of the tribes and local groups, however, the family remained the fundamental unit of aboriginal society. A man might have several wives simultaneously, a woman might have several husbands consecutively, and it was not unusual for wives to be borrowed or exchanged; but the family was, nevertheless, a recognised and economically self-sufficient unit: parents were interested in their children and passed their knowledge down to them.

After British settlement began at the end of the eighteenth century, the life of the Aborigines was gradually disrupted, but a few were able to exercise their talents in the service of the intruders. Pastoralists employed them as stockmen and shepherds on their runs, where their tracking skill was useful in keeping herds and flocks together. Their knowledge of the country and their extraordinary ability as trackers were invaluable in police work, and in the 1840s a native police corps was formed in the Port

Phillip District. Explorers envied the way the natives moved around barren bush country without starving, and admired the dexterity with which they drained pure water from the roots of the mallee scrub. An aboriginal member was always an asset to an exploratory expedition. When the pearling industry grew in Western Australia after the middle of the nineteenth century, male and female aboriginal divers were employed in lifting pearl-shell from depths of up to sixty feet, but the Legislative Council intervened and prohibited their employment in this work. Thereafter divers were introduced from Timor, Java and, later, Japan. The pearling industry grew until at the turn of the century it was earning over £100,000* a year, and by 1913 was the fifth largest exporting industry of Western Australia. The prohibition on the use of aboriginal divers was necessary to prevent their exploitation by unscrupulous pearlers, for by the 1860s it had become manifest that, however useful the natives might be to white settlers in certain fields, unsupervised contact between the two races was invariably detrimental to the Aborigines.

When Governor Phillip and the First Fleet arrived at Sydney Cove in January 1788, there were probably no more than 300,000 Aborigines in Australia, and from that time on their numbers steadily declined. Their decimation was due as much to the upset in their hunting and dietary habits and to the undermining of their customs and beliefs by christian missions as to the casualties and infections that white settlers inflicted upon them. Although Governor Phillip, in accordance with his instructions, did his utmost to prevent the settlers from antagonising the natives, depredations and murders on each side ruined any hope of establishing permanent friendly relationships from the outset. In January 1802, Lord Hobart, the Secretary of State for the Colonies, wrote to Governor King lamenting the failure to culti-

* At federation in 1901, the currency in Australia consisted of United Kingdom coins, notes issued by the banks, and, in Queensland, Treasury notes. An Australian currency was introduced by federal legislation in 1909. The Australian pound was on a par with sterling until the depression of 1930, when it began to depreciate in terms of sterling. All currency figures cited in the text until Chapter 7 are therefore at the full sterling value for the relevant period. See note on page 98.

vate the goodwill of the natives: 'The evils resulting from this neglect seem to be now sensibly experienced, and the difficulty of restoring confidence with the natives, alarmed and exasperated by the unjustifiable injuries they have too often experienced, will require all the attention which your active vigilance and humanity can bestow upon a subject so important in itself, and so important to the prosperity of the settlement.'

Various governors attempted to eliminate inter-racial troubles, but no matter what success they had, the fact remained that the damage had been done by the act of settlement itself, which deprived the Aborigines of their traditional hunting grounds and made them trespassers on Crown property if they continued to subsist in the manner to which they were accustomed. They lost their game and their water-holes, and when they slaughtered and ate the sheep and cattle introduced to their old hunting grounds by the white invaders, they naturally provoked retaliation from the pastoralists and stockmen. Both sides committed minor outrages that would sometimes culminate in an atrocity such as the massacre at Myall Creek in New South Wales in 1839, when white settlers, seeking revenge for depredations among their stock, went out in force to murder and burn Aborigines, including women and children. It was the same story elsewhere, notably in the north-western districts of Western Australia, where pastoralists whose stock was speared or stolen organised punitive expeditions to 'teach the natives a lesson'. It was found impossible for the two races to live peacefully together within the confines of Tasmania, and what amounted to a state of war lasted sporadically for nearly thirty years. There was fearful slaughter in some areas of Tasmania, and one observer recalled a settler who preserved the ears of his aboriginal victims in a pickle tub.

It is clear that the natives, with reason, distrusted the settlers, and that the whites, especially those on the far frontiers of settlement where they were few in number and widely scattered, feared the natives. Mutual distrust was accentuated by the inability of either race to understand the practices of the other. It was not unusual for white men in the outback to take advantage of the aboriginal custom of lending wives to visitors as a mark of hospitality, and trouble would occur when the white men omitted to offer in return gifts to the husbands and families as they were expected to do. Moreover, venereal disease originally transmitted to the natives by the settlers would occasionally be remitted to a white man, and reprisals were likely to follow. A squatter from Scotland noted that several men on one station had been infected by the natives: 'Notwithstanding the bad name they had here', he remarked, 'I am told it is no uncommon thing for these rascals to sleep all night with a lubra [native female], and if she poxes him or in any way offends him perhaps shoot her before twelve next day.' It was impossible for government policy at this time to ensure fair and sensible relations between the races when so many of the settlers regarded the natives with contempt and disdain.

The attitude of Europeans towards the Aborigines was not always contemptuous. The Dutch navigators of the seventeenth century had held them in low estimation, but after the middle of the eighteenth century the influence of the concept of the noble savage led to an admiration of primitive existence that coloured the writings of Captain Cook and Sir Joseph Banks. 'These people may truly be said to be in the pure state of nature', wrote Cook in his journal, 'and may appear to some to be the most wretched upon earth: but in reality they are far more happier than we Europeans, being wholly unacquainted not only with the superfluous but of the necessary conveniences so much sought after in Europe, they are happy in not knowing the use of them.' After the first settlement had been established, English opinion in New South Wales reverted to the concept of the treacherous savage, possessed of a certain primitive nobility perhaps, but unreliable. Captain Watkin Tench, the most acute observer of the natives under Governor Phillip, qualified his professed affection and respect for them with doubts about their nature and status in the human scale.

Of their intrepidity no doubt can exist [Tench declared]; their levity, their fickleness, their passionate extravagance of character, cannot be defended. They are indeed sudden and quick in quarrel, but if their resentment be easily roused, their thirst for revenge is not implacable. Their honesty, when tempted by novelty, is not unimpeachable, but in their own society there is good reason to believe that few breaches of it occur. It were well if similar praise could be given to their veracity, but truth they neither prize nor practise. When they wish to deceive, they scruple not to utter the grossest and most hardened lies. Their attachment and gratitude to those among us whom they have professed to love have always remained inviolable, unless effaced by resentment from sudden provocation: then, like all other Indians, the impulse of the moment is alone regarded by them.

By the beginning of the nineteenth century, the doubts evident in Tench's account had grown to a reaction against the idea of noble primitivism; native society was now considered an abomination and the Aborigines were regarded as a fallen race in need not of sympathy or study but of christian redemption. 'In the licentiousness of their lives', wrote a New South Wales assistant protector in 1848, 'they are as the men of Sodom, sinners exceedingly.' The gradual elimination of the inferior race by the superior was widely accepted as the necessary work of Providence, and to deplore the disappearance of the Aborigines, wrote the Scottish statistician and political economist, John Ramsay McCulloch, in 1847, was 'hardly more reasonable than it would be to complain of the drainage of marshes or of the disappearance of wild animals'. Implicit in all opinions, whether of ordinary settlers or of learned investigators, was an assumption that the Aborigines were mentally retarded, that they represented what an English anthropologist in 1822 termed, 'the childhood of humanity itself, revealing to us the condition of mankind, if not in primeval times, yet when the original potentialities of man's being had been slightly developed by the struggle for existence'. An effective policy towards the natives was impossible when the white people despised and exploited them, possessed only a perfunctory knowledge of their language and little understanding of their customs, and lived in self-centred, materialistic and acquisitive communities where any considerable expenditure on the evicted natives was politically impracticable.

The failure of native policy in the nineteenth century was not due to indifference on the part of the British government. It is true that instructions to the early governors to propitiate the Aborigines and punish British subjects who interfered with them were a formal repetition of instructions despatched to governors in the old American colonies, but the correspondence between the Secretary of State and the colonial administrations indicates that there was some genuine concern in official quarters over the ill-treatment of the native peoples. Governor Macquarie, in particular, possessed for the Aborigines a sympathy and respect which, though shared by few of his compatriots in New South Wales, was not altogether unproductive. In 1814 he opened at Parramatta a native school which seldom contained more than twenty children but survived until 1823, and in 1815 he settled sixteen adults on a reserve about six miles from Sydney where he hoped, he said, they would 'become industrious, and set a good example to the other native tribes residing in the vicinity of Port Jackson'. In his policy towards the Aborigines, Macquarie was the humane, rather than the practical, administrator, and his views were the product of simple concern rather than of careful study. 'It seems', he wrote, 'only to require the fostering hand of time, gentle means, and conciliatory manners, to bring these poor unenlightened people into an important degree of civilisation.' Macquarie's idealism, however, was exceptional among the people of New South Wales, where, except for the creation of a few native reserves and assistance to only partly successful missions, the expropriation of the Aborigines was regarded with equanimity.

While complacency and indifference predominated in the colonies, the concern in the mother country over the weak and dispossessed races of the empire intensified, especially after 1833, when the abolition of slavery released the energies of the humanitarian movement for greater attention to the problems of subject peoples. British colonial policy at this time was strongly influenced by the humanitarian movement. Lord John Russell conveyed to Governor Gipps at the end of 1839 the British government's feelings of responsibility for the depletion of the native population, adding that it was impossible 'to contemplate the prospects of that unfortunate race without the deepest commiseration'. Reports of racial clashes and punitive expeditions in Western Australia led the Colonial Office to insist in 1835 that the Aborigines be treated as British subjects and be punished only on the order of a competent authority. Thus it was made a principle of native administration that the Aborigines should enjoy the full protection of the normal processes of British justice. But observance of the principle was difficult to enforce, and a traveller in 1839 described 'the professed recognition of the blacks as British subjects (however well intended in England) as practically a sort of blind to the British public as to the real state of these injured people'.

The United Kingdom's interest went further, however, with the appointment of a select committee of the House of Commons to examine the whole question of native peoples in British territories. Its report in 1837 condemned the appropriation of the natives' lands and the failure to protect them from unscrupulous handling by white settlers, and recommended the introduction of protectors, who were to facilitate friendly understanding between the races, and the creation of reserves where the Aborigines could support themselves without being molested. Accordingly, in 1838, an aboriginal protectorate was established in the Port Phillip District of New South Wales, representing the most important experiment in native administration attempted in Australia in the nineteenth century.

For the first six years of its existence, the Port Phillip protectorate flourished; central stations were set up in the several districts, schools were organised, land was tilled, and food was distributed to the aboriginal inhabitants. After 1843 the New South Wales government reduced its annual appropriation for the protectorate from an average of £5,000 to an average of £2,000, with the result that the protectorate declined, few improvements or extensions were made, the number of assistant protectors was halved, and by 1850 it had come to an end. Among the reasons for its demise were the apathy of the settlers and the hostility of the press, notably the *Sydney Morning Herald*, which despised the Aborigines and scoffed at what it called 'exaggerated philanthropy'. Moreover, the superintendent of the Port Phillip District, La Trobe, disliked the scheme and was supported in his views by Governor Gipps who, in May 1842, wrote to Lord Stanley expressing his doubts of the efficiency of the chief protector's assistants. 'I am painfully convinced', he remarked, 'that the protectors have as yet effected no good that can be put in comparison with the irritation which they have created; though at the same time I feel very reluctant to put a stop to their proceedings so long as the remotest hope can be entertained of a better result from their labours.' In his reply Lord Stanley deplored the malevolence of the settlers and refused to concede the extinction of the Aborigines as an inevitable corollary of white advance, but admitted: 'it seems impossible any longer to deny that the efforts which have hitherto been made for the civilisation of the aborigines have been unavailing, that no real progress has yet been effected, and that there is no reasonable ground to expect from them greater success in the future.' Lord Stanley gave no precise instructions on the policy to be pursued towards the protectorate, thereby leaving Gipps and La Trobe free to reduce expenditure on it and ensure its ultimate dissolution. By 1860, when legislation was passed creating a Board for the Protection of the Aborigines, the process of eradicating the Aborigines had gone further in what had become Victoria than in any other of the Australian colonies except Tasmania.

In every colony a significant, and sometimes effective, part in caring for the Aborigines was played by the christian missions. In New South Wales, attempts to establish missions for the natives had been made as early as 1814; in Queensland an Anglican mission was started at Moreton Bay in 1837 and a Roman Catholic one on Stradbroke Island in 1842; but none of these lasted more than a few years or enjoyed much success. More memorable was the mission founded in 1846 by Spanish Benedictine monks among the tribes of the Victoria plains at New Norcia, eighty miles or so north of Perth in Western Australia. Its work was generally agreed to be of a high order, but, as with most of the missions, its achievements were not always as valuable as well-wishers liked to suggest. To remove Aborigines from their customary environment, to clothe them with the trappings of civilisation, and even to convert them to christianity, was to produce a drastic readjustment in their ways of living and thinking that could not easily be sustained. The tribal life of the Aborigines was destroyed, their traditional beliefs and totemistic ritual upon which they leant in the past were dismantled

32

and replaced by a creed which they could not properly appreciate and which could not provide them with the spiritual support it provided Europeans. The missions were well-intentioned, but, instead of giving the natives a religion to which they could cling and turn for comfort and moral uplift, they too often merely succeeded in destroying the Aborigines' will to live. In 1914 the last of the full-bloods at New Norcia died.

By the second half of the nineteenth century, the failure of attempts to civilise the Aborigines was apparent, and native policy became a negative one of protecting their physical welfare, ensuring they were not maltreated but were supplied with food and medical treatment and permitted to die out as gradually and painlessly as possible. Western Australia, which possessed the largest aboriginal population of any of the colonies, established in 1886 an Aborigines Protection Board financed by a statutory and inadequate one per cent of the gross annual revenue, and elevated it in 1905 to an Aborigines Department with a chief protector. Although in the years that followed there was no substantial decline in the 25,000 Aborigines of Western Australia, little was done effectively to improve their working and living conditions or to devise a positive plan for their future. In New South Wales, legislation of 1909 provided for a Protection Board, educational institutions and safeguards against exploitation and alcoholic liquor, while thousands of acres were reserved and centres were set up from which food and medical treatment could be obtained. In South Australia, where many tribes lived in the far, inaccessible inland and consequently flourished, legislation was drafted in 1911 along similar lines to that of Western Australia. In Queensland, protective legislation in 1897 and 1901 provided for reserves, control over the employment and wages of Aborigines, and supervision of their service in pearl-shell fishing and on cattle stations. In the Northern Territory, responsibility for the Aborigines was transferred in 1911 from the South Australian to the commonwealth government, and protective measures were introduced in the style of those of the states.

The native policies of the commonwealth and the states were sometimes criticised, but it was generally accepted by the 1930s

C

that the paramount object should be the preservation of unfettered tribal life and that the principal contact between the
Aborigines of the reserves and white civilisation should be through
the missions. Thus when, in 1932, Aborigines of Arnhem Land in
the Northern Territory east of Darwin murdered a party of five
Japanese trepang fishers and, later, a white police trooper, the
federal government rejected suggestions of a punitive expedition,
and accepted an offer by the Church Missionary Society to send
experienced missionaries to demand the peaceful surrender of the
culprits. The inadequacy of governmental policies was evident to
serious observers, however. Educational facilities were meagre and
often operated by untrained part-timers in conditions that were
seldom satisfactory. Six different administrations were dealing
with not one problem but with a complex series of related problems, none of which had ever been properly studied. Many tribes
appeared to have lost the will to survive. Thousands of Aborigines
lived in a limbo on the outskirts of cattle stations or country
towns, leading the life of dispirited and detribalised parasites.
Those who displayed a veneer of western civilisation were not truly
assimilated and were unable to understand their new way of life,
as in the cases where spectacles were worn with the lenses removed
so that glass should not interfere with their naturally keen eye-
sight. Many thousands were in organised reservations and mission
stations, but thousands more lived as they had for centuries in the
Kimberlies, in the monsoonal flats of the Northern Territory, in
Cape York and in the arid country of Western Australia and the
centre of the continent.

A little had been done for the Aborigines, but generally they
were a neglected and largely forgotten people facing the prospect
of eventual extinction. The census of June 1936 showed that there
were fewer than 59,000 full-blood Aborigines in Australia and
some 23,000 half-castes, representing a decline in the proportion
of full-bloods since 1921 from 82 per cent to 69 per cent. Despite
the efforts of missionaries and the Protection of Native Races
Association, there was a notable lack of public concern over the
uninterrupted decline in the aboriginal population. In a farewell
address to the Victorian Anthropological Society in November
1937, Professor F. Wood Jones of Melbourne University accused

the Australian governments and the Australian people of having never wished to preserve the Aborigines, and charged the missionaries with believing the salvation of one aboriginal soul to be worth the death of the remainder. Much of the criticism occasionally levelled at native policy was unjust, and the difficulties that missions and administrations had to face were not always fully appreciated. Nevertheless, the ineffectiveness and inadequacy of native policy were uncomfortably obvious. Funds were extremely limited, the Northern Territory administration in 1934 having to manage on the annual sum of ten shillings for each native, some of which the natives themselves contributed, and the lack of properly trained staff was a glaring weakness.

In February 1939, the federal cabinet promised a new deal for the Aborigines that would include the appointment of patrol officers, the establishment of a native constabulary, and the creation of special courts to deal with native offences. In an editorial commending the proposals, the *Sydney Morning Herald* pointed out that past failures had been due partly to the want of a specialised administration fortified by expert knowledge. 'The task of administering a policy for Aborigines in differing stages of culture, ranging from the primitive tree-dwellers of Arnhem Land to the sophisticated half-castes of Darwin, is one which calls for an expert.' The defect was now to be remedied by the creation in Darwin of a 'native affairs branch' of the department of the Interior and the appointment of a director of native affairs. It was a sad commentary on native policy in Australia, however, that the minister of the Interior, in sponsoring the proposals, should have had to confess that the achievement of the objective of raising the Aborigines to the responsibilities of full citizenship was envisaged in terms not of years hence, but of generations. The aboriginal population in 1939, after a century-and-a-half of contact with white civilisation, had been reduced to less than 20 per cent of its original number, and the remnant had little to hope for in the future. The tragic and sordid feature of the history of native policy in Australia was not that it had failed, but that so few of the Australian people had ever really cared.

CELEBES

WEST NEV
GUINEA
(Dutch until 1962, n
part of Indonesi

TIMOR

Darwin

Arnhem
Land

Kimberley
Ranges

NORTHERN
TERRITORY
(To South Australia,
1863: to the
Commonwealth, 1911)

WESTERN
AUSTRALIA

SOUTH
AUSTRAL

Kalgoorlie
Coolgardie

PERTH, 1829
Fremantle

Swan R.

ADELAIDE,

St. Vincent G

INDIAN OCEAN

MILES

0   1000

(W) GUINEA

(J)an, 1884: Australian
(J)andate, 1920)
(J)A

sh-Protectorate,
Australian, 1906)

— C O R A L —
— S E A —

Inset map:

Bathurst o   SYDNEY •

NEW SOUTH WALES

Murray R.

Australian
Capital
Territory

CANBERRA

V I C T O R I A

o Bendigo
(Separated from N.S.W., 1851)

Ballarat o   MELBOURNE

Geelong o

Port Phillip Bay, 1835

0   Miles   200

Main map:

P A C I F I C

New
Caledonia

O C E A N

ENSLAND
(sep)arated from
(N.)S.W., 1859)

Moreton Bay
• BRISBANE, 1824

Norfolk I.
(Aust.)

(N)EW SOUTH
WALES

(Bro)ken
(Hi)ll   Bathurst o

Blue Mts.

o Newcastle, 1804
• SYDNEY, 1788

• CANBERRA, 1911

For Victoria,
see inset map

(VI)CTORIA

MELBOURNE

Sydney to Wellington
1233 miles

T A S M A N

S E A

(La)unceston o
1804

VAN DIEMEN'S LAND
(TASMANIA after 1856)

• HOBART, 1803

N E W Z E A L A N D

WELLINGTON

3

The Federation at Work (1901-1914)

WHEN THE first federal Parliament was elected in March 1901 all but five per cent of the nearly four million people of the commonwealth were of British extraction. It was a maxim with all Australians that their country should remain a preserve for European, preferably British, stock and that the only coloured element in the community should be, of necessity and on sufferance, the declining and neglected Aborigines. This determination to keep the population white was expressed in restrictions on immigration which became known as the White Australia policy; a terse but accurate title not favoured in official circles. In the Immigration Restriction Act of 1901, the commonwealth adopted a formula used by Natal in South Africa whereby intending coloured immigrants were required to submit themselves to a test in any prescribed European language, meaning, in practice, one of which they were known to be ignorant. Every political party subscribed to a policy that successfully kept Australia white—an objective the importance and propriety of which the Australian people have never seriously questioned.

Behind the determination to restrict immigration there was undoubtedly a certain amount of colour prejudice. The matter at issue, said J. C. Watson, first leader of the Labour party in the federal Parliament, was 'whether we would desire that our sisters or our brothers should be married into any of those races to which we object'. Among more sober arguments used to justify the policy was the inability of a relatively small white population to assimilate large numbers of Asians, who would threaten the stability and future of a society which, it was hoped, would remain democratic and English-speaking. Asians possessed ideas, social habits and morals repugnant to westerners, and it could not be expected that, different as they were from Australians in customs, language and colour, they would be able to fit amicably into Australia's society and accept its political practices. The economic structure of the nation would be dislocated and the living standards of its people would be jeopardised by immigrants prepared to work in inferior conditions for lower wages. Moreover, there was a security danger in permitting the entry of races who were products of another, and distinct, civilisation, to which they owed a loyalty they might not renounce in times of war or international tension. The exclusion of coloured races was regarded, therefore, as an essential and permanent feature of commonwealth policy, to tamper with which would be to risk destroying the fundamental unity of the nation. The Asians, declared the *Sydney Morning Herald* in August 1910, 'are representative of a civilisation older than our own, and the centuries of heredity which this implies have evolved thoughts which are not our thoughts, and ways which are not our ways. And hence we, as being in greater degree than any other Western country under the shadows of Asia, have to choose between exclusion or extinction of our own type of civilisation. And in this we have the justification of the white Australia doctrine.'

[The federal government legislated to prevent non-whites entering the country, but the necessary concomitant measures to encourage desirable immigrants from Europe it left, until 1920, to the six state governments. Drought and bad seasons during the first five years of federation lost to Australia nearly 17,000 more people by emigration than it gained by immigration, but the process was reversed after assistance to immigrants was restored in New South Wales in 1906 and in Victoria, South Australia, and Tasmania by 1912, so that when war broke out in 1914 some 200,000 newcomers had reached Australia. Nevertheless, the need for a national immigration system to replace the six independent systems operated by the states was obvious, but the suggestion was rejected by nearly all the state governments, and no political party fully appreciated yet the importance of a sustained and co-ordinated immigration program in securing the future that Australians envisaged for their country.

Immigration was not a contentious issue in the early days of the commonwealth, therefore, and all political groupings subscribed to the White Australia principle. The chief question which aroused controversy and divided political opinion was that of a federal tariff. The elections in 1901 had been reported in terms of High Tariffists and Low Tariffists, and in Parliament the protectionists formed a Liberal government and the free-traders became the Conservative opposition. The Labour party, though initially divided within itself over the tariff, was united on other issues and able to secure concessions as the price of its support for the administration. The tariff was not a political issue for long. In one of his first statements as prime minister, Edmund Barton indicated that there would be a moderate protectionist tariff and probably preferential duties in favour of the mother country. This was to take a middle position in a Parliament divided broadly into those favouring a high protective tariff and those favouring as low a tariff as possible, free trade having been made impracticable by the obligation of the commonwealth not only to meet its own expenses but also to compensate the states for the revenues they surrendered on federation. It was clearly impossible also to embark upon a policy that would destroy industries which had been fostered in several states by existing protective tariffs. The compromise tariff of 1902 was designed, therefore, to 'operate protectively as well as for the production of revenue'. In 1908, after an inquiry by a royal commission into the operation of the tariff, the rates imposed in 1902 were increased, the number of articles on the free list was reduced, and a preference of five per cent on British goods was introduced.

The inclusion in the 1908 enactment of the five per cent preference on goods of the mother country was due largely to the insistence of Alfred Deakin, then coming to the end of the second, and longest, of his three terms as prime minister. Deakin is generally considered to have been the outstanding political leader in Australia between federation and the outbreak of the first world war. Born in Victoria in 1856, Deakin trained to be a barrister but took to journalism under David Syme, entered colonial politics in Victoria and, with the creation of the commonwealth, became attorney-general in Barton's cabinet, in which his personal magnetism and charm, his sympathy and persuasiveness, were invaluable in reconciling the diverse temperaments of such formidable colleagues as William Lyne, George Turner, John Forrest and J. G. Drake.

When Barton retired to the High Court in 1903, Deakin succeeded him as prime minister. Although his first term was a short one, he emerged as prime minister again in 1905 with a small following of his own and a promise of support from the Labour party. The second Deakin administration lasted over three years and was not defeated until November 1908, when Labour resumed office. Deakin joined forces with his former opponents led by Joseph Cook and defeated Labour in 1909, only to be routed at the election of 1910. Thereafter he gradually withdrew from parliamentary affairs and finally left politics in January 1913. Deakin's greatness was founded upon personal popularity among all parties, a clear-headed administrative competence, a magnificent voice and an eloquence that none of his contemporaries could equal, a conviction of high purpose, and a selfless devotion to service. Tall, erect, bearded, immaculate in dress, Deakin was a towering presence in cabinet for over seven of the first ten years of the commonwealth's history, but with all his talents, he lacked the toughness and zeal of a great parliamentarian and seldom engaged in the stormy moments of parliamentary life. Nevertheless, he recklessly disregarded his known physical limitations and spent his energies in the task of helping to make the infant federation a success.

Deakin's quality was impressed upon the statesmen of Britain and the empire at the Imperial Conference of 1907, when he contributed to the discussion of proposals to strengthen imperial unity and repeated the Australian government's wish to construct a small naval squadron of its own to operate in conjunction with the British fleet. Australia's continuing dependence on the Royal Navy for defence was a source of anxiety among Australian leaders after the formation in 1902 of the Anglo-Japanese alliance, which implied that Britain was relying in some degree for the security of its interests in the Pacific on a power from which, it was believed, any challenge to the White Australia policy would most probably come. When Barton suggested an Australian navy to the Imperial Conference of 1902, he found the British government wedded to the idea of a single navy under one authority with the self-governing Dominions contributing to its manpower and cost. The creation of local Dominion squadrons was regarded as wasteful and inefficient, involving a dispersal of control that, in the event of a widespread or global war, might weaken British naval strategy if one arm was inactive and tied to a particular coast. Barton was obliged to yield to the idea of centralised imperial control, and it was agreed that Australia and New Zealand should find half the cost of a strengthened British fleet in Australian and New Zealand waters, and that some Australian personnel should be employed under officers of the Royal Navy on ships in the Australian squadron.

The agreement was not well received in Australia, and it was with difficulty and under a barrage of criticism that it was ratified by the commonwealth Parliament. After Deakin returned to the question in 1907, events in Europe intensified the need for a review of imperial defence and naval strategy. Britain's attempts at the Hague Conference of that year to secure limitations on European armament were opposed by other powers led by a Germany fearing any check on the growth of the German navy. In April 1908, a new German navy law increased Germany's annual program to four capital ships, and in an interview with Sir Charles Hardinge at Cronberg in August, the German emperor refused to consider the possibility of any reduction. In October 1908, Germany loyally supported Austria's annexation of Bosnia and Herzegovina: a breach of the Treaty of Berlin of 1878 that brought Europe close to war. A large increase in Britain's naval program in 1909 was now regarded as imperative by the British government; after heated debate, eight capital ships were planned. These developments affected imperial naval strategy in two important respects. They led to an offer from Australia and New Zealand of two dreadnoughts for the Royal Navy, and to the replacement of the old idea of a single navy with central control by the new concept of local Dominion squadrons.

When a special Imperial Defence Conference met in London in July and August 1909 in order 'to discuss the general question of naval and military defence within the Empire', both Australia and New Zealand displayed a keen desire to participate more in the maintenance of their own security. Australia's concern at the potential threat to the White Australia policy from Japan had been accentuated by the Japanese victory over Russia in 1905 and by the withdrawal of British ships for concentration in the North Sea area to meet the menace from Germany. Feeling in Australia ran strongly in favour of a local fleet under the control of the commonwealth government, and it seemed probable that Australian public opinion would not support the dreadnought promised to the mother country unless some gesture were made towards the creation of an Australian navy. Britain formulated a plan for a Pacific fleet of three squadrons: an East Indies, a China, and an Australian squadron, each to consist of a battle cruiser, three light cruisers, six destroyers and three submarines, and each in time of war to come under the direction of the Admiralty in London. Australia undertook to maintain the whole of its squadron and furnish most of the capital for the construction of its battle cruiser. The commonwealth Parliament authorised a loan of £3,500,000 for establishing the Australian squadron, the ships to be built in British shipyards, and the crews to be recruited in Australia and led by officers provided by the Admiralty. At the same time compulsory military training was introduced with the aim of producing a citizen force for land defence. (The regulations for this remained in force until 1929.)

When an Imperial Conference next met in 1911, the tension in Europe had not abated, and political leaders in the parliaments of Australia and New Zealand had expressed apprehension over the worsening international situation. The representatives of the Dominions were invited to attend a separate conference of the Committee of Imperial Defence where, for the first time, they were given important information bearing on British foreign policy. Sir Edward Grey, the British Foreign Secretary, told the Dominion representatives that sea-power determined the foreign policy of the United Kingdom: 'It is the naval question which underlies the whole of our European foreign policy.' From this it followed that the establishment of local Dominion navies made it more necessary than ever that there should be a foreign policy common to the whole British empire and accepted by all its parts. It was also made clear that the Admiralty retained its conviction that a single, centrally controlled imperial navy would be the most efficient and manageable striking power at sea, although the Royal Navies of Canada and Australia were recognised as under the authority of their respective governments. None of the three Pacific squadrons projected in 1909 was yet at full strength, however, and both Australia and New Zealand were still concerned at Britain's naval weakness in the Pacific, especially as the opening of the Panama Canal might soon facilitate the passage of hostile warships into eastern waters. Nevertheless, when war began in August 1914, Australia, with Japan a British ally and the United States a likely friend, possessed a naval force which, though small, provided at least a token of national security.

The creation of the Royal Australian Navy was the achievement largely of a Labour government led by Andrew Fisher, who continued Australian defence policy along the lines laid down by Deakin. Fisher had been minister for Trade and Customs in the short-lived Labour administration of 1904, and in 1907 he succeeded J. C. Watson as leader of the federal Labour party. In this capacity he was prime minister from November 1908 to June 1909, when he was replaced by Deakin at the head of his so-called 'fusion government', but the Labour party gained a parliamentary majority at the general election of April 1910 and Fisher remained prime minister for the next three years. The sincere and solid leadership of Fisher combined admirably with the vigour of his colleague, W. M. Hughes, to produce a balanced government with policies to which Deakin could take little exception. Labour lost ground in the elections of June 1913 but returned to power with a working majority at the war-time election of September 1914. Fisher's cabinet was not a harmonious one, however, and in October 1915 he resigned in favour of Hughes, later becoming Australian High Commissioner in London, where he quietly passed the last years before his death in October 1928. Fisher's greatest service to Australia was undoubtedly in the years from 1910 to 1913: a period of immense legislative output, when his wise leadership gave him a political stature nearly equal to that of Deakin. He lacked Deakin's polish and eloquence, but his clear, plain and vigorous language, embellished with a pronounced Scottish accent, conveyed a sense of honesty and reliability that inspired confidence beyond the ranks of his own party. His determination to improve the lot of the working class was rooted in his origins and in a career that took him from pit-boy to prime minister. Fisher had been born in Scotland, worked in the local collieries of Ayrshire from the age of ten, and, after emigrating to Queensland at the age of twenty-three, continued as a coal-miner while reading economics and social science. He owed his success to character: what he lacked in personal magnetism he made up with diligence, tenacity and moderation, qualities that won general respect, notably at the Imperial Conference in London in 1911, when his speeches belied a popular view that a Labour prime minister must be revolutionary. Slow-moving and hard-headed Fisher may have been, but his strength of will, shrewdness and humble dignity were a source of strength to his Labour government.

During Fisher's administration, the social reforms begun under Deakin were pressed on with more speed and urgency. In 1908 Deakin superimposed on the various state schemes then operating a federal old age and invalid pensions scheme, which Labour amended in 1912 to apply its benefits to naturalised subjects also, and to permit pensioners to possess a home and receive allowances from their children without reducing the pension to which they were entitled. Maternity allowances of £5 on the birth of a child were introduced, and a Commonwealth Bank was established which provided both general and savings business and was to become the dominant financial institution in the country.

The most significant developments so far as Labour was concerned, however, were in industrial arbitration, conciliation and wage regulation. Among the matters upon which the constitution gave the federal Parliament power to make laws for the peace, order and good government of the commonwealth were 'conciliation and arbitration for the prevention and settlement of industrial disputes extending beyond the limits of any one state'. The Labour party wished to create as soon as possible a federal arbitration court to determine conditions for unions organised on a federal or national basis. After intense debate and several changes of ministry, the Arbitration and Conciliation Bill introduced by Deakin in 1903 emerged the following year in a form acceptable to the Labour party. The presidency of the new Court of Conciliation and Arbitration went to Henry Bournes Higgins, who had been in the first commonwealth Parliament and attorney-general in the Labour cabinet of 1904, although he refused to join the party. In his new office Higgins delivered a judgement in 1907 of profound importance to the economy and industrial conditions in that it established the doctrine of the basic wage. Recent legislation had provided for the remission of excise duties on articles manufactured in conditions certified by the Court as fair and reasonable. The question of what Parliament meant by 'fair and reasonable' arose almost at once with the application by H. V. McKay for exemption from the payment of excise duties on goods produced in his Sunshine Harvester works at Melbourne. Higgins estimated the wage that would be considered fair and reasonable by reference to the normal needs of an average employee with a wife and three children, and declared £2 2s per week to be the minimum amount to be paid to unskilled workers. The Excise Act by which remissions were allowed was soon found unconstitutional, but the principle of the Harvester Judgement of 1907 was incorporated into Labour philosophy. The basic wage it annunciated became the criterion upon which later calculations were made, and from 1913 onwards figures compiled by the Commonwealth Bureau of Census and Statistics were used to determine the current equivalent in purchasing power of the wage laid down by Higgins in 1907.

The Harvester Judgement encouraged the Labour party in the hopes it entertained of the Arbitration Court, but enthusiasm was dimmed somewhat by the actions of the High Court of Australia in declaring important federal legislation invalid and setting aside certain judgements of the Arbitration Court and curtailing its powers. Higgins complained of an extending 'Serbonian bog of technicalities' around the Arbitration Court, and expressed the opinion that the High Court's decisions affecting the Arbitration

Court's powers, 'with all the corollaries which they will involve, will make it impossible to frame awards that will work; will entail, indeed, a gradual paralysis of the functions of the Court'. Moreover, although it was the Labour party that was particularly incensed by the High Court's rulings, none of the invalidated laws had been introduced by a Labour government, but all had been carried between 1905 and 1907 by Deakin's government with Labour support, so that the rejected measures could not be described as purely party legislation. There was widespread concern, therefore, that it should appear that the freely elected representatives of the people were not supreme in the land but were second to a small body of non-elected and irremovable judges who were known to disagree among themselves. Of the five justices on the High Court, three believed the constitution should be so interpreted as to preserve the federal balance between the states and the commonwealth, each of which should be kept within its respective legislative confines, but the remaining two believed the constitutional authority of the commonwealth should be interpreted in broad terms and without reference to the restraint imposed upon it by the supposed powers of the states.

In 1911 Fisher's Labour government attempted to overcome the judicial barrier to legislation upon which it was determined by a referendum, seeking the people's sanction for constitutional amendments designed to extend the powers of the commonwealth over matters relating to corporations, monopolies and industrial disputes. It was hoped to make the issue a non-party one, but in practice the sides divided into Labour and anti-Labour, or Liberals, except in New South Wales, where a section of the Labour supporters led by several state ministers declared that the questions being decided were outside the official party platform and that they would not vote for the proposed amendments. Fisher was in London to attend the coronation of King George V, and in his absence the leadership of federal Labour fell on W. M. Hughes, who argued that without an extension of the commonwealth's powers it would be impossible to enact important parts of the Labour program. Deakin, leading the opposition, admitted that changes were necessary but argued that they could be effected without recourse to the drastic measures advocated by the government. The electorate might have been prepared to grant the commonwealth the powers needed to pass the recent invalidated legislation, but it would not grant the extensive powers desired by the government, whose proposed amendments were heavily defeated, only Western Australia of the six states returning a favourable vote.

The referendum of 1911 and another held in 1913, when South Australia and Queensland joined Western Australia to reduce the majority opposing the amendments, tended to link the Liberal party with the doctrine of state rights which, as commentators pointed out, the example of the United States suggested would be difficult to maintain undiluted. The anti-Labour forces were beginning to realise their disadvantages when compared with the positive phalanx presented by the Labour party, whose vision of Australia as one nation rather than as a collection of separate states infused it with a certain nationalistic appeal. Labour's program could be criticised on many points, but at least it was concrete and explicit. The Liberal party, on the other hand, was based on the fusion in 1909 of Labour's various opponents whose common ground was merely hostility to particular aspects of Labour's policy, but this was a negative position which made it difficult to frame a definite policy acceptable to all the members and offered little assurance of vigorous government. In 1912 W. H. Irvine, a prominent Liberal from Victoria, said his party's program 'appeared to have been arrived at by the simple process of elimination, by the taking out of it of anything that could offend the susceptibilities of anyone. All the bones had been carefully removed, and nothing left but a kind of gelatinous compound, political food for infants and invalids, warranted not to cause the slightest inconvenience to the weakest digestion.'

These deficiencies had to some extent been remedied by 1913, when Labour was defeated in the general election, and Joseph Cook, who had succeeded Deakin as leader of the Liberals, was invited to form a government with a parliamentary majority of one and a minority in the Senate of seven to Labour's twenty-nine. To break the deadlock, Cook decided on the bold policy of forcing measures through the House of Representatives that he knew the Labour majority in the Senate would reject, thereby producing the circumstances required by section 57 of the constitution for a double dissolution and the election of all members of both Houses of Parliament at the same time. Cook proposed to introduce electoral reforms including the revival of postal voting, to repeal the provision in the Arbitration Act relating to the grant of preference to trade unionists in government employment, and to restore the exemption of rural workers from the operation of the Act. All of these proposals represented a reversal of the recent Labour government's policy. The Senate duly rejected twice the measures sent to it by the House of Representatives, and the governor-general agreed to a double dissolution in accordance with the terms of the constitution. The elections took place in September 1914, after war had broken out in Europe. Both parties pledged themselves to support the mother country, but the Labour campaign carried the greater conviction, and the result was a Labour victory and the return of Andrew Fisher to head the government for the third time. The Australian federation that in 1901 had been successfully conceived in a troubled world was now to be called upon to prove itself in the matrix of war.

4

The First World War (1914-1919)

AUSTRALIA WAS a nation of four and a half million when, in August 1914, Britain committed its empire to war with Germany. None of the Dominions had been consulted in the crisis diplomacy that had preceded the rupture in Europe, but all pledged themselves to contribute fully to the imperial war effort. The Australian government immediately placed its new navy under the orders of the Admiralty in London and began recruiting an expeditionary force of 20,000 men for service overseas. In the initial moves against German colonial territories in Africa and the Pacific, the seizure of north-eastern New Guinea was an easy exercise for the two Australian battalions which went ashore near Rabaul in the island of New Britain on September 11, for the German land force there was negligible and the naval squadron at Tsingtao in China was powerless to intervene. Within a week of the Australian landing the Germans in New Guinea capitulated. The only disconcerting element in the situation was the Japanese seizure of other German islands in the Pacific a few degrees from the equator and close to Australia, but the commonwealth government suppressed its misgivings and accepted Britain's advice to confine its operations to the islands south of the equator and, for strategic reasons, to allow the Japanese to occupy those north of the equator until the whole question could be settled at the end of the war.

In the meantime there had been an enthusiastic response in Australia to the call for service, and the large numbers seeking enlistment in the expeditionary force enabled the original offer of

20,000 men to be increased. As the war went on and the needs of the Allies grew, the Australian contribution in men was extended until in 1918 over 400,000 volunteers had been recruited of whom 330,000 served overseas. The organisation of the expeditionary force was entrusted to Major-General W. T. Bridges, the first commandant of the Australian Military College established in 1911 at Duntroon, and his chief of staff Major C. B. B. White, who had studied at the staff college at Camberley in England. After preliminary training in Australia, the first contingents of what became the Australian Imperial Force disembarked in Egypt in December 1914 and completed their training with New Zealand troops in the desert near Cairo. At the request of Lord Kitchener, Secretary of State for War in the British cabinet, and with the consent of the governments of Australia and New Zealand, the contingents from the two Dominions were joined together under the command of Lieutenant-General W. R. Birdwood, a British cavalry officer, and under the name of the Australian and New Zealand Army Corps were soon to earn for its abbreviated title of ANZAC a permanent place of honour in the Australian and New Zealand national traditions.

When the second Australian contingent began to arrive in Egypt in February 1915, the British government was already considering action in the eastern Mediterranean in order to answer Russia's request for a diversion to relieve its troops fighting in the Caucasus against the Turks, who had entered the war on Germany's side in October 1914. Winston Churchill, the First Lord of the Admiralty, urged the forcing of the Dardanelles, and after Kitchener's reluctance to spare the necessary troops had been overcome and a naval attack on the Turkish land batteries in the Straits had been repulsed, the idea was accepted and plans were laid to capture the Gallipoli peninsula. General Sir Ian Hamilton was put in command of an Allied army comprising the 29th British Division, which had recently been organised in England from regular troops recalled from overseas, a French Division, and the Australian and New Zealand Corps. Apprised of the intended assault, the Turks accepted the supreme command of a German general, Liman von Sanders, who in a few weeks built up a good defensive system on the peninsula, and the Allied forces which began landing just before dawn on April 25, 1915, met a prepared enemy in entrenched positions.

The principal blow came from the British and French troops who went ashore at Cape Hellas, the toe of the peninsula, where they were expected by the Turks and were greeted with heavy machine-gun fire which on the first day killed or wounded a third of the 3,000 men who landed, but after desperate fighting a beachhead was effected. A diversionary attack was intended to be delivered by the Australian and New Zealand troops at a beach near the promontory of Gaba Tepe, thirteen miles northwards on the coast of the peninsula opposite the narrows, but unfortunately the landings were made in error a mile further north with the result that, after the surprised defenders had been scattered, the Anzacs found themselves on strange ground for which they were unprepared and confronted by precipitous scrub-covered ridges instead of the open undulating country they had expected. In the new and confused situation tactics had to be hastily improvised, but by the end of the day an irregular line was established. Nevertheless, the landing had secured only a foothold and none of the original objectives. There was some doubt whether the decimated divisions were in a condition to withstand sustained counter-attack, but the suggestion of a withdrawal was rejected by General Hamilton, who bluntly declared that there was nothing for it but to dig themselves in and 'stick it out'. The Turkish counter-attacks were repelled and thereafter for three months the operation became largely a holding one with some attempts to improve on the narrow beachhead that had been retained. A determined effort to break out and cross the peninsula was begun on August 6, when the 29th British Division at Cape Hellas made a feint and fought a costly action for several days while the Australian 1st Infantry Brigade engaged in bloody and ferocious hand-to-hand fighting in the enemy trenches before capturing the Turkish stronghold at Lone Pine and holding it against repeated counter-attacks. In no place, however, was the Turkish defence broken, and hopes of a break-through by a new British force established on a beachhead at Suvla Bay, four miles north of the Anzac position, were erased by the lethargy of the commanders. The campaign relapsed into intermittent skirmishing, and when Lord Kitchener visited the scene in November 1915 he agreed that evacuation was the only sensible course. Troops were laid low with sickness, especially dysentery, and late in November many were smitten with frost-bite when a blizzard descended, while others were drowned in the rains that flooded the low-lying trenches at Suvla Bay. Orders for the evacuation were given in December, and during the second half of that month and the first week of the next the operation was conducted with such skill and efficiency that, contrary to general expectations, losses were negligible.

Of 35,000 Allied soldiers killed in the Gallipoli venture, 8,500 were Australian; of 78,500 wounded, 19,000 were Australian. It would be an idle exercise, even if it were possible, to apportion the contributions made by the various nations or divisions to the campaign. French and Indian contingents played their part along-side the British, Australian and New Zealand forces, and the hero-ism, endurance and skill at arms so much in evidence among the 29th British Division and the Anzacs were exhibited on all sides and not least on that of the enemy. Nevertheless, Gallipoli was of particular significance to the Australians and New Zealanders because it established for them a reputation as the equal of the best soldiers of older lands. An Australian military tradition was founded on the battlefields of Gallipoli, at Lone Pine where the dead and dying of both sides clogged the trenches, at Quinn's Post where enemy grenades were caught and returned before they could explode, at Courtney's Post where Private Albert Jacka displayed the fighting valour that was to earn him the first Victoria Cross in the war awarded to an Australian, and at the Nek where, as one line of Australians was wiped out by intense machine-gun fire, another line would clear the parapet to meet the same fate. The Gallipoli campaign was the first great baptism of fire for the Australian soldier, and from it he emerged a proud and undaunted warrior. More than this, there was no bitterness in any responsible quarter at the gruelling to which the Australian troops had been committed, nor resentment against the British government and generals, although it was realised that some terrible blunders in strategy had been perpetrated. It was as much in the unflinching and uncomplaining acceptance of the failure of the Gallipoli expedition as in the courage and fighting qualities revealed by its men that Australia's maturity was demonstrated and its stature enhanced.

The defeat at the Dardanelles punctured British prestige throughout the Near East and a Turkish attack was expected against Egypt, to which the Australian and New Zealand forces returned from Gallipoli in order to reorganise their ranks, now greatly increased by new contingents from the home countries. The Anzac infantry were transferred to France, but the mounted troops remained in the Sinai peninsula where, in August 1916, they were involved in an encounter with a Turkish army that Kress von Kressenstein, a German officer, had brought across the desert from Palestine with the idea of defeating the British garrison at Romani, only twenty miles east of the Suez Canal. In five days' fighting, the British, Australian and New Zealand mounted troops killed or captured half the enemy's army and forced the remainder to retire towards Katia and then to El Arish, fifty miles back on the coastal approaches to southern Palestine. The Turkish defeat transformed the military situation in the Near East, enabling the British to clear the Sinai peninsula and reassert their control of the desert.

While the mounted troops were distinguishing themselves in the desert, the infantry divisions were experiencing their first taste of warfare on the Western Front. On July 1, 1916, eighteen British and five French divisions hurled themselves against the German entrenchments to begin the expensive Battle of the Somme, on the first day of which 57,000 British troops were lost and the Newfoundland regiment, the only unit from the Dominions then taking part, was virtually annihilated. In the series of attacks that followed, every division in the British army was employed until the German line was pressed in, but progress was slow, and it was felt necessary to prevent the enemy from diverting forces elsewhere to his precarious position on the Somme. On July 19, therefore, an Australian and a British division attacked along the quiet sector south of Armentières and penetrated the German lines in parts, but eventually had to withdraw after sustaining heavy casualties, over 5,000 of them Australian. On the Somme, where the Allied offensive was now three weeks old, troops of the

THE FIRST WORLD WAR

1st Anzac Corps captured the strongly fortified village of Pozières after a week's fighting and held it against a German attack in August. On August 10, an arduous struggle began for possession of Mouquet Farm, which the Australians seized and lost again several times before they were withdrawn from the line on September 5, leaving the farm in German hands until the Canadians captured it three weeks later. The Australians had lost 20,000 men in only a few weeks of unproductive fighting, and the Allied offensive subsided before the end of the year having strained the enemy heavily but not defeated him.

As the exhausted Australian troops settled down for a grim, cold winter in the muddy trenches and shell-holes on the Somme, a change took place in the nation's political leadership. In October 1915, Andrew Fisher retired as prime minister and was succeeded by W. M. Hughes, who for long had been the most dynamic member of the cabinet in the prosecution of the war.

While attorney-general in the Fisher government formed in September 1914, Hughes had been responsible for the commonwealth legislation placing newspapers under censorship and providing for stern measures against sedition, espionage and any activities that might encourage disloyalty to the British empire or cause public anxiety. Precautions were also taken in the early months of the war against persons of German origin, some of whom were truculent and were interned, but the majority of whom had been largely assimilated into the Australian environment and were not seriously disturbed except for the formal necessity to report their presence. Commerce was quickly brought under federal control for the purpose of prosecuting the war, and the export of important commodities such as copper, tin, wheat, flour, wood and meat was prohibited except under the licence of the government, which channelled the goods to the United Kingdom market. The state governments undertook to prevent the hoarding of foodstuffs and to control prices, but they failed to achieve the promised uniformity of legislation and their divergences occasioned the introduction in 1916 of a federal control that produced a more satisfactory situation. The commonwealth government also attempted to reduce Australia's dependence on the United Kingdom for military equipment and established clothing factories in spite of opposition from the trade. The small-arms factory set up in 1912 at Lithgow, less than 100 miles from Sydney on the north-western edge of the Blue Mountains, maintained a supply of rifles, but ambitious schemes to manufacture shells and artillery had to be abandoned. Of more permanent significance was the Broken Hill Proprietary Company's iron and steel works that came into operation in 1915 at Newcastle, New South Wales, and rapidly extended its activities both during the war and after. Nevertheless, Australia remained essentially a primary producer exporting wheat, wool, meat, sugar, fruit and dairy products. Its economy was geared to overseas markets and dependent upon imported capital, so that, although its financial position was strong in 1914, Australia could not meet the cost of its contribution to the Allied campaigns during the war years without heavy borrowing both locally and from the British government. The adoption of the loan method of financing the war effort did not obviate the need to secure more funds from taxation, and direct taxes were levied on entertainments, while the land tax that had been introduced in 1910 was steadily increased. These enlarged federal revenue, but in some instances they were superimposed on taxes already being levied by the state governments and consequently raised the problem of double taxation that was eventually to lead to a reorganisation of the financial relationship between the commonwealth and the states.

These extensions of federal authority were prompted largely by Fisher's attorney-general and successor as prime minister, William Morris Hughes, who, after October 1915, gave his country a strong and aggressive war-time leadership no other Australian politician of the time could have hoped to emulate. Hughes had been born in Wales and had migrated to Australia at the age of nineteen. He tried a variety of occupations in Brisbane and Sydney before achieving prominence in the trade union movement, organising the waterside workers of Sydney and becoming president of the Waterside Workers' Federation. In 1894 he entered the New South Wales legislature and in the elections of 1901 transferred to the new federal Parliament, where his administrative talent, energy, determination and quickness in debate earned him some influence with the Labour leadership. He was a tiny, elfish man who could command attention and sway an audience with his flailing arms, sharp repartee, ostentatious fervour and waspish phrases; he nonplussed both colleagues and opponents with his defective hearing which, in difficult moments, was sometimes pretended. Hughes, said an opponent, was 'too deaf to listen to reason, too loud to be ignored, and too small to be hit'. He became the most important figure by far in Australian politics for many years, affectionately admired by one part of the population and bitterly denounced by another. In England he was universally popular and during his visit in 1916 won acclaim with his impassioned speeches on the conduct of the war. Hughes was a vigorous exponent of Australia's national rights, but he did not succumb to the parochialism that characterised most of his contemporaries. He saw Australia's interests not in isolation but as an integral part of those of the British empire, and in so doing detached himself from the narrow partisans who sat in the federal Parliament. His very brilliance lost him friends and his cantankerousness and cruel tongue gained him enemies, for popular as Hughes was with many people, his was not an attractive personality. Overweening, unpredictable, inordinately ambitious, he was a rude and autocratic parvenu, a petty and ungenerous opponent, and a difficult and untrustworthy colleague, as the Labour party was soon to discover.

Hughes was determined that Australia should contribute its utmost to the Allied war effort, and he doubted whether voluntary recruitment for the Australian Imperial Force would satisfy his concept of Australia's military obligations. Conscription for military service overseas was a contentious issue throughout the British empire, but it was adopted by the United Kingdom in January 1916, by New Zealand in the following August, and by Canada in September 1917. In Australia the government had been adamant in its opposition to conscription since the beginning of the war, but a change to compulsory service was now being canvassed in the country by representatives of all sections of the public and found influential advocates among the clergy, the universities, the trade union movement and the press. The

57

Sydney *Bulletin*, which campaigned for conscription from the very start, appealed in August 1915 for the abandonment of a recruitment policy it described as an anomaly. 'The business of wailing for recruits by means of posters, politicians' speeches, white feathers, and so forth', it declared, 'is as degrading as those other appeals by which our hospitals are periodically rescued from insolvency. Speaking broadly, the system gets the wrong men, the best, leaving the bad patriots and the cowards behind. There is everything against voluntary service as a means of raising a national army, and nothing but a few deceptive old catchwords in its favour.' It was argued that only with conscription could Australia adequately support the mother country, upon which its security fundamentally depended and to the protection of whose navy the Dominion owed the freedom and unhampered development it had enjoyed for over a century. A league was organised in several states and allied itself with the Australian Natives' Association to press for the adoption of universal military service.

A decline in the figure for voluntary enlistment in the middle of 1916 was the signal for Hughes to announce that a referendum would be taken at the end of October to enable the electors to decide whether the government's compulsory power over recruitment for service at home should be extended to cover service abroad. There followed a bitter campaign in which the ignoble art of vituperation was practised by Hughes on the one side and by Dr Daniel Mannix, the Roman Catholic coadjutor-archbishop of Melbourne, on the other. Mannix, for whom Ireland rather than Australia was the national interest and England, not Germany, the principal enemy, was opposed not only to conscription but also to voluntary enlistment. He was not supported by any other prelate and his speeches were so charged with anglophobia that his deportation was suggested, but his forcibly expressed views undoubtedly weighed much among the large numbers of Catholic Irish in the ranks of the trade unions and the Labour party. Opponents of conscription believed that Australia was already doing its share for the Allied cause (more than its share according to Mannix), that the voluntary system provided all the troops that were necessary, and that to resort to compulsion would bring militarism into the country and lead to the subordination of industry to army rule. Those with relatives in the trenches in France were exhorted not to commit others involuntarily to the same ordeal, and those who, on account of age or disability, were not suitable for service were cautioned against selfishly willing it upon such people as were.

It is impossible to judge whether it was the reasoning of the opposition or an idiosyncratic distaste for conscription that decided the Australian people to reject Hughes' request by 1,160,033 votes to 1,087,557: a negative majority of 72,476. Victoria, Tasmania and Western Australia returned majorities in favour of conscription, and New South Wales, Queensland and South Australia returned majorities against. Many responsible Australians regarded the result as an illustration of their countrymen's inability to look beyond their own secluded corner of the globe and appreciate the critical significance of the war. It seemed to be a renunciation of obligations incurred during a hundred years of protection by the Royal Navy, which had enabled the people of Australia to enjoy uninterrupted exploitation of their soil and forge for themselves a standard of living that would have otherwise been unobtainable. It looked as if Australia was not prepared to follow less fortunately endowed nations and make the ruinous sacrifices necessary in a common cause upon the success of which the continuance of its prosperity depended. The referendum cast a shadow over Australia's war effort; its politics became vulgar and confused, and, Gallipoli notwithstanding, it lost the opportunity of kindling the public spirit that older nations find in the collective discipline and sacrifice required in times of national adversity.

Hughes accepted the people's verdict on the conscription issue, but the antagonisms aroused during the referendum campaign destroyed the unity of his party. He walked out of a meeting of the Labour caucus in November 1916 when a motion of no confidence in him was moved, taking with him twenty-two members whom he called the 'National Labour Party' and brought into a reorganised Cabinet. The forty-two members who refused to follow him elected Frank Gwynne Tudor their leader, took the title of the 'Australian Labor Party',* and became the

*See note on page 15.

AUSTRALIA IN THE TWENTIETH CENTURY

parliamentary opposition. Hughes now led the smallest political grouping in Parliament; he was confronted by a hostile majority in the Senate and depended in the House of Representatives on the support of the Liberals. The motives behind his determination to hold office in a highly unsatisfactory political alignment are debatable: he may have been sincerely reluctant to allow the management of Australia's war effort to slip into the hands of a party not only glaringly defective in leadership but also susceptible to narrow and prejudiced outside influences which were opposed to fighting for what they thought to be the interests of British capitalism. Nevertheless, a majority of the Australian people had agreed with the Australian Labor Party's belief that the country's military obligations could be satisfied without conscription, and it would have been logical to let the people have the government they deserved and permit the Australian Labor Party to implement the policies it had advocated and take the responsibility for the consequences of them. Hughes, however, clung tenaciously to power, and in January 1917 took his following into the ranks of the Liberals to form a new Nationalist party, from which in the February he reconstituted his cabinet so as to include six former Liberals and five former Labour members. These tactics triumphed in May 1917 at a general election which Hughes unsuccessfully attempted to defer but which reduced the Labour opposition to a negligible quantity, increasing the Nationalist party's majority in the House of Representatives from twenty-three to thirty-three and replacing its minority in the Senate with a majority of twelve.

While Hughes was bending all his energies to a bitter election campaign and the task of confirming his ascendancy in Australia, plans were being formed for a renewed Allied offensive in France. In April 1917 British troops over-ran the German front near Arras, the Canadians achieved their most spectacular success with the capture of Vimy Ridge, and an Australian division penetrated the German defences at Bullecourt but was taken in the flank and, lacking artillery support, forced to withdraw after suffering heavy casualties. Three weeks later the attack was renewed: a British division fought its way into the Hindenburg Line, and the Australians, after nine days' fighting, seized Bullecourt and bloodily repulsed a counter-attack on their right flank. When the French offensive seventy miles away in Champagne became a fiasco and the French army hovered on the brink of disintegration, the burden of keeping the enemy occupied during the middle months of 1917 fell entirely on the British, who prepared for a determined onslaught on the Flanders front.

In June, troops of the Australian and New Zealand Corps participated in the seizure of the Messines ridge near the battered Belgian town of Ypres—a preliminary to what was intended to be a break-through into the coastal plain of Flanders. At the end of July, the British launched an attack in the Ypres salient that was soon drowned in heavy rains. Men and equipment were engulfed in the mud, but in spite of the appalling conditions and fearful carnage, the offensive was maintained in order to relieve the Russian and Italian fronts of German pressure and give the French army time to complete its recovery.

The Australian troops were being rested in the first phase of this struggle, but they distinguished themselves in the next phase which commenced in September when the weather had cleared and the ground was less treacherous. Australian infantry pushed the enemy back and before the end of the month captured Polygon Wood, reached the outskirts of the devastated village of Zonnebeke, and early in October joined British and New Zealand forces in the advance on the Broodseinde ridge. There they outfought German infantry in hand-to-hand combat and participated in the move against the village of Passchendaele, but they were caught by German machine-gun and rifle fire which exacted a heavy toll and obliged the survivors to fall back through the quagmire that renewed rains had produced.

The gaps produced in the strength of the Australian army by the slaughter in France were difficult to fill, for recruitment had been declining since the referendum on conscription. Any hope there may have been of changing the outlook of the electorate was dimmed by opposition from sections of organised Labour and by the preoccupation of discontented industrial workers with the failure of wages to keep pace with the rising cost of living. Skilled labour objected to the dilution of its ranks with unskilled, and the

unions increasingly insisted on the principle of absolute preference to unionists and complained at delays in the issue of new
awards by the wages boards. In November 1916 the coal industry
was disrupted by a dispute that a special tribunal settled by conceding most of the employees' demands, and in the middle of 1917
industrial unrest, overlapping state boundaries, spread among
railwaymen, waterside workers and seamen, as well as among the
miners. The strikes collapsed in September 1917 after an un-
bending government had employed volunteers to man essential
services, and a period of industrial peace followed which lasted
until the end of the war.

Nevertheless, the fact remained that the Australian Imperial
Force had been depleted in the costly campaign in France in 1917
and that voluntary enlistment was failing to satisfy its requirements. The government decided, therefore, on a second referendum on the conscription issue, and the end of the year was
consumed in another acrimonious campaign. Mannix reappeared,
condemning Britain's 'sordid trade war' and exhorting Australians
to put their own country first and the British empire second: a
rallying cry widely interpreted as meaning Ireland first, Australia
second, and the empire nowhere. Hughes' caustic speeches were
on the same ungraceful level as those of Mannix, and were
peppered with intemperate and envenomed language more
typical of the born agitator than of a man with pretensions to
statesmanship.

The vote on December 20 rejected conscription even more
decisively than on the previous occasion: a severe rebuff to Hughes
that put in doubt his position as prime minister. In the peroration
to his speech opening the campaign at Bendigo in Victoria on
November 12, he had declared that the government must be
granted the power it asked for. 'It cannot govern the country without it', he said, 'and will not attempt to do so.' This was a specific
pledge, reiterated during the succeeding five weeks, and one that
could hardly be dishonoured. After some hesitation he tendered his
resignation in January 1918.

It is a fair assumption, however, that Hughes and his cabinet
colleagues had had no intention of allowing the pledge to bind
them, for they had long persuaded themselves that it was their

patriotic duty to keep the Labour party out of office at any cost, even if it meant the breaking of a public promise. The result was some unedifying political manoeuvring which culminated in the issue of a new commission to Hughes to form a ministry, and he and all his cabinet colleagues returned to office. The governor-general perhaps acted correctly in the circumstances, for it was undesirable to precipitate another election within ten months of the previous one, and only the Nationalist party led by Hughes possessed the cohesive elements necessary to form a stable government. On the other hand, it is doubtful whether Hughes acted properly in accepting the invitation in defiance of his declaration during the referendum. If he believed it absolutely essential to keep the Labour party out of office at this time, he should not have made so specific a pledge; but having done so, the honest and democratic course was either to let the Labour party attempt to govern or to advise a dissolution and an election in which the people could decide the matter for themselves. Political expediency and personal ambition motivated Hughes in January 1918, and Australian politics took on an ignoble and uninspiring mien.

Meanwhile in France, by contrast, the reputation of the Australian soldier was yet further enhanced in the defence against the German offensive launched in March 1918 against the St Quentin sector. The British Fifth Army was driven back forty miles and suffered crippling losses, but when the enemy attempted to swing his attack northwards he was checked by the resistance of the British Third Army. In April, though weakened by bombing and machine-gunning from Allied aircraft which included two Australian scout squadrons, the Germans renewed their pressure and penetrated as far as Villers Bretonneux, south of the Somme ten miles from Amiens, but the British and Australian troops on this front kept their line intact, conducted a successful staying action, and delivered a brilliant counter-attack that is counted as among the greatest Australian actions of the war.

The final and decisive Allied offensive on the Western Front was started east of Amiens on the misty morning of August 8, 1918, when the British Third Army, the Canadian Corps and the Australian Corps swept quickly through the enemy defences on a broad front. The bastion of Mont St Quentin overlooking the town of Péronne was audaciously stormed by Australian units on August 31, and by the middle of September the advance had reached the area of the Hindenburg Line from which the German offensive the previous March had begun. British and Australian troops successfully carried the difficult Hindenburg Outpost Line on September 18 and cleared the way to the main Hindenburg Line. The assault was made on September 29, but the plan for new American divisions to lead and for the Australians to follow through and take the final trenches was upset when fierce German machine-gun fire wrecked the advance of the inexperienced American infantry. Nevertheless, the Australian troops proceeded to fight their way through line after line of German trenches until, aided by an extraordinary feint in the south by troops of the 46th British Division (who swam the St Quentin canal in lifebelts, scaled the brick wall on the opposite bank, and struck well into the country beyond), the enemy resistance was broken. On October 5, Australian infantry took the village of Montbrehain, which lay behind the Hindenburg Line, and were then withdrawn from the closing stages of an offensive that had smashed the German defences and was soon to lead to the signing of an armistice.

In four years of war Australia put into the field 330,000 men, of whom over 59,000 lost their lives. It was not to be expected that this contribution should equal proportionately that of the mother country, but it was a worthy one from a nation whose population did not pass the five million figure until 1918 and lived in a continent far removed from the principal areas of conflict. Although Australia did not make as much progress in the production of munitions as did Canada, it was the only Dominion to provide a sizeable naval force, which soon distinguished itself in the sinking of the *Emden* in 1914. Its soldiers had established a fine military heritage at Gallipoli against the Turks and along the Somme against the Germans, and with the New Zealanders they had made ANZAC for ever a symbol of gallantry and dependability. The success of the soldiers abroad contrasted with the failure of the politicians at home, where the national glories achieved in battle were frittered away in barren party polemics and subterfuge.

Militarily, Australians had shown themselves to be among the best in the world; politically, they had given evidence of being petty and immature.

In the peace conference that opened at Paris in January 1919, Australia filled a role befitting the contribution made by its soldiers to the Allied victory. The enhanced status of the Dominions was recognised in the conference procedure, their representatives influenced the policy of the United Kingdom, one of the five Great Powers, and they participated in the work of the committees set up to deal with particular subjects, Hughes sitting on the Commission for Reparations and Joseph Cook sitting, with what an official adviser described as an attitude of benevolent boredom, on that for Czechoslovakia. The most statesmanlike performance among the Dominions' representatives undoubtedly came from J. C. Smuts of South Africa, but in adopting an aggressively nationalistic approach Hughes probably secured for Australia a more effective voice in the negotiation than it would have had from a reasonable and restrained leadership. Hughes was particularly concerned with the fate of the former German colonies in the Pacific and New Guinea, on the northern route to Australia. At a meeting of the Supreme Council of the Allies on January 24, 1919, he supported Smuts in advocating annexation. President Wilson of the United States was opposed to annexation, however, and Smuts, with the support of Lloyd George of England and Sir Robert Borden of Canada, drafted the three-class mandate system as a compromise. Hughes heatedly objected to it and in the Supreme Council on January 30 he was involved in some spirited exchanges with President Wilson. But the compromise was approved and eventually appeared as Article 22 of the Covenant of the League of Nations. The former German colonies in the Pacific south of the equator went to Australia as 'C' class mandates: territories that could be administered as an integral part of the mandatory nation; and Australia therefore extended its existing commitments in New Guinea to become a colonial power in the full sense with all the responsibilities and difficulties associated with the government of backward peoples overseas. Australia had proved itself in the stress and danger of war; it had now to discharge the obligations placed upon the Dominion by the peace.

E

5

A Colonial Power (1888-1940)

NEW GUINEA in 1921 was divided into two; the Dutch continued their long established control over the western half of the island, while over the remainder Australia now added its mandate for the 93,000 square miles of the former German territory in the north-east to the 90,000 square miles in the south-east which had been under Australian control since 1888. Although only 100 miles of water separated the island from the Australian mainland at their closest point, New Guinea, lying in the equatorial region, presented an inhospitable front to the stranger, its coasts sometimes running into wide swamps or rising precipitously to the mountains and the dense tropical rain forests of the interiors. Its climate was hot, humid and unhealthy, productive of malaria, tuberculosis, intestinal parasites and dysentery.

The wisdom of Australia's assuming additional colonial responsibilities was questionable at a time when it was deficient in trained civil servants experienced in tropical administration and when the country's own resources were still undeveloped and its finances in a straitened condition. Fortunately, the Australian government was not entirely ignorant of the conditions in which it was now called upon to govern in trust. After the annexation in 1888 of south-eastern New Guinea—the portion to be known later as Papua—general supervision over the administration had been exercised by the government of Queensland acting in consultation with New South Wales and Victoria and sharing the cost with them. Sir William MacGregor, a doctor of Scottish birth, formerly chief medical officer in Fiji and subsequently governor in turn of Lagos and Queensland, was appointed administrator of the colony in 1888. It was intended that he should be guided by the Queensland government and assisted by an executive and a legislative council each of nominated members, but in the following ten years he personally charted the course for the development of Australian colonial policy.

MacGregor strove gradually to bring the elements of civilisation to the native population while preserving, so far as the requirements of good government would permit, the indigenous culture, tribal forms and customs. The theory of indirect rule associated with British colonial administration, more particularly at the beginning of the twentieth century and in Nigeria under Lord Lugard, found an application in New Guinea under Mac-Gregor, whose methods were influenced by his experience under Sir Arthur Gordon in Fiji and Mauritius. MacGregor organised a native constabulary, officered by Europeans and recruited at first from among the Solomon Islanders but later from among the local inhabitants themselves. The village constables appointed in each native settlement were usually the most aggressive members of the community and sometimes notorious murderers, but Mac-Gregor believed that 'the native who could carry out a successful murder under savage conditions, and escape the wrath of injured kinsmen, had exactly those qualities of determination and fore-sight and energy which, if rightly directed, would make him a reputable member of society and an instrument of native regeneration'. MacGregor also encouraged the activities of the various missionary societies, which exercised a considerable social and educational influence among the natives in New Guinea and were invaluable in the preservation of order; he made cheap land available to them and facilitated the erection of new mission stations in areas to which they had not yet penetrated. The danger of sectarian competition among the missions he removed by prompting a conference in 1890 between representatives of the Anglican Board of Missions, the Wesleyan Conference and the London Missionary Society, who negotiated a private arrangement to respect three agreed spheres of influence. MacGregor was indifferent to denominational differences between the missions and was concerned only with the practical matter of their assisting his administration. 'To me in my official capacity', he said, 'all Christian churches are exactly alike, and that which does the best work will be most appreciated.'

MacGregor was succeeded as lieutenant-governor by Sir George Ruthven le Hunte, a genial and handsome Irish barrister, educated at Eton and Cambridge, who had served as private secretary to Sir Arthur Gordon, governor of Fiji, held office in the West Indies and Mauritius, and was to be successively governor of South Australia and of Trinidad and Tobago before ending forty years in colonial administration. He brought to his New Guinea appointment in 1898 an ability and experience that ensured efficient government during his four years' tenure and some necessary improvement in the territory's financial affairs. When Hunte relinquished office in 1903, provision had been made for the commonwealth Parliament to assume sole responsibility for the New Guinea colony, which in 1905 was given the name of Papua and a new constitution for its government. A lieutenant-governor holding office during the pleasure of the Australian governor-general was to be assisted by an executive council of six officials who, in association with three non-officials, were also to make up the legislative council, but, as under MacGregor, the lieutenant-governor was empowered to over-ride the advice of his councils. Within the federal government responsibility for Papua belonged to the Department of External Affairs, whose secretary, Arthur Attlee Hunt, took an informed interest in its development, maintaining an extensive correspondence with people working there, of whom the most important was soon to be John Hubert Plunkett Murray.

The Papuan administration of Hubert Murray was remarkable not only for its duration (thirty-two years), but also for the personal identification of the lieutenant-governor with the policies pursued and the humanity of their enforcement. Born in New South Wales in 1861, Murray had won athletic as well as academic distinction at university in England before returning to Australia to practise law. At the end of the century he had taken a commission in the Australian army, served in the Boer War and retired with the rank of lieutenant-colonel. In 1905 he was appointed chief judicial officer in Papua; in 1907 he became the administrator, and in November 1908 he was promoted to lieutenant-governor: a position he held until his death at Samarai on February 27, 1940, while on a tour of inspection. During his long rule, Murray won the confidence of the people under his control. He emphasised the need to protect the indigenous peoples and opposed forced labour, corporal punishment, exploitation and interference with harmless native customs. He attempted conscientiously to further the interests of the Papuan population as he understood them, and in so doing made the colonial administration the instrument of his personal convictions.

When Australia accepted a Mandate over the former German colony in north-east New Guinea after the first world war, the question was raised of an administrative union with Papua, for the two territories were adjacent and their needs sufficiently alike to call for a common policy. Such a union was advocated by Murray, who served on a royal commission set up in 1919 to inquire into the government of the areas it was anticipated would fall to Australia in the peace terms, but his two colleagues on the commission rejected the idea. The decision prevented the Territory's profiting from the experience of Murray and his officers in Papua and condemned the Mandate to administration by returned soldiers who, admirable as they were in many ways, lacked knowledge and sometimes interest in native affairs, with the result that the government of New Guinea took on a noticeably amateur appearance. To this separation of authority at the outset may be attributed in part Australia's unsatisfactory performance in the Mandate in the following twenty years. Australia attempted to satisfy the principle laid down in Article 22 of the Covenant of the League of Nations that the well-being and development of backward peoples in the colonies constituted 'a sacred trust for civilisation', but its rule was vitiated by the failure to devise a definite policy for its Territories, by the indifference to them generally shown in the federal Parliament, and by the innumerable difficulties that any modern western nation encounters when made responsible for dispersed and varied primitive tribes.

Among the problems that confronted the white ruler in Papua

and New Guinea was the absence of a strong tribal organisation, a superior caste or a system of chieftains with a tradition of authority upon which to erect an administration. The enforcement of justice was complicated by native customs and taboos. Sorcery and witchcraft still existed and were often blamed for influenza and other evils; killing was regarded not as a heinous crime but as a proof of valour, so that a native murderer might be basking in the admiration of his kith and kin or sweetheart when colonial officials arrived to place him under arrest. Punishment had to be made to fit the crime and take into account the extent of the criminal's absorption of western principles; a graduated series of penalties was therefore contrived varying with the degree of civilisation attained in the different areas. In both Papua and New Guinea, dependence was placed on local agents for the execution of justice and governmental orders, and the village constables who had been appointed in Papua by MacGregor in the nineteenth century had their New Guinea counterpart in the *luluais*, who were nominated by the natives, acted as their spokesmen, and ensured the observance of the regulations laid down by the administrator. After 1923 Murray improved on the system of village constables in Papua by establishing village councils, elected by the inhabitants themselves and charged with the function of advising on local requirements and conveying the wishes of the villagers to the government. Although the village councils in Papua never came up to Murray's expectations, they were a form of municipal government that was totally lacking in the Mandate, where, except for the limited activities of the *luluais*, all administrative duties were carried out by district officers, each of whom headed a field staff in one of the seven districts into which the territory was divided. Patrol officers stationed in the districts travelled from one village to another, usually over extremely difficult terrain, and inspected village development, supervised the maintenance of order, and spread the customs of the civilised world as extensively as native resistance would allow.

In both the Territories the administration was cramped by inadequate finances. The million pounds which the commonwealth government had granted to Papua in the fifteen years after 1906 had barely sufficed to balance the budget of the restricted administration. An ordinance of 1918 introduced into Papua an annual tax on all males between the ages of sixteen and thirty-six inhabiting those areas with resources deemed adequate to meet it, but remission of the tax was permitted to all who completed a quota of work on native plantations. The proceeds of the tax, which averaged £14,000 a year, were paid into a special account distinct from general revenue and devoted solely to welfare services for the natives themselves. In the Mandated Territory the Australian government continued the policy of the former German colonial establishment which, in 1907, had instituted a head tax on all adult males and followed it up three years later with a graduated tax, exemptions being granted in favour of those who worked at least ten months in the year for Europeans or taxed natives. In New Guinea the tax could be justified as a device to ensure a stable labour supply, but in Papua, where native labourers under contract were not exempted, it was designed principally to obtain revenue and illustrated the financial stress under which Murray was compelled to operate. The parsimony of the commonwealth government towards its colonial responsibilities reflected the indifference of the Australian nation, whose interest in Papua and New Guinea was confined to the strategic necessity of preventing them from falling a prey to a potential enemy. But with that contingency secured against, neither the Australian people nor their government evinced more than a casual concern over the discharge of a trust that was specific in the case of the Mandate and should have been implicitly understood in the case of Papua.

In the matter of native labour the commonwealth government sought to avoid exploitation of the inhabitants without hampering employers or prejudicing the economic development on which great store was laid. Although the terms of the Mandate permitted the use of forced labour for essential public works and services, the commonwealth prohibited it under any circumstances in both of the New Guinea Territories and relied instead on indentured or contract labour. Under the indenture system the recruitment of native labour was strictly controlled and licensed by the administration. A maximum term was set for a contract, which had to be witnessed and sanctioned by a magistrate or other qualified official, upon whom fell the onus of ensuring that the native was acting voluntarily and freely and would be employed on a plantation in satisfactory conditions. Wages under the indenture system varied upwards from five shillings a month: a small enough sum, but it was supplemented by free food, clothing, lodging and medical attention. The system gave the native labourers some security, but it drained the economic life of the villages, whose family and social organisation was disrupted by the absence of their young men for long periods. Greater use of casual labour was encouraged after 1926 by allowing natives whose work was within twenty miles of their home to be employed for an indefinite time without indenture. Although the immediate effect of this amendment to the Native Labour Ordinance was only slight, there was a tendency during the 1930s for contracts in Papua and New Guinea to cover shorter terms and, by 1940, to be replaced by the casual employment, at daily or weekly rates, of labour from villages within easy walking distance of the European township.

It was held as axiomatic among an influential section of the European population in the Territories that the amenability of native labour might be imperilled by the improvement of native education. This apprehension was allayed as it became apparent that governmental interest in education was small and progress slow. The multiplicity of languages presented a tremendous obstacle to any systematic educational policy, but the Australian government made little attempt to tackle the problem seriously or even to study and learn from the policies pursued by western administrations in other backward countries. The money devoted to schools was meagre from the start and diminished to pathetic proportions: New Guinea in 1940, after twenty years of Australian rule, possessed only six elementary schools, one technical school and one agricultural training centre. The business of education was left largely to the missions; much of the teaching was done by unqualified Europeans and semi-literate natives; it seldom went beyond the elementary stage, and the content bore no relation to the life the pupil was going to lead and was quickly forgotten after he had returned to his village. Native education in Papua and New Guinea was a sterile and unimaginative feature of the Australian administrations, and by 1940 educational progress there was probably the slowest of any European-controlled territories anywhere in the world.

The commonwealth government was a little more generous towards medical assistance than it was towards education in the Territories, although in this, as in education, the missions relieved the civil authorities of much of the responsibility, but it was only with sustained governmental interest and adequate financial expenditure that the challenge of caring for native health could be properly met. In the Mandate after 1921, the old German system was revived of training selected natives at district hospitals, supplying them with elementary medicines and dressings, and making them responsible for the health and sanitation of their villages. The work of these locally trained medical assistants, or *tul-tuls*, was supplemented by medical patrols which, acting sometimes in conjunction with the administrative patrols, carried hygiene instruction and medical aid to villages situated at a distance from the native hospitals. Each district had its hospital, a medical officer and medical assistants, and the health of the natives was protected as carefully as these facilities would allow. But the establishment of a satisfactory medical service was impossible until the commonwealth government increased its financial subsidy.

In a report published in 1924, Colonel John Ainsworth, formerly Chief Native Commissioner in Kenya, who had been appointed by the Australian government to investigate the New Guinea Mandate, declared that neither the necessary public works nor an effective administration could be maintained from the Territory's existing resources. He pointed out further that most of the plantations were held by the Expropriation Board set up in 1920 to manage expropriated German property, which employed a large and expensive staff but was in no way committed to a scheme of progressive development. The freehold tenure preferred by the Germans was replaced by leasehold, and the German plantation interests were bestowed by the Board principally on Australian returned soldiers, who in many instances were ignorant of cocoa production and permitted the crop to decline in importance and in some places to go out of cultivation. In Papua the sole right of acquiring native land belonged to the Crown, and the administration could grant to settlers only land not required by native owners. The settlers obtained the land under a lease not exceeding ninety-nine years, paid an annual rent based on its unimproved value, and were liable to have their lease cancelled if certain improvements in it were not achieved within five years. In both Territories, therefore, economic development was dependent on private enterprise conditioned by government policy. This was illustrated also in 1921 in the application to Papua and New Guinea of the Commonwealth Navigation Act restricting their external trade to carriage in Australian ships. As a royal commission of inquiry into the operation of the Act reported in 1924, the effect so far as Papua and New Guinea were concerned was to eliminate foreign competition and enable the shipping services of Burns, Philp and Company, a firm founded in Queensland in 1883, to monopolise the passenger and cargo traffic to Australia and charge excessive freights. The necessity of first shipping all produce for overseas markets to Sydney in order to be transshipped to overseas vessels, helped to make freight and handling charges prohibitive, and the economy of the Territories was throttled until the Navigation Act was removed in 1925. The following year the commonwealth government introduced bounties and preferential duties on certain products from Papua and New Guinea, and the plantations began to recover from the economic depression of the earlier years, but they suffered another reverse in the world economic crisis of 1929 and revived only slowly after 1932 despite encouragement from additional bounties and preferential duties.

In both Territories the chief products were gold and copra (the dried kernel of the coconut palm). By 1936 copra from Papua was being exported to a value of £100,000 a year, and from the Mandate to a value of £761,000; desiccated coconut also brought £42,000 to Papua and £65,000 to the Mandate. Gold mining had grown enormously in importance, Papua exporting £81,000, making gold second only to copra in its list of exports, and the Mandate exporting £,704,498, which represented over 62 per cent of its total exports and enabled it to achieve a favourable trade balance of £1,283,000. Gold mining had flourished in the valley of the Bulolo and at Edie Creek since 1926, and miners had penetrated dense bush and jungle to dig among the almost inaccessible mountains and valleys of the gold-bearing districts. In the early days their food and supplies were carried to the diggings from the port of Salamaua by native bearers, an arduous trek of ten days, but the manifold advantages of air transport were quickly perceived, and all travel to and from the goldfields was eventually by aeroplane: an adventurous service that eliminated the gruelling journey by land but included the hazard of a forced landing and a fortuitous meal for cannibals. In addition to the production of gold, copra and desiccated coconut, trochus shell, coffee, rice and peanuts were cultivated in small quantities, and in Papua copper mines were still operating and a start was made with the production of paper pulp from native grass. The search for oil was conducted by the commonwealth government as a national undertaking with the help of experts from the Anglo-Persian Oil Company, but commercial production remained only a hope for a distant future.

The progress made in the economy, in medical care, in education and in local administration during the Australian rule had no determinable effect on the numbers of the native population before 1940. The separation of womenfolk from the young men who left the villages to work on the plantations may have contributed to a decline in the birth rate, and to this factor must be added an infant mortality rate that was still high, and such lingering practices as the strangling of widows on the death of their husbands or their abstention from food for a long period after. The perpetuation of barbarous practices, however, represented only one of the many enormous obstacles in the way of bringing order, justice and economic advance to Papua and New Guinea. The Territories harboured a multiplicity of languages; external influence had been so weak that cannibalism still existed; only in a few areas was the soil suitable for cultivation; communication was so difficult that the first motor roads were not commenced until 1935; and knowledge of the interior was so thin that the island became an explorers' paradise and a prolific source of travellers' tales.

In these conditions it is impossible not to admire the untiring efforts of Hubert Murray and his devoted staff in Papua and of their counterparts in the Mandate. Murray's death in February 1940 ended an epoch in the Australian administration of Papua and New Guinea, for his nephew's succession was terminated abruptly by the Japanese invasion in the second world war. Massive as were Murray's services to native administration, however, they were nonetheless a pernicious influence on the development of an Australian colonial policy. His benevolent police rule envisaged no future for the natives beyond that of labouring service to their white overseers. His hostility towards the administration in the Mandate became almost an obsession with him, and his dominance was so sure and long that the commonwealth government allowed his paternal gradualism to take the place of the long-term government planning that was patently necessary. Australia's public opinion was so disgracefully uninformed that politicians could not only praise the Australian record in Papua and New Guinea as comparable with that of any other colonial administration, but even suggest that it was a model for others. The tragedy of Australian colonial rule between 1920 and 1940 was that, with the people in the Dominion uninterested in their overseas responsibilities, the government, lacking either experience or incentive, permitted its judgment to be affected by the one man who had devoted all his energies and the best part of his life to the problem. Murray was in control for so long that his shadow fell across the years after his death, and his opposition to the creation of a native intelligentsia was inherited by the commonwealth government and evolved into a concept of uniform development that was to be pursued long after it had been outmoded by changing circumstances. Australia's performance as a colonial power was undermined from the end of the nineteenth century by indifference, both public and governmental, and impaired after the middle of the twentieth century by the refusal to understand the lesson of a world-wide colonial revolution, and by the failure to revise the old colonial policy to meet the new times.

6

Inter-War Problems (1919-1932)

THE PREOCCUPATION of Australia's inter-war governments was not with international covenants or idealistic concepts of civilising backward peoples, but with the immediate and practical problems of reorganising the economy for peace-time and curbing renewed outbursts of industrial discontent. Hughes returned from the Versailles Conference in Europe to be met by a three months' maritime strike repudiating industrial arbitration in favour of direct action. 'I adhere to the policy that a union is not to have arbitration and strikes too', declared Mr Justice Higgins from the Bench, and the commonwealth government dealt firmly with the strikers and prosecuted their secretary. This antagonised militant Labour, but Hughes' popularity was already on the wane, and although his Nationalist party was returned to office in the elections of December 1919, its absolute majority in the House was reduced to a margin of only two after providing the Speaker.

Hughes had been spoilt by the authority he had enjoyed during the war, and he was reluctant to lose the emergency powers invested in the government by the War Precautions Act, the continuance of which in peace-time could perhaps be justified in that Australia was still technically at war with Austria, but this was a juridical nicety that could not be expected to impress the layman. There was resentment and surprise, therefore, when as late as 1920 Hughes defeated a strike of maritime engineers by invoking the Act in order to confiscate the union's funds and prevent their distribution for the maintenance of the strike. Labour's indignation at the frustration of a strike in this fashion was accompanied by an uneasy feeling among other sections of the community that the federal government had acquired powers more extensive than were good for it. Hughes, fundamentally the autocrat, tended increasingly to regard legitimate criticism of his government as something akin to treason. He was absent too often from Parliament and grew indifferent to its feelings and temper; and a bureaucratic trait appeared in his interference with the routine administrative functions of his colleagues. For the moment, however, he remained the undisputed leader of the largest party and turned his undoubted talents to the problems of post-war Australia.

The twin questions of defence and the conduct of external affairs were inextricably interlocked with the question of relations within the British empire. The Imperial Conference that met in 1921 was concerned largely with the future of the Anglo-Japanese alliance. The Canadian prime minister, Arthur Meighen, demanded its termination on the ground that its continuance would offend the United States, while Hughes, speaking on behalf of an Australia for whom Japanese antagonism would be a more direct threat, advocated its renewal in a form inoffensive to the United States. The issue was settled later in the year at the Washington Conference, to which the Imperial Conference had been, in effect, a preliminary, and where, on the insistence of Smuts of South Africa, the Dominions were represented as they had been at Versailles. The Anglo-Japanese alliance was replaced by the Four-Power and Nine-Power treaties to regulate international relations in the Far East. This outcome was well received in Australia, where it was believed that the danger of war in the Pacific had been removed and a peace and security confirmed that would enable Australia to save money on defence and concentrate on economic affairs. 'While the news will be welcomed in all countries', said Hughes, on the Four-Power agreement, 'to Australia it has a special significance. It ensures our security, for it guarantees peace and harmony in the Pacific.' It was a comforting, but in the long run ill-founded, expectation, and the unity of British imperial diplomacy that the Washington Conference had exemplified was soon to undergo a severe test in another quarter.

At the Imperial Conference in 1921, Hughes had emphasised the necessity of making more effective arrangements for 'continuous consultation in all matters of common imperial concern'. Nothing was attempted towards this end, and in September 1922, when the British government was left by France and Italy to protect Constantinople and a neutral zone above the Dardanelles against a Turkish revolutionary army under Mustafa Kemal, it appealed for assistance from the Dominions, none of which had been kept informed of the developments leading up to the crisis. In a cable to the Dominions' governments just before midnight on Friday, September 15, Lloyd George, the British prime minister, outlined the situation and asked whether, in the event of war with Turkey, they would send contingents to help resist an attack on the Straits.

Hughes received the cable late in the afternoon of Sunday, September 17. After consulting such of his ministers as were available, he returned an affirmative answer but requested fuller information; he also declared that Australia regarded her obligations as being limited to the preservation of the freedom of the Dardanelles and not extending to the support of any reckless national ambitions that might be entertained by Greece. Hughes' action in the crisis was generally approved in Australia, but debate in Parliament and the press revealed considerable discontent with an imperial system that evidently excluded the Dominions from active participation in the formulation of foreign policy and exposed them to the risk of war merely out of loyalty to the mother country. The crisis passed within a few days when the Turks agreed to confer with the Allies, but closer co-operation and mutual consultation in determining imperial policy now became a permanent objective of the Australian government, pursued not only by Hughes but also, after his resignation in February 1923, by his successor, S. M. Bruce. 'If we are to take any responsibility for the Empire's foreign policy', said Bruce, in the Australian Parliament, 'there must be a better system so that we may be consulted and have a better opportunity to express the views of the people of this country.' He expressed satisfaction with imperial conferences as a means of harmonising the general outlook of the empire, but called for the creation of improved machinery to facilitate consultation in urgent and specific matters. As a move in this direction he established a liaison officer in London to be in daily communication with the Foreign Office and reporting direct to the Australian prime minister: an initiative that was later copied by governments in the other Dominions.

The downfall of Hughes did not mean a reversal of his policies in the domestic field any more than it did in the imperial. His successor as prime minister had been federal treasurer in his cabinet which lost its absolute majority in the general election of December 1922. Hughes' unpopularity had been growing, and the election campaign was conducted on a highly personal note, some Liberals and the recently formed Country party joining Labour in the cry that 'Hughes must go'. His own Nationalist party, born of a wartime coalition between Liberals and those of the Labour party who followed him on the conscription issue, was not completely united behind him, and included a section inclined to follow W. A. Watt, a former treasurer and acting prime minister who had resigned from the cabinet in 1920 after a quarrel with his leader. Hughes made no attempt to conciliate the County party, which he despised and ridiculed but upon whose support the Nationalist party depended after the 1922 election had eliminated its absolute majority in the House of Representatives. The Nationalists and the Country party were at one in their determination to keep the Labour party out of office, but the formation of a coalition government was delayed by the Country party's refusal to support any administration of which Hughes was the head. During several weeks of negotiation between the parties, Hughes strove to retain his power, but on February 2, 1923, he resigned his office and advised the governor-general to call upon S. M. Bruce, the federal treasurer, to form a government.

Bruce had a comparatively short political career behind him, having not yet been five years in Parliament, but his youthful energy, coolness and business efficiency, combined with the culti-vation of an excellent public personality from which even the wearing of spats could not detract, enabled him to lead a difficult partnership to success in two subsequent general elections. In the cabinet which Bruce formed in February 1923 the Nationalist party filled six places and the Country party five, but it was agreed that, if any matter before it were to be decided on a strict party vote, the decision would be regarded as negative. The separate identities of the two parties were to be preserved and they were to continue to meet in separate party rooms, but they would act together on the floor of Parliament and the administration was to be known as the Bruce-Page Ministry, with the positions of Bruce, the Nationalist leader, and Earle Page, the Country party leader, as nearly equal as possible, although Bruce held the title of prime minister and was, in fact, to become the dominant figure.

The formation of the Bruce-Page administration signified the advent into Australian politics of an important third party, fundamentally conservative, opposed to Labour and holding to policies of a distinctly sectional character. It was composed mostly of people from rural areas, whose interests it was designed to protect, and was known variously as the Country party, the Farmers' party, and the Progressive party. It had been organised towards the end of the war as a protest against the wartime improvisation of control over primary products and the attempts to fix their prices for domestic consumption. It objected to the extension of governmental activity in the economy, to the growth of public expenditure, to increases in taxation, and to tariffs imposed to foster Australian manufactures. It believed that Australian government was influenced unduly by financial, industrial and trade union interests in the cities, and that primary producers had to be organised politically if their problems were to be properly considered in Parliament and rural development preserved and fostered. It was against socialism because it deplored high taxation, rejected urban reforms such as the forty-hour working week or industrial unemployment benefits, and resented government interference except when it assisted country people with conservation projects and guaranteed prices. Although Country party support went predictably to the Nationalists or Liberals in normal circumstances, especially in the early days when its landowning members were nervous of socialist ideas in the Labour party and feared the dissemination of the doctrine of the eight-hour working day among farm labourers, it nevertheless

F

formed at times part of the swinging vote and obliged both the main parties to pay more respect to rural interests. Its flirtation with the Labour party ruined whatever chance the anti-socialist forces had of defeating the Labour government in the Queensland elections of 1923, and precipitated the resignation in 1924 of the premier of Victoria, where the breach with the Nationalists was demonstrated in by-elections in which many Country party followers gave their second preferences to Labour candidates and where at one time the Country party governed with the support of Labour.

The Bruce-Page administration governed during 1924 and 1925 in the shadow of an unmistakable Labour revival coinciding with a threatened rift in the Nationalist and Country party coalition. State elections brought the Labour party into power in South Australia, Western Australia and Tasmania, as well as in Queensland, and even, for a brief period, in Victoria also. It had expelled Communists from its ranks; it was no longer bedevilled by the conscription issue, the memory of which was now becoming blurred; and in 1925 its federal leadership was strengthened by the addition of E. G. Theodore, who abdicated the premiership of Queensland in order to enter national politics. This was the second time a Labour premier of Queensland had transferred from the state to the federal sphere, Theodore's immediate predecessor, T. J. Ryan, having taken a similar step in 1919 and become immediately the deputy leader under Tudor and the spearhead of the opposition's attacks on the government after Hughes returned from the peace conference in Europe.

In 1925 Theodore was widely regarded as the capable helmsman the federal Labour party greatly needed. Son of a Rumanian father and an Irish mother, Theodore had worked as a youth among the goldfields of Western Australia and the lead and silver mines at Broken Hill in New South Wales before moving to Queensland. There he organised the Amalgamated Workers' Association, became president of the Australian Workers' Union, entered the state parliament, and in 1919 became the youngest premier in the British empire. In 1927 he won a New South Wales seat in the federal Parliament, where he was to continue to be a controversial figure, his commanding presence, unruffled dignity, financial skill and forceful fluency adding power to the Labour front bench.

The prime minister, on the other hand, was being hard pressed by industrial disturbances and openly expressed dissension among his supporters. During 1925 a series of seamen's strikes embarrassed the commonwealth's communications with the outside world, and scenes of violence occurred on the waterfronts at Fremantle, Brisbane and Cairns. In a speech on September 9, Bruce said that the troubles in Australia were traceable to the influence of Russian Bolsheviks, and it now became his principal objective to remove the stranglehold which he believed extremists had on trade union machinery. The House of Representatives was dissolved before its full term had run, and the government went into the elections seeking a mandate to deal effectively with outbreaks of industrial unrest. Opening his campaign with a speech at Dandenong in October 1925, Bruce affirmed his government's determination to defeat 'the nefarious designs of the extremists, and', he continued, 'when armed with the necessary mandate of the people, it will take all necessary steps to that end.' The election resulted in a victory for Bruce all the more decisive because the Nationalists gained seats when it had been freely prophesied that the usual reaction against the party in power would bring Labour back after nearly ten years out of office. Nevertheless, at the referendum the following year, Bruce's plan to confer on the federal government new powers to enable it to deal with industrial disturbances was firmly rejected. The Australian public could not be persuaded to consent to alterations in the regulation of industry, a highly technical matter which few laymen could understand, nor could leading lawyers, including the attorneys-general of the commonwealth and Victoria, agree on the likely effects of the proposed changes.

Bruce had a little more success in achieving another objective upon which he also felt strongly, namely, to meet the manpower shortage of the early 1920s by peopling the vast empty spaces that many believed were a standing provocation to densely populated neighbouring countries who might be tempted to violate the White Australia policy. Australia's population at the end of 1922 was

5,634,000—an increase on the year of 124,000, of which 38,000 was due to the excess of arrivals in the country over departures. This represented a substantial improvement in immigration compared with the preceding years. The rate, however, was still below that which had been reached during the last few years before the war, and it was certainly not high enough to satisfy impatient critics, both within the country and without, who deplored the failure to settle the inner continent but usually disregarded the question of the economic viability or attraction of its admittedly extensive but remote and mostly arid soil. Hopes that immigration would be accelerated after the war were raised in 1920 by the difficult trade and employment situation in England, one which recalled the situation following the Napoleonic wars a century before and had led to large-scale emigration.

At a special conference in February 1921, the British government proposed to the Dominions a co-operative policy of imperial development and offered to assist the emigration of approved settlers provided the Dominions undertook to contribute to the same degree. Only South Africa found the scheme unattractive and rejected it, and in April 1922 the Empire Settlement Act was passed authorising the British government to make loans for a period of up to fifteen years to meet half the cost incurred in transporting settlers overseas. The scheme was received enthusiastically in Australia, but its results were disappointing and at no stage during the 1920s was immigration from the British Isles to reach the level achieved in the years immediately before the outbreak of war in 1914. The Act of 1922 was intended to make Britain and the individual Dominions equal partners in developing the empire's resources and distributing its population more equitably. In pursuance of this objective, a £34 million agreement between Britain and Australia in 1925 provided for loans by the two governments to the Australian states over a period of ten years for approved developmental works in return for a guarantee from the states to absorb one assisted migrant for every £75 received.

The following year Bruce established a Development and Migration Commission to manage the related problems of development and immigration and to consider schemes submitted by the states under the £34 million agreement. The Commission was to be a co-ordinating and advisory body of four members, including at least one representative from Labour, and act as liaison machinery between the states and the commonwealth in the investigation of what industries Australia could sensibly establish and what it could not. In introducing the Bill to establish the Commission, the prime minister emphasised that development should come before immigration, and that expansion in the country's absorptive capacity was an essential preliminary to a successful settlement policy. 'We cannot develop unless we have more population, and we cannot absorb more migrants unless we develop', he declared, and reiterated the unfounded, or at least premature, optimism characteristic of Australians in the 1920s: 'Australia is the greatest undeveloped country in the world. Its resources, if brought to full development, would probably solve most of the economic problems that face the world today.' Unfortunately, the Commission was presented with few developmental schemes that were economically sound and only a small portion of the £34 million available to it under the agreement of 1925 was spent. The states experimented with several projects with money borrowed overseas, but with little success. A group settlement scheme in Western Australia which aimed to settle 6,000 farmers at a cost of £6 million in fact settled fewer than 2,000 at a cost of £9 million; the failure of a land settlement scheme in Victoria obliged the state government to pay out £400,000 in compensation; and a proposal to settle 6,000 farmers in New South Wales petered out after establishing only thirty-eight. The immigration program brought a net increase of some 250,000 to the commonwealth's population during the 1920s: about half the number that had been hoped and planned for; in that time twice as many Britons migrated to the Greater London area than to Australia, and in the 1930s the migration between Britain and Australia was even to go into reverse.

There was never any difference of opinion in Australia on the policy of keeping the population white and ensuring an immigration predominantly of British stock. Australians, indeed, regarded themselves as a people not only independent and possessing distinctive national traditions, but also essentially British, combining a youthful and aggressive national sentiment with a racial pride and sense of belonging to a world-wide Anglo-Saxon community. Obvious ties with the mother country of ancestry and family, language, literary heritage, economic and strategic interest, constitutional government, and common outlook on fundamental issues made Australians the patriots of two lands: the predominantly British character of their population and the imperial connection with the United Kingdom being as precious to them as the individual Australian ethos and their independence of external interference.

This dual loyalty was illustrated in the Australian government's attitude towards the Balfour Report which emanated from the Imperial Conference of 1926 and was to culminate in the Statute of Westminster in 1931. The Balfour Committee, appointed by the Imperial Conference of 1926 to study the question of Dominion status and imperial relations, reported that the British empire, considered as a whole, defied classification and bore no resemblance to any other known political organisation, and that nothing would be gained by attempting to lay down a constitution for it. Nevertheless, in a famous passage that has been well described as reading like a clause from the Athanasian Creed, an attempt was made to define the relationship of the Dominions and the mother country: 'They are autonomous communities within the British Empire, equal in status, in no way subordinate one to another in any aspect of their domestic or external affairs, though united by a common allegiance to the Crown, and freely associated as members of the British Commonwealth of Nations.' It was not certain what this declaration meant and its full implications were not immediately recognised; but conferences in 1929 and 1930 endeavoured to clarify obscure points, and in 1931 the Statute of Westminster gave some legal definition to the changes that had been taking place in the imperial relationship. It gave the Dominions power to repeal or amend United Kingdom legislation applying to them, and to make laws having extra-territorial application; it also declared that no future Act of the British Parliament should extend to any of the Dominions unless the Act stated they had requested and agreed that it should do so. The unqualified extension of these provisions of the Statute might

86

have conferred on the Australian Parliament a power to amend the Commonwealth of Australia Constitution Act of 1900 otherwise than in accordance with the procedure set down in section 128 of the constitution, with its safeguards for the rights of the states. At the request of the commonwealth government, therefore, it was stipulated that these provisions should not apply to Australia unless adopted by the federal Parliament, and that the power to legislate should not include the power of amending the constitution or the Constitution Act of the Commonwealth of Australia 'otherwise than in accordance with the law existing before the commencement of this Act'.* In 1936 and 1937 Bills introduced in the commonwealth Parliament to adopt those sections of the Statute inapplicable to Australia unless adopted were not given a second reading, and it was 1942 before the requisite legislation was passed, its provisions being made retroactive to September 3, 1939.

Australia's nationhood found its permanent expression in the federal capital that was being built with incredible slowness at the foot of the Australian Alps in New South Wales. It was in 1912 that the commonwealth government had awarded the first prize for a design of the intended city to an American landscape architect, Walter Burley Griffin, but the intervention of the war and differences between ministers and departmental officials delayed the construction of a national capital which had been originally conceived at the time of federation but had aroused little enthusiasm among Australians since. However, on May 9, 1927, the Duke of York, later King George VI, opened in Canberra the new provisional building of the commonwealth Parliament: a large white structure, architecturally simple, but dignified and pleasant, and containing a replica of the Speaker's chair in the House of Commons at Westminster—a reminder of the affinities and interlocking histories of the mother country and the Dominion. The Australian Capital Territory comprised some 900 square miles of mountainous, well-watered country, much of it previously devoted to grazing, and the planners hoped that the city laid out within it would become a garden city. Canberra was eventually to become just that: beautiful

* There were provisos also for Canada, New Zealand and Newfoundland.

in its dispersed symmetry and the shifting colours of its hills, a microcosm of Australia itself in its near-excellence and in its lonely, almost unreal, defiance of the blank horizons and the vast spaces beyond them.

Canberra, indeed, was one symbol of a national consciousness that took pride in the growing evidence of Australian accomplishment. This appeared, for example, in much of the poetry of the period, not only in that which expressed an intense love of the Australian soil and confidence in its future, such as Dorothea Mackellar's *My Country*, but also in that which strove for a maturer idiom that could be appreciated more for real merit and less for the mere evocation of patriotic emotions. The verse of Hugh McCrae, Mary Gilmore, Vance and Nettie Palmer, and Christopher Brennan testified to the quest by a dedicated minority for a culture that should be distinctive and no longer palpably derivative. It was not a particularly creative period in Australian cultural history, but standards were beginning to improve. Arthur Streeton led the landscape painters in oils, and Max Meldrum in Melbourne and George Lambert in Sydney were gaining recognition. After a long struggle the Sydney Symphony Orchestra was established, and the universities in Sydney, Melbourne and Adelaide had their conservatoria of music. Percy Grainger became the best-known of Australian pianists and composers, and Florence Austral and Frederic Collier sang at Covent Garden, though Nellie Melba remained Australia's greatest and sweetest contribution to opera.

Although the general level of imaginative work remained low, and higher aspirations seldom went beyond the now traditional contentment with something less than excellent, a small coterie of cultivated persons laboured to add a civilising balance to an excessively materialist society and occasionally succeeded in rising above the mediocre average so entrenched in the national affection. In this task the new federal capital in Canberra was to play its part, for around the new Parliament House were to grow not only dull suburban bungalows and civic and governmental buildings, but also a national university devoted primarily to research, laboratories of the Commonwealth Scientific and Industrial Research Organisation, a national observatory, and the headquarters of the

Australian Academy of Science founded in 1954 to promote scientific knowledge.

The Parliament that met for the first time in Canberra in May 1927 was aware that the most pressing problems before it would be financial and economic. The banks were obliged to restrict credit, for deposits were not increasing at a satisfactory rate and gold was leaving the country. The immigration schemes were not achieving the success anticipated of them; unemployment was beginning to spread; and the commonwealth budget of 1928 revealed a deficit of over £2,600,000, which the federal treasurer, Earle Page, proposed to place in suspense and liquidate out of the surpluses of future years: a policy that made political, if not economic, sense with a general election in the offing.

The need to end the practice of state and federal governments' acting independently and sometimes competitively in the loan market had become urgent by 1927, and in June and July of that year a conference between Bruce and the state premiers reached a financial agreement that terminated a long-standing controversy. Under the terms of the constitution, the commonwealth had been required to return to the states three quarters of the customs revenue, but this had been altered to a fixed annual grant of twenty-five shillings per head of population in each state. This system had been maintained throughout the war, when the commonwealth introduced an income tax in addition to that levied by the states, and had continued on through years of frictional debate until the agreement of 1927, which, it was hoped, by ending competition between the various Australian governments in the loan market, would enable them to secure better terms. All future borrowings were to be supervised by the Loan Council, which had been created in 1924 and included representatives from all the states and the commonwealth, although voting on it was weighted in the commonwealth's favour. The commonwealth took over the public debts of the states as at July 1, 1929, and agreed to contribute towards the interest on them the equivalent of the capitation payments for the year 1926–7, leaving the states to find the balance. In addition, a sinking fund at the rate of three eighths per cent was established on the net amount of the existing state debts in order to provide for their extinction in fifty-eight years, the commonwealth contributing one eighth per cent annually and the states making up the balance. To provide for new loans contracted in the future, a sinking fund at the rate of one half per cent was set up, the commonwealth and the states contributing from revenue equal shares for a period of fifty-three years from the date of raising the loans. The agreement signified a severe blow to the rights of the states, for the commonwealth had, in effect, trimmed their financial independence, but it meant also a great measure of much needed discipline in what had been a confusing federal financial system.

After an eventful year in 1927, Bruce's government enjoyed few successes. It was returned to power for the third time at the election of November 1928, but the Nationalist party's majority was reduced and its continuance in office made dependent on the support of the Country party, its coalition partner. Moreover, there were signs of a cleavage within the Nationalist party itself over what the relationship with the Country party should be, some members urging closer association and some preferring to sever what they regarded as a mistaken and entangling alliance. Bruce had been in power a comparatively long time and among his backbenchers were several disgruntled at his failure to recognise their talents. Moreover, the irrepressible Hughes had been antagonised by the decision to dispose of the Commonwealth Shipping Line that he had brought into being when prime minister in 1916. The line had lifted Australian wheat and picked up return cargoes, but it ran at a loss for several years, until in 1927 the government accepted the recommendation of the Public Accounts Committee that the remaining ships be sold.

Industrial unrest added to Bruce's troubles, and it was the attempt to deal firmly with the unions that brought his administration to defeat within eleven months of its electoral victory of 1928. His trade union opponents were now better organised than they had ever been, having accomplished at a congress in Melbourne in May 1927 the dream of one big union that had been eluding them since the end of the nineteenth century. The achievement, however, was not complete, for the sectional rivalries and struggle for control between the most powerful unions which had for so long impeded the movement towards greater cohesion were not entirely overcome, and the Australian Workers' Union, the largest in the country, remained aloof. The Australian Council of Trade Unions established in 1927 was a federal organisation, its executive handling disputes and industrial matters of an interstate character that affected the trade union movement as a whole.

Of central concern to the unions was the process of industrial arbitration, and it was Bruce's undoing that he offended them on this very issue. The constitution had preserved for the states their courts of compulsory arbitration and the right of determining conditions of industrial employment, limiting the commonwealth to the arbitration of disputes that extended beyond the boundaries of a single state. It had soon become evident that there were few industries which did not overlap state borders, so that employers and workers generally had a choice between the state and the federal courts, and the unions naturally availed themselves of the court from which they anticipated most sympathetic consideration, sometimes going backwards and forwards between the state and federal courts and abiding by the award they preferred, or even blending selected portions of the various awards into a hybrid award of their own concoction. The commonwealth government had made several attempts to revise this confusing system, but on each occasion the necessary constitutional amendment had been rejected in a referendum. After Bruce failed to carry an amendment in 1926, it had become abundantly clear that opinions differed almost irreconcilably on what the true functions of the arbitration system should be. Employers saw in the courts a means of ending strikes and consequently advocated heavy penalties for defiance of court awards, whereas Labour saw in the courts an alternative weapon to the strike in the struggle to improve working conditions, but with the strike remaining as the ultimate sanction. Arbitration awards to the Timber Workers' Union and the Waterside Workers in 1928 resulted in strikes, and in the following year coalowners of northern New South Wales defied an award and locked out employees in order to reduce wages.

The government, maintaining that the two-fold jurisdiction of the commonwealth and the states was detrimental to the country's welfare, decided that, since the states were not prepared to surrender their rights in the matter, the commonwealth should re-nounce its rights, abolish the federal court except in regard to the maritime industries, and return the main business of arbitration to the states. In September 1929 in the House of Representatives, Bruce carried the second reading of his Bill to abolish the Federal Arbitration Court, only to be thwarted in committee by an amend-ment, moved by Hughes and carried by a majority of one, to the effect that the Bill should stay in abeyance until the people had been consulted. Bruce thereupon applied for a dissolution of the lower House and in the ensuing election of October 1929 was decisively defeated. The Nationalist party, which Bruce had led for over six years, was reduced from twenty-nine seats to fourteen, Bruce himself failing to secure re-election. The Country party, its coalition partner, lost three of its thirteen seats, while the Labour party, which had campaigned in defence of the existing arbitration system, gained fifteen seats and the largest majority since federation.

The Labour party leader and new prime minister was James Henry Scullin, a slightly built, cautious, sober man of moderate views, lacking ministerial experience but respected on all sides. He had been a small grocer and editor of a newspaper in Ballarat before taking to politics. His studious, deeply religious outlook, austere way of life, modesty and gentleness matched ill the very heavy burden and worries that were to fall upon his shoulders. The new treasurer, E. G. Theodore, was commonly regarded as the driving force in the cabinet, though much was expected also of J. A. Lyons, the postmaster-general and formerly premier of Tas-mania.

But before long the ministry was to be torn by internal dis-sension as the effects of a world-wide economic depression spread to Australia. The Scullin government was confronted not only with a crisis that baffled economists and financiers everywhere but also with a hostile Senate, where, in contrast to its large majority in the House of Representatives, the Labour party held only seven of the thirty-six seats, rendering the government powerless to put several of its proposals into effect unless it decided on a double dissolution, and this it would not do after having already fought two elections within twelve months. Furthermore, it was embarrassing for the Labour party to come to power at this juncture, for during its long period in opposition it had made promises that could not now be kept, and was obliged in office to assume responsibility for deflation, retrenchment and a reduction in wages and the standard of living. It was a measure of Scullin's courage that he frankly repudiated pledges given in better times and in vastly different circumstances.

Throughout 1929 and 1930, world prices of Australia's export commodities fell, the sources of its overseas capital dried up, and pressure on its overseas exchange reserves increased to a degree that was to lead, at the end of 1931, to a devaluation of the Australian pound in terms of sterling. Although Australia expanded its production of wheat, butter, meat and sugar between 1930 and 1932 and the volume of exports grew, their value was reduced to below the level obtaining before the depression by the decline in world prices. Drastic cuts were made in imports by means of higher tariffs and complete prohibitions, but little could apparently be done to check the growth of unemployment and the serious decrease in government revenue. In June 1930 Sir Otto Niemeyer of the Bank of England visited Australia to investigate the economic problems, and in August he attended a financial conference of federal and state ministers in Melbourne. Niemeyer's visit was viewed in a sinister light by some Labour parliamentarians who were now in revolt against the government's policy, and their suspicions were accentuated by his unpalatable report. Niemeyer maintained that the Australian policy of tariff protection and heavy external borrowing was an attempt to support a standard of living higher than was justified by economic conditions abroad and production at home.

By the middle of 1930, the government was harassed by political difficulties arising out of its management of the economic crisis. In New South Wales J. T. Lang, the leader of the state Labour party, a big man with a snarling voice who dominated the Labour movement in the state for a decade or more, fought and won an election on a platform opposing both retrenchment and the agreement to balance their budgets which the premiers had reached at the Melbourne conference in August. The effect of Lang's election was not only a sharp drop in Australian securities on the London stock exchange but also a split in the federal Labour party, where support was spreading for Lang's policy of repudiating or postponing debt payments. During Scullin's absence at an Imperial Conference in London, the federal Labour party resolved that holders of bonds in a maturing loan should be compelled to retain their securities for a further twelve months, but postponed action until after Scullin had returned from abroad. Although Lang's plan was widely criticised by conservatives as unethical, it succeeded in drawing attention to the need for an equality of sacrifice from the community in the task of reducing costs and balancing budgets and for ensuring that bondholders' interest as well as workers' wages were affected.

When Scullin returned to Australia, his parliamentary following was already divided, and soon there was outright defection. One of his first moves was to restore Theodore to the federal treasury from which he had resigned after a royal commission in 1930 found that, while premier of Queensland in 1919, he had conspired to defraud the government of £30,000. Theodore did everything legally possible publicly to refute this charge, but his reinstatement in the cabinet was the signal for the disruption of the federal Labour party. Five New South Wales members left and formed themselves into a Lang group and five others followed J. A. Lyons, who resigned from the ministry, and joined the opposition. Not for the first time, changing sides at the critical moment brought its reward to the renegade in Australian politics, in whose atmosphere principle and loyalty count for less than self-aggrandisement. When the government was obliged to risk an election at the close of 1931 it was faced by a consolidated opposition led by Lyons and composed of his small ex-Labour following and the former Nationalists, all of whom now coalesced under a new label and called themselves the 'United Australia Party'. In the polling in December 1931, the United Australia party swept the crippled Labour government out of office making large electoral gains everywhere except in Queensland, and Scullin was replaced as prime minister by his former lieutenant. Inside a few months, with an act of poetic justice, the militant Lang in New South Wales contrived his own downfall as state premier.

94

Lang's tenure of office had been a particularly stormy one. He attempted to destroy the state's Legislative Council by requesting the governor to appoint sufficient new members of the right persuasion to ensure assent to its own abolition, but was foiled by the refusal of the additional nominees to end their role as legislators although promised retention of the privilege of free transport in the state if they complied. Lang further outraged conservative interests by what they regarded as his extreme measures and evident hostility towards banks, insurance companies and the business world in general, and some of the wealthy classes organised themselves for their own defence.

Their most dramatic success was the deflation of the premier's glory at the opening of Sydney's harbour bridge in March 1932. The single-arch bridge was not only a magnificent adornment to a lovely harbour comparable with that of San Francisco, Rio de Janeiro or Hong Kong, but also a practical necessity, for the fleet of ferry steamers was incapable of carrying the rapidly increasing traffic between Sydney and the thickly populated suburbs on the northern side of the harbour. Although it had been commenced under a previous state administration, Lang was naturally gratified that it should have been completed under his. In the ceremony of cutting the ribbon across the southern end of the bridge, however, Lang was forestalled by a military officer who galloped in front of him, severed the ribbon with his sword, and declared the bridge open. The interloper was charged with offensive behaviour, with threatening a police officer, and with 'maliciously damaging a ribbon worth two pounds'. Newspapers in the state were asked to omit the incident from their columns, and cinemas were prohibited from exhibiting a film of it.

The final drama of Lang's premiership came a few weeks later when he defied federal legislation ordering the banks to pay over to the commonwealth money held on state account. The governor, Sir Philip Game, warned Lang that he was defying commonwealth law and gave him the opportunity to alter his stand and comply with the law. When Lang refused, Game dismissed him from office and called on the leader of the opposition to form a ministry pending a general election. The constitutional propriety of the governor's action was open to question, and if Lang had won the

95

ensuing election a highly embarrassing predicament might have arisen, but, as was expected, he was overwhelmingly defeated, his representation being more than halved. By the end of 1932 only one Labour government remained of the six which had held office in the seven state parliaments two years before.

By this time there were signs of a recovery from the troubles of the depression, and in the slow economic revival that now began to take place the imperial preference provided for at the Ottawa Conference of 1932 was a contributing factor. Bruce headed the Australian delegation to the conference, where the conflicting aims of Britain and the Dominions were soon apparent, and it was only after hard bargaining that agreements were reached. The essence of the agreements was the reciprocal exchange of preferences either through the imposition of higher duties on foreign goods, or by a lowering of rates on imperial goods, or by a combination of the two: the overall effect being the maintenance by Britain and the Dominions of high protection against the foreigner and of moderate protection between themselves. The system agreed upon at Ottawa was to be the subject of incessant discussion and repeated modification during the succeeding years, and at an Imperial Conference in 1937 the Dominions emphasised the need to co-operate with other nations in removing obstacles to the free flow of trade. According to the report of the 1937 conference, the outstanding feature of the discussion on general economic questions 'was the emphatic desire expressed by the representatives of every part of the British Commonwealth that all practicable steps should be taken to secure the stimulation of international trade. It was recognised that in the last resort the prosperity of the countries of the Commonwealth depends on that of the world as a whole, and that a healthy growth of international trade, accompanied by an improvement in the general standard of living, is an essential step to political appeasement.' The world economic crisis of the early 1930s had now been overtaken by a political crisis of such proportions that it threatened the whole fabric of international security.

7

The Breakdown of International Security (1932-1939)

IN 1931, when Australia and most countries of the world were grappling with the economic crisis, Japan attacked Manchuria, successfully defied the League of Nations, and exposed deficiencies in the machinery of international security that it and other nations were to exploit with devastating consequences in the next decade. For Australians a long-standing apprehension was now given substance, and whatever relief they felt that Japanese expansionism had found its first major outlet elsewhere in the 1930s, they were to be concerned with national defence and external problems to an extent greater than ever before in peace-time. It was to be the task of the new ministry that took office in January 1932 under J. A. Lyons to guide Australia out of the economic depression and prepare the country for the renewed world war towards which the events of the period were leading.

Joseph Aloysius Lyons possessed few of the outstanding qualities that would normally be expected of a prime minister. A Tasmanian by birth and upbringing, he had been state premier between 1923 and 1928 and a member of Scullin's Labour cabinet after his entry into federal politics in 1929. His desertion of the Labour government at a time of crisis and reappearance in the front rank of the opposition perhaps demonstrated, among other things, an acute appreciation of where the interests of his own career truly lay. His elevation to the leadership of the conservative, landed and capitalist influences to which he had hitherto been opposed was a tribute, not to an aggressive temperament such as that of Hughes, nor to any gifts of oratory, intellect or wit, for he was lacking in all

G

these things, but to his sincerity, patriotism, tact, political experience and sheer plainness, which won the confidence both of the country and of his amorphous party. Lyons failed, however, to secure the co-operation of the Country party because it insisted that the ministry for Trade and Customs should be given to one of its members as a pledge that the government would lower the tariff: an attempt at dictation by a minority that Lyons was able to refuse on account of the absolute majority which the United Australia party at this time enjoyed.

Nevertheless, in February 1932 the minister for Trade and Customs tabled a new tariff schedule that was commonly recognised as the first move in a steady downward revision. It cancelled most of the prohibitions and special duties imposed by the Scullin administration and reduced the duties on a number of items that in normal times covered a trade amounting to over £6 million. The budget of October 1933 provided for further reductions in the protective tariff to the benefit of British and Canadian exporters and the satisfaction of the Country party and Australian primary producers. Moreover, indications of recovery from the depression which had been evident before the Lyons ministry came to power were being realised by 1933, when the financial year closed with a surplus of £3½ million instead of an estimated deficit of £1¼ million.* There had been a sustained rise in wool prices and Australian industrial stocks had appreciated about 30 per cent over their value the previous year. In the budget, therefore, the government was able to remit both direct and indirect taxation on a scale which it was hoped would stimulate employment, lighten the burden on industry and reduce the cost of living. The state governments also attempted to stir the economy. Victoria, for example, made use in 1934 of its centenary celebrations in order to attract visitors and improve business, notwithstanding the embarrassment of a tramway strike in Melbourne at the very moment of the Duke of Gloucester's ceremonial arrival. The poorer states—Western Australia, South Australia and Tas-

* From here on currency figures quoted are in Australian pounds except where otherwise stated. The Australian pound had been identical to the pound sterling until depreciation during the depression led, on December 3, 1931, to its stabilisation at the rate of £125 Australian to £100 sterling.

mania—were helped by the establishment of the Commonwealth Grants Commission which examined the financial needs and claims of any state and made recommendations on them to the federal government.

With the process of recovery considerably advanced, the nation's credit at a high level, unemployment declining, and interest rates greatly reduced, by 1934 circumstances appeared to the government to be favourable for an election. Accordingly Parliament was dissolved some six months earlier than was strictly necessary. The campaign revolved naturally around economic issues, the United Australia party's propaganda claiming for Australia 'the most spectacular economic recovery the world has known', and the prime minister attributing to his own wise management Australia's emergence from 'the valley of gloom' and approach towards 'the sunshine of prosperity'. The government's admiring opinion of its own achievements did not unduly impress the electors, who, though returning the ministry to office in the September election, deprived it of its absolute majority, thereby compelling it to seek a renewed understanding with the Country party. After their first negotiations had failed, the United Australia party and the Country party succeeded on a second attempt in forming a composite ministry in which the Country party held four places and its leader, Earle Page, was deputy leader of the government and acting prime minister whenever Lyons was absent. Lyons regarded the election result as an endorsement of his government's economic policies, although the improvement in the economy of which he boasted was less than had been confidently predicted in the Premiers' Plan of 1931. Moreover, the birth rate was declining, the immigration program had been discarded, and social welfare was still very much neglected.

It was not purely on economic matters, however, that the policy of the government now differed in important respects from that of the Labour opposition. Although the election of 1934 revolved almost entirely around economic issues, the next election three years later was to be fought largely on the urgent problem of national security, defence and rearmament. The Lyons government kept to the traditional reliance on the Royal Navy as the principal arm in the country's protection, and therefore pursued a policy of associating Australia as effectively as possible with the general scheme of imperial defence.

In a speech in Sydney in September 1933, the minister for Defence, Senator G. F. Pearce, emphasised that Australian defence would be chiefly naval and would dovetail with Imperial policy. 'To give effect to this policy', he said, 'Australia's primary aim should be the provision of an efficient squadron of ships able to co-operate efficiently with the Royal Navy.' Both Pearce and his successor, Archdale Parkhill, argued that participation in the naval defence of the empire was the best means of ensuring Australia's own security, for an attack on Australia's trade was more likely than an attack on Australia itself. 'If Australia's markets were closed', declared Pearce, 'and her imports and exports stopped by enemy action, she could be forced to sue for peace without a single enemy soldier coming within sight of her shores.' There was as yet no strong public feeling on defence, except perhaps an understandable belief that money should be saved on it if possible, but in October 1933 the government announced an increase of over £1 million in defence expenditure and a three-year program of expansion in the defence services was inaugurated. For its part, the Labour opposition was beginning to question the value of increased expenditures on a navy whose use would necessarily be beyond the borders of Australia, and to lay more stress instead on home defence by air power. This concept was only in its formative stages in 1933, but during the next four years it developed into a well-considered and logical policy which the government could not entirely ignore.

Dependence on the United Kingdom for defence meant almost inevitably following the United Kingdom's lead in foreign policy. The department of External Affairs, which was expanded and reorganised in 1935, continued to rely heavily on the Foreign Office in London for information and guidance, and the few debates on international issues in the federal Parliament tended to be miniature reproductions of the debates at Westminster. When Italy revealed its designs on Abyssinia in 1935, the commonwealth government warmly supported Britain's attempts to secure a settlement of the dispute without recourse to war, being anxious lest the mother country should become involved in a European conflict that might encourage Japan to unleash its ambitions in the western Pacific and so endanger an Australia denuded of British protection. The Australian delegate at Geneva was instructed to co-operate closely with Britain in the maintenance of League of Nations principles, and Lyons told the House of Representatives that he had assured the British government that, in its policy of doing everything possible to avoid another European war, Australia would support Britain 'up to the hilt'. Australia joined with the League and the rest of the British Commonwealth in the imposition of economic sanctions against Italy, though the Bill to implement the policy was strenuously opposed in Parliament by the opposition. The Labour party denounced Italy's attitude and denied charges of isolationism, but criticised the use of sanctions as liable to drag Australia into war on an issue that was not its concern, while the Lang extremist group led by J. A. Beasley, which had fewer inhibitions, urged the government to withdraw from the League and adhere to a policy of complete neutrality. The opposition failed to shake the government's determination to follow the United Kingdom in support of collective security. But the Italian conquest of Abyssinia destroyed what remaining confidence Australia had in the efficacy of the League of Nations and accentuated Australian doubts about the degree of protection the Royal Navy would be able to afford the Dominion if a European war cut the Mediterranean communication with the Pacific and kept all Britain's might fully occupied around its own shores. Australia was now made more than ever conscious of the importance to its security of events in Europe, and consequently it was its policy both to assist any moves to keep the peace in Europe and also to remain on good terms with Japan, whose militaristic bent had already been demonstrated.

A friendly Japan was necessary for commercial as well as security reasons. Australia's recovery from the depression in the early 1930s had been due partly to the increase in Japanese purchases of wool and wheat at the time when Australia needed additional markets for its exports. By 1935 Japan had become second only to the United Kingdom as a customer for Australian wool, and, although there was an increase in the importation of cheap Japanese textiles, the balance of trade between the two countries was very much in favour of Australia. In April 1934 the minister for External Affairs led an Australian mission to the Pacific countries in an attempt to improve relations, and in 1935 discussions were held with Japan in order to obtain greater economic co-operation.

Then suddenly, on May 22, 1936, the government changed its tune and introduced new tariffs and an import licensing system with the object of stimulating trade with the United Kingdom and of restricting imports from Japan and the United States. The revision of the cotton duties, for example, was intended to limit the value of the textiles being bought from Japan and to promote the importation of textiles from Lancashire by about another £1 million a year. The new trade diversion policy was a conscious assertion of the principle of preference and was naturally popular in Lancashire, but it provoked retaliation from Japan, which cut its purchases of wool, with the result that trade between the two countries was drastically reduced. The Australian government made little attempt to anticipate the likely consequences of its action on the attitude of Japan, and although a new agreement in December 1936 brought the trade war to an end, not only had Japan been antagonised but the evidence of 1936 helped to convince its leaders of the unreliability of foreign sources of supply and of the need to become economically self-sufficient.

Having damaged commercial relations with Japan in 1936, the government adopted a conciliatory approach during the following year in the hope of recovering some of the loss sustained by Australian exporters, so that when the Japanese invaded China in July 1937, the government was determined not to criticise Japan more than was strictly necessary. Furthermore, it would not condone unofficial demonstrations of disapproval, and in 1938 successfully broke the boycotts by Australian waterside workers of ships loading scrap metal for Japan. The waterside workers acquired public sympathy by their stand, but the government declared the Australian economy would be endangered by the serious interference with Asian trade which the boycotts would provoke. It put forward the usual argument in such cases that it was the duty of the government, not of private citizens, to decide what the national reaction to Japanese aggression should be. 'The question is not whether the waterside workers are right or wrong in their views on what the international policy of Australia should be', said Menzies, the attorney-general; 'it is whether that policy is to be determined by the duly constituted government of the country or by some industrial section.' The delayed ships sailed with their cargoes to Japan and the government maintained its detached policy towards the Sino-Japanese conflict.

While preserving a cordial front to Japan, the government was under no illusions about the danger from Japanese militarism. The need for improved local defence was recognised and closer co-operation with the United Kingdom seemed more essential than ever, especially as little could be expected of America, where isolationist sentiments still prevailed. At the Imperial Conference in London in 1937, Lyons pointed out that the experience of recent years had shown the impracticability of achieving the ideas embodied in the League of Nations Covenant, and that therefore the Australian government believed 'an examination of the basis of British Commonwealth foreign policy and of the position of the League should be one of the major considerations of this conference with a view to the formulation of a consistent and unified Empire policy'. The discussions at the conference confirmed the Australian government in its attitude towards defence and world problems in the succeeding two years, particularly the conference's profession of faith in the virtues of international appeasement and its assumption that in the event of war there would be co-operation between Britain and the Dominions.

The problem of defence became the dominant issue in the general election of October 1937, when John Curtin, the Labour party leader, accused Lyons of having entered into an engagement while in London to introduce conscription if war came: a charge that was hotly denied. The campaign was conducted in a tense atmosphere generated by the Japanese attack on China, and each party undertook to provide handsomely for Australian defence. The government offered no departure from established policy, and in his speech of September 28, the prime minister reiterated the belief that 'the Australian people stand for Empire co-operation; that they prefer to a policy of isolation the benefits of their traditional association with Britain and the assurance that in the event of aggression her strength is ours'. The government proposed to increase the air force and provide what it estimated to be adequate defences for the coast, but it would fit these local undertakings into the wider schemes of imperial defence and would co-operate with Britain and the other Dominions in keeping open the long sea communications vital to Australia's existence.

The Labour party questioned the wisdom of this conventional trust in British naval power, arguing that in a world war England would be unable, at least for a time, effectively to help Australia, and that therefore the main requirement of a sound defence policy was not the maintenance of a navy, whose immediate value to Australian defence would be slight, but the construction of an air force capable of repelling any attempt to invade Australian soil. Labour's policy was carefully thought out and for over a year had been convincingly expounded by Curtin. In November 1936 he had claimed in a parliamentary debate that dependence 'upon the competence, let alone the readiness, of British statesmen to send forces to our aid is too dangerous a hazard upon which to found Australia's defence policy'. This was the basis of the program that he and the Labour opposition put to the country in the election campaign of 1937, after three years of recurring international crises during which the capacity of the British fleet to protect interests in both Europe and the Pacific if war had come had not by any calculation been certain.

Logical as Labour's defence platform appeared to be, however, it was not such as to commend itself to the Australian electorate. There was disagreement about it in the ranks of the Labour movement itself, and although the discordant Lang faction had been reabsorbed, the party failed to win the public support it had confidently predicted. Lyons became the first Australian prime minister to survive three general elections and remain in office. Nevertheless, the government's majority was reduced, the ministers for Defence and External Affairs being significantly among those who lost their seats. Although the result was interpreted as an endorsement of the government's defence policy, a reshuffled ministry modified the rearmament program to bring it more into accord with the views enunciated by the opposition.

As Australia prepared for the possibility of a renewed world conflict, the country continued to recover from the earlier economic crisis. In spite of the differences with Japan in 1936, Australia's trade had rallied from the depression by the end of 1937. There was a considerable growth of manufacturing, but primary products still made up over 90 per cent of the nation's exports. The wool industry remained the basis of the economy, boasting over 100 million head of sheep, half of them in New South Wales. The merino retained its primacy, but Corriedale and Polwarth flocks were gradually replacing finer woolled sheep in areas where rainfall was high. During the depression, wool-growers had been obliged to accept prices below the cost of production, but the policy of disposing of the entire output within each season had prevented the embarrassment of stocks' accumulating.

Wheat cultivation was not so successful. Its acreage declined, production fluctuated, and prices were unusually low; and both the commonwealth and state governments were called on to give the wheat-growers financial assistance. A commonwealth royal commission in 1934 described the main problems of the wheat industry as the uncertainty of overseas prices, the high cost of production, and inadequate farming methods that in some cases had damaged soil fertility and caused declining yields. Nearly all harvesting was now done by machinery, a great advantage to an industry in which it was essential to maintain a low ratio of labour to acreage, but the horse remained the principal source of power, tractors being used only in districts where speed was essential to control weeds and gather the crops in time.

The most conspicuous economic development, however, was in secondary industry, especially in New South Wales and Victoria which between them possessed over 70 per cent of Australia's factories, and more specifically in the four main centres at Melbourne, Sydney, Newcastle and Port Kembla, the last two producing practically the whole of Australia's steel output. A motor industry had appeared in Victoria, where as early as 1925 the Ford Company of Canada had erected a large assembly plant at Geelong, and in 1936 General Motors Holden Limited opened a factory at Fishermen's Bend and became the largest motor manufacturing concern in Australia. In South Australia after the depression the state government had embarked upon an ambitious program to expand industry, reducing company tax and offering special credit facilities in order to encourage the investment of private capital. In 1937 over half a million people were employed in Australian factories, and since 1932 some £14 million had been invested in secondary industry. The total value of Australian manufactures was now rapidly overhauling the total value of agricultural, pastoral and other rural production.

The population of Australia by 1938 was 6,900,000, and more than ever before the vast majority clustered in the capital cities, whose attraction continued to deprive rural areas of the increase that government policies intended. People were beginning to live in houses which no longer deliberately excluded the sun, and the appearance of garages alongside was evidence of prosperity, or, where the garage was empty (as it often was), of the hope of affluence to come. Most city houses were connected with water mains and sewers, and possessed gas and electricity. The radio had become an almost universal adjunct, and national and commercial stations brought entertainment, information and education to communities in every part of the continent. Air transport had improved with the help of government grants, and in 1939 there were twelve subsidised services operating under contracts with the Civil Aviation department. More railways had been constructed, and even in the rural areas there were few farmers who had a longer haul than ten miles to the nearest siding. Each state possessed its university, each Education department tried to provide schooling in remote inland places where the assemblage of a dozen pupils was often difficult, and an elaborate system of teaching by correspondence was being devised for those beyond the reach of a proper school. Nevertheless, expenditure on education was below that of most western countries, and financial difficulties prevented a more progressive educational policy and seriously handicapped the universities in their struggle to meet the growing requirements of modern tertiary education.

Generally, the state governments adopted cautious policies during the 1930s, especially in New South Wales, where, after the downfall of Lang, the anti-Labour forces held office for nine negative years, winning successive elections by the grace of a divided opposition. The most cautious policy of all, however, was that of the commonwealth towards the neglected Northern Territory, whose aboriginal population had declined to about 20,000 and whose total number of settlers was less than 5,000. The inauguration in 1934 of the first regular air service between England and Australia led to Darwin's becoming an important air base and port of entry, but the progress of the Northern Territory was appallingly slow, its arid isolation deterring the responsible authorities in Canberra from effective action. Dissatisfaction with its progress caused the appointment in March 1937 of a committee to investigate methods of developing and utilising its resources, but the committee's report in October was not acted upon. The federal government was then too preoccupied with defence and a worsening international situation that seemed likely to plunge the world, including Australia, into another war more terrible even than the last.

The Australian government preserved its faith in appeasement throughout 1938 and fully supported, indeed encouraged, the efforts of the British prime minister, Neville Chamberlain, to placate Germany even at the price of conceding a great part of Hitler's demands on Czechoslovakia. The government was comforted in its policy by the views of its attorney-general and minister for Industry, R. G. Menzies, who headed an Australian trade mission to Germany in July 1938 and returned impressed by the Nazi achievement, persuaded that nobody in Germany wanted war, and convinced that in the European crisis the faults were not all on the one side. Few people in Australia expected a policy other than that of support for the mother country, and there was very little questioning of the morality or expediency of appeasing the fascist nations. The Labour party, it is true, was somewhat more critical of British statesmanship, fearing subordination of Australia's interests to those of the United Kingdom, and its industrial left wing outside Parliament called for more active measures against totalitarianism. The government appreciated the increasing precariousness of world peace, and in the budget of September 1938 imposed, for the first time since 1932, widespread tax increases: a reversal of previous budgetary trends which was occasioned principally by a rise in defence expenditure to nearly £17 million for the ensuing year. A week after the introduction of the budget, the House of Representatives debated the events leading up to the Munich conference between Chamberlain and Adolf Hitler. Lyons stated that his government had been in constant communication with the British prime minister and had called him out of bed in the early hours of the morning to acquaint him with its views. The Munich Agreement was well received in Australia, and Lyons congratulated Chamberlain on his successful handling of the problem.

Australia's confidence in appeasement began to fade in the closing months of 1938. As the realisation grew that the preservation of peace might become impossible, there was increasing uneasiness at the lifelessness of the government, and in the press and on the public platform the pressure mounted for an infusion of new blood into the cabinet. In October, Menzies spoke to a luncheon meeting in Sydney of the need in Australia for 'leadership as inspiring as that of the dictator countries': a thesis commonly interpreted as a broad hint to the prime minister. In an attempt to capitalise on public feeling, the Labour opposition submitted a censure motion in Parliament: 'that by lamentable lack of leadership regarding urgent national problems the Government have forfeited the confidence of the House.'

On November 7, 1938, Lyons reconstructed his team to include Brigadier G. A. Street as minister for Defence—a change clearly designed to restore the public's shaken confidence in the government's capacity to provide for the country's security. Any good effect the alteration might have had was initially weakened by the new minister's exclusion from a senior cabinet group which Lyons announced would deal with major policy matters of national significance. The error was retrieved the next day at the expense of the resignation of T. W. White, the minister for Customs, who objected to his omission from the inner coterie and signified his annoyance both at the swearing-in ceremony at Government House and in an undignified altercation with Lyons on the floor of Parliament. The ministry was plainly not a happy one, and the opposition taunted it on the changes, Curtin predicting that the prime minister would soon 'engage once again in that most popular pastime of his, the game of political musical chairs', and commenting on the instability inherent in the prime minister's frequent cabinet reconstructions. 'As a matter of fact', said Curtin, 'I should say that, sitting behind him today, the number of ex-Ministers almost totals the number of his present Ministry.' In the event, the new administration was not to last long, and there were soon unmistakable indications that it was not united within itself.

In March 1939 Lyons decided to postpone the introduction of a national insurance scheme which the government had prepared in order to honour promises made in the 1937 elections; instead, he proposed to satisfy critics of the scheme in the Country party and in a section of his own United Australia party by beginning work on a modified version of it. Menzies, who had been a difficult member of cabinet since its last reconstruction in November 1938, made this abandonment of the national insurance scheme his excuse for resigning from the government. His action was widely applauded at the time as a manifestation of his political principle and respect for election pledges, though an unkind observer might have interpreted it as an astute move to enhance his prestige both in the country and among the large section of the United Australia party that the party conference of February 1939 had shown to share his views. His resignation was almost certain to strengthen his personal standing at a crucial time, for the coalition with the Country party seemed about to disintegrate, Lyons was ailing and was thought to be considering retirement, and the federal treasurer, R. G. Casey, was rapidly becoming a dangerous rival to anyone contemplating the party's leadership and the office of prime minister. Only three weeks later Lyons died at the age of fifty-nine and Menzies was elected leader of the United Australia party by a narrow majority over Hughes, Casey and White, the rival candidates.

Menzies thus became prime minister at the early age of forty-four. Despite his previous hostility towards the Country party, he announced his readiness to maintain the existing balance between the two parties in cabinet. The coalition was destroyed, however, when Earle Page, the Country party leader, delivered in the House a malevolent personal attack on the character of the new prime minister, citing instances from Menzies' past in an attempt to prove that he possessed none of the qualities of loyalty, judgement and courage required to lead the nation in critical times. Menzies answered with dignified restraint, and disgust with the highly personal abuse in Page's speech brought about a change in the Country party leadership. Nevertheless, Menzies was obliged to form a minority government from the ranks of the United Australia party alone: an unsatisfactory situation for a country preparing for war.

The prime minister announced at once that the government's preoccupation would be with improving national defence. In addition to the program inherited from the recent coalition, he introduced legislation establishing a department of Supply and providing for a register of manpower, though he was compelled to accept amendments in order to get it passed. Any lingering belief in Australia in the virtues of appeasement had already been destroyed by the German annexation of Czechoslovakia in March 1939, when, only a fortnight before his death, Lyons broadcast to the Australian people that the time for making concessions in the hope of preserving peace had passed. 'We cannot rely now on negotiation and consultation', he declared, 'as means of adjusting international disputes.' Australia's close association with the mother country in defence and international affairs was reiterated with increased emphasis both by Lyons and his successor. 'I cannot have a defence of Australia', said Menzies in April 1939, 'which depends upon British sea power as its first element; I cannot envisage a vital foreign trade on sea routes kept free by British sea power, and at the same time refuse to Britain Australian co-operation at a time of common danger. The British countries of the world must stand or fall together.'

The government continued its efforts to placate Japan and improve Australian interests in the Pacific as a whole, and it was announced in April that legations would be created in Tokyo and Washington, with ministers of full diplomatic status. During the next four months, as the war shadows gathered over Europe, the government accelerated rearmament and there was no disagreement on the need for Australia to prepare to fight alongside its British Commonwealth partners when the conflict came. On the evening of Sunday, September 3, 1939, Menzies spoke for a united nation in his broadcast announcement that 'in consequence of a persistence by Germany in her invasion of Poland, Great Britain has declared war upon her and that, as a result, Australia is also at war'. After less than twenty-one years of uneasy peace the world war was renewed on an even greater scale, and without hesitation Australia stood once more at Britain's side.

8

The Second World War (1939-1945)

AFTER ASSOCIATING itself with Britain's declaration of war against Germany, the Australian government hastened to nerve an unprepared and bewildered nation for the task that lay ahead. Parliament reassembled on September 6 and the following day the government introduced a National Security Bill modelled on the War Precautions Act of the first world war and authorising the executive to prohibit public meetings deemed likely to disturb public order, to order trials in closed courts, and to arrest persons without warrants and keep them in custody without being charged. The legislation conferred on the government extensive powers of regulation widely recognised as necessary for the effective prosecution of the war, but many liberal observers regarded them with some apprehension as potentially dangerous to democratic rights and liberties.

In his speech on the second reading of the Bill, the prime minister intimated his respect for the opinions of those who feared it could mean the surrender of democratic principles and the imposition of the sort of totalitarianism against which the British Commonwealth was fighting.

> We are asking Parliament to hand over to the executive a very great reservoir of power [Menzies confessed], and it may well be said that in doing so we incur grave risk in the limitation of freedom of the individual and in the limitation of parliamentary control. I frankly admit that we do. Legislation of this kind can be made an instrument of repression in

bad hands. The greatest tragedy that could overcome a country would be for it to fight a successful war in defence of liberty and lose its own liberty in the process. There is no intention on the part of the government to use these powers when they are granted, as I am sure they will be, in any way other than to promote the security of Australia.

War, however, changes people, as the parliamentary critics of the Bill pointed out; while no one questioned the good intentions of the ministry, there was no guarantee that its integrity and moderation would survive all the exigencies of a prolonged conflict. Nevertheless, the Bill was passed, and in June 1940 amended to empower the executive to make regulations requiring all persons to place themselves, their services, and their property at the commonwealth's disposal except in regard to military service abroad. Conscription for overseas was still a sensitive issue, and in October the prime minister stated categorically that service abroad remained voluntary, but compulsory military training, which had been suspended in 1929, was reintroduced with the aim of maintaining a force of 75,000 militiamen.

In February 1940 the first detachments of the 6th Australian Division under the command of Lieutenant-General Sir Thomas Blamey began to arrive in the Middle East; airmen of the Royal Australian Air Force reached England, joined immediately in reconnaissance operations with British Coastal Command, and later participated in the Battle of Britain and the night bombing of Germany; while the Royal Australian Navy, which was placed under British orders, assisted in the protection of convoys and took part in engagements off Dakar and in the Mediterranean. By the middle of 1940 Australia was accelerating its military preparations, but the German violation of Dutch and Belgian neutrality, the entry of Italy on the side of the enemy, the downfall of France, and the evacuation at Dunkirk left Britain alone to face an aggressor that now bestrode the European continent from the Pyrenees to the Arctic coast of Norway and eastward as far as Russia's portion of Poland.

All political parties in Australia were agreed in their determination to assist the beleaguered mother country to the utmost, but they continued to deny the Dominion the positive government the urgency of the hour demanded. The Menzies government was neither secure in Parliament nor contented within itself, and it suffered a tragic loss on August 13 when three of its most active ministers were killed in an aviation disaster near Canberra. With only a precarious majority in the House of Representatives, the depleted cabinet failed to win unqualified public confidence in its ability to prosecute the war efficiently. The prime minister tried hard to inspire the nation, but he had never been a popular figure and there was a growing suspicion that his fine words were not always followed by resolute action. The department of Supply and Development, which had been created in April 1939 to prepare industry and the economy for the exigencies of war, had been affected by the transference of its first ministerial head, R. G. Casey, to the newly established diplomatic post in Washington, and it was no longer functioning smoothly, partly because too heavy a load of work was placed on it. The 'Economic Cabinet' which had been constituted in November 1939 to direct the business side of the war failed to exercise the duties expected of it and within a few months began to crumble away as a useful body. A department of Munitions was not set up until June 1940; Essington Lewis, the general manager of the Broken Hill Proprietary Company, was appointed its director-general under the ministerial supervision of the prime minister himself. The maintenance of amicable labour relations was not the subject of serious consideration by the government until July 1940, over ten months after the war had started, and the department of Labour and National Service did not emerge from the planning stage until October of that year, when it co-ordinated what an official described as 'a constellation of predominantly pre-war and part-time committees and boards'.

The cabinet's numerous reshuffles and resignations, the need to bestow portfolios on the Country party again, and the evidence of individual discontent in the ranks of the United Australia party itself, all combined to give the government an unhealthy and unstable appearance. The Labour party, on the other hand, was more confident than it had been for a long time, and although its unity was not yet complete, it was assuming a more cohesive and responsible image under the patient guidance of John Curtin.

In the general election of 1940, an electoral swing in New South Wales reduced the government's majority to only one after it had provided the Speaker and compelled it to rely for its continued existence on the support of two independents. This inconclusive result clearly made necessary a measure of co-operation between the government and the opposition if war policy was to be conducted with decision, and at the end of October an Advisory War Council was constituted on which the government and the opposition possessed equal representation. The Council was designed to keep the Labour party leaders acquainted with major questions of war policy and ensure their co-operation in implementing any action which it would be undesirable to make a subject of open controversy. It was also hoped that the association of the Labour party in the conduct of the war would contribute towards the pacification of industrial disturbances. The prime minister, no doubt, harboured some expectation that membership of the Council might eventually reconcile the opposition leaders to a national government in which they would share responsibility for policy as well as enjoy the privilege of confidential knowledge of the circumstances in which it was formulated.

The new Council was soon apprised of the dangers to which Australia was becoming exposed. In Europe the German run of success had been checked by the Royal Air Force in the skies over England and the tension there had begun to ease, but the United Kingdom's predicament intensified the fears in Australia that Japan would seize this opportunity to imitate the dramatic victories of its Axis partner. The British government had already warned Australia of this contingency in June 1940, at the height of the disasters in Europe, admitting that, although defence policy in the Pacific was based on the presence of a fleet at Singapore, it could not both send naval forces to the Far East and retain sufficient in European waters to match the German and Italian fleets combined. Nevertheless the British prime minister, Winston Churchill, assured the Australian and New Zealand governments that in the event of their countries being invaded by Japan 'we should then cut our losses in the Mediterranean and sacrifice every interest, except only the defence and feeding of this island'. There were many in Australia, however, who were justifiably sceptical of Britain's ability to safeguard its imperial interests in the Pacific. A conference in the last week of October called by the United Kingdom chiefs of staff to consider the Far Eastern situation disclosed what Menzies described to the Advisory War Council as an 'alarming position in regard to the defence of Singapore', and anxiety over it prompted him to visit London early in 1941.

On his way to England, Menzies visited Australian troops in the Middle East, which had been transformed into a theatre of operations by the entry of Italy into the war on Germany's side in June 1940. In September of that year a large Italian army had crossed the Libyan frontier into Egypt and moved cautiously across the desert as far as Sidi Barrani, but in December it was hurled back in disorder by a British armoured division and an Indian infantry division. The British followed up this success, and in January 1941 the 6th Australian Division penetrated the Italian defence perimeter around Bardia, fought off a counter-attack by enemy tanks, and captured the little town with the loss of fewer than 500 casualties. Little more than a fortnight later Tobruk, the main Italian fortress on the coast of Cyrenaica, was stormed and taken, and at the end of January the town of Derna, at the edge of the desert, was entered. In the first week of February, columns of the British armoured division crossed 150 miles of desert, intercepted the retreating Italian army, and destroyed it; on February 7 British and Australian troops entered Benghazi, the capital of Cyrenaica.

Unfortunately, any plans to press further west along the road to Tripoli were thwarted by the need to transfer troops to Greece, which had been attacked over the Albanian frontier by an Italian army the previous October and was now threatened with an attack by a German army which had penetrated Rumania and Bulgaria and seemed likely to come to the support of the as yet unsuccessful Italians. On February 8, 1941, the Greek government requested British help; it was decided to send an expeditionary force from the troops recently successful in Cyrenaica. The greater part of this force would necessarily comprise the Australian and New Zealand troops, and the consent of their governments was sought.

Menzies reached London on February 20 and took part in the War Cabinet's discussions on the proposed expedition. Although evidently apprehensive about it, he agreed to it and telegraphed to his colleagues recommending that his conditional consent should be ratified. The Australian War Cabinet felt it had no alternative to concurring in the plan, but sought assurances that the expedition would be adequately equipped and suitable preparations made in advance for its evacuation in case of necessity. The army of over 57,000 men began to disembark at Piraeus on March 7, but it arrived too late to be of use, and when the Germans attacked in April the campaign was short-lived. Before the end of the month the Germans were in Athens, and the British, Australian and New Zealand troops had to be hastily evacuated from small ports and open beaches, leaving behind about 15,000 killed or captured and all the heavy equipment.

The failure of the Greek expedition gave rise to some adverse comment in the Australian press on the apparent lack of consultation between the British and Australian governments, and there were suggestions that a purely British decision had sacrificed Australian troops in what had been predictably a futile campaign. German and Japanese propaganda seized on this criticism to invent stories of disaffection within the British Commonwealth, and even in the United States there was talk of the possibility of Australia's refusing to participate further in the war. To its credit the Australian government emphasised the continuing unity of the British Commonwealth and declared that it had been fully consulted at every stage before any Australian troops had been moved into a new action or theatre of operations. The principal misunderstanding, indeed, appears to have been between the prime minister and the Australian military commander, General Blamey, each of whom apparently agreed to the Greek expedition in the belief that the other had already consented to it. In fact, Blamey had viewed the whole idea with uneasiness, feeling that the defeat he regarded as probable would harm the morale and reputation of his troops.

Whatever the military prospects, however, the decision to help Greece was primarily a political one taken after discussions in London in which Menzies himself had been involved, though admittedly only in their closing stages. Greece had fought with remarkable success against the Italians and at this period of the war was the sole fighting ally of the Commonwealth nations, which were consequently honour-bound at least to demonstrate awareness of their obligations towards Greece.

Some of the forces evacuated from Greece were taken to Crete, the defence of which was entrusted to Major-General Freyberg of the New Zealand division. On May 20 a German airborne invasion of the island began, and although attempts at landing from the sea were smashed by the Royal Navy, within a week 20,000 enemy airborne troops had captured the three aerodromes. At the end of the month the British, Australian and New Zealand troops carried out another evacuation. These defeats were offset a little by the campaign in Syria which began at daybreak on June 8 with British, Indian, Australian and Free French troops crossing into Syria over the Palestine border, and in six weeks overcoming the Vichy defence and checking the spread of German influence.

Although the invasion of Syria brought welcome success to British arms, it reinforced the Australian government's feeling that it was not participating in military decisions taken by the mother country on the conduct of the war in theatres where Australian troops were very much involved. The Greek, Cretan and Syrian episodes seemed to the Australian leaders evidence of the poor regard shown by the British government to the rights of the Dominions and the proper courtesies of the Commonwealth relationship. Respect for Winston Churchill's qualities of wartime leadership could not allay the doubts that now existed about his conception of free association and full consultation between the members of the British Commonwealth. Menzies greatly admired Churchill, but was perturbed at what he described to the Advisory War Council as Churchill's 'unsatisfactory state of mind' on matters affecting the interests of the Dominions. It was difficult to square the desire of Australia and other Dominions to participate directly in the formulation of major decisions with the domination over war policy exercised by a British prime minister who was preoccupied with the main problems in England and Europe and disposed perhaps to think of the Dominions in nineteenth rather than twentieth-century terms. Differences between Churchill and the Australian government were to recur later in 1941 after the fighting in North Africa had been renewed by the arrival of German troops to help their battered Italian allies.

The first units of the German reinforcements had begun to reach Tripoli in February 1941 and by March their commander, Erwin Rommel, was prepared to advance against a British army weakened by the recent transfer of contingents to Greece. Benghazi was reoccupied by the enemy in April and the British forces withdrew in good order to just west of Tobruk. By April 11, the advancing Germans had completely invested Tobruk, where four Australian infantry brigades, four British artillery regiments, and a British armoured car battalion and machine-gun battalion prepared to resist a siege. Rommel's attempts to penetrate the defences were repulsed by severe British artillery and anti-tank fire and by the resolution of Australian infantry patrolling the perimeter and remaining in their position after it had been over-run by enemy tanks. Efforts to relieve the beleaguered garrison failed in May and June and it became clear that a long siege was in prospect.

It was at this juncture that an unfortunate controversy began between the British and Australian governments. In July, Menzies received a telegram from the Australian commander, Blamey, asking for his troops in Tobruk to be withdrawn and reassembled in Palestine with other Australian units as a single force, adding that the physical condition of those in Tobruk was now a source of considerable anxiety to him. The government naturally backed the judgement of its commander and forwarded his request to London. Churchill and the new British commander-in-chief in the Middle East, General Sir Claude Auchinleck, demurred, pointing out that to implement the Australian suggestion would impose an added burden on the fleet that might affect other naval operations. On Australia's insistence, however, Churchill regretfully agreed that the proposed relief should be undertaken, 'irrespective of the cost entailed and the injury to future prospects'. In August the 18th Australian Brigade was relieved by a Polish brigade group. In September and October the 9th Australian Division was replaced by the 70th British Division, which the following month drove a gap three miles wide through the enemy's position encircling Tobruk, and, after the fiercest fighting yet seen in the desert, compelled the besieging German and Italian forces to withdraw.

The communications with the British government on the Australian withdrawal from Tobruk had been conducted by three successive Australian prime ministers who followed one another rapidly between August and October. The political situation had been unstable since before the war began, and although Curtin led the Labour opposition with moderation and avoided unduly embarrassing the government during critical times, there were ambitious elements among his followers who were hungry for office and wished to use every opportunity to secure it. Dissatisfaction with the administration was rife among other sections of the community besides the Labour party, however, and by the middle of 1941 there was a movement in the press and the United Australia party itself to depose Menzies. Many responsible people in public life believed that the prime minister was incapable of providing the vigorous and inspiring leadership for which the hour called. 'It is being freely questioned among his supporters', said a *Sydney Morning Herald* editorial on Menzies in July 1941, 'whether his judicial tolerance, his keen analytical brain and the sparkling dialectic are not better suited to the higher council chambers of the Empire rather than to the post of man of action, which demands rapid decisions, the devolution of responsibility, and hasty improvisations.' To sober criticism of the country's leadership was added some unseemly manoeuvring among the members of the United Australia party that reflected little credit on the condition of Australian politics, and indicated a good deal of selfish disregard both of party and of national interests.

Menzies was aware that he did not command the unwavering devotion of the whole of his party, and the mounting criticism led him to revive the idea of an all-party national government in which the Labour and non-Labour parties would serve equally. Labour rejected all invitations to enter a national administration and brought upon itself the wrath of the predominantly conservative press, but Curtin sensibly gauged that what was good for

England was not necessarily good for Australia and he was determined to consolidate his party: the one hope the country possessed of a strong and efficient government prodded by the democratic processes of party opposition in Parliament. By the last week of August 1941, Menzies realised that he could no longer continue in office with his own cabinet rent by personal animosities and the Labour opposition adamant in its refusal to join an all-party administration. At a meeting of the cabinet on the evening of August 28, the prime minister announced his intention to resign. 'A frank discussion with my colleagues in the cabinet', he stated afterwards, 'has shown that, while they have personal goodwill towards me, many of them feel that I am unpopular with large sections of the press and the people; that this unpopularity handicaps the effectiveness of the Government by giving rise to misrepresentation of its activities; and that there are divisions of opinion in the Government parties themselves which would or might not exist under another leader.' The resignation was offered with a dignity and absence of rancour that contrasted strikingly with the obvious wrangling and self-indulgent manoeuvring of a large number of his party, some of whom entertained inflated notions of their own abilities and value to the nation. The United Australia party was in an unhealthy condition and had been disintegrating ever since it took office, and of this Menzies was perhaps as much the cause as the victim. He had proved to be temperamentally unsuited to the delicate task of winning the confidence and trust of those upon whom he depended; a lesser man might well have succeeded where he had so clearly failed.

Menzies was succeeded by the treasurer, A. W. Fadden, leader of the Country party, an affable, popular, hard-working accountant from Queensland, who possessed many of the qualities that his predecessor had lacked but was hardly the man to provide the national leadership required in war. A month later he was defeated in the House of Representatives on the opposition's vote of censure on his budget, and on October 4 he tended his resignation to the governor-general, who now turned to the only person with any chance of forming a coherent government.

John Curtin had been an excellent leader of the Labour opposition in Parliament since 1935, when he had been unexpectedly elected by a majority of one to succeed J. H. Scullin, who had resigned on account of ill-health. He was to become a commanding and competent war leader of the Australian people, among whom he inspired that trust and respect which they had withheld from Menzies. He acquired a reputation as a sincere, thoughtful and devoted party man, who was yet big enough to rise above the demands of party to answer the urgent national need for supreme and unprovocative leadership. His simple and forthright approach gave him strength in the eyes of the community, and if he was not exempt from the human weaknesses of impatience, aloofness and a certain melodramatic bent, he was far closer to deserving the people's affection and confidence than any of those around him.

Even before Curtin became prime minister, the danger of Japanese aggression in the Pacific had been growing rapidly, and in the closing months of 1941 it dominated the thinking of the new Australian government. On December 7 the Japanese attack on the American base at Pearl Harbor transformed the whole balance of the war in so far as it affected Australia, and the Japanese southward drive in the weeks following eliminated all controversy in Australia as to where its troops would in future be deployed. After December 1941 the war was primarily with Japan and only secondarily with Germany so far as the commonwealth government was concerned, and this fact was the source of its reappraisal of the traditional concept of the foundations of Australian defence policy. Curtin declared that the struggle in the Pacific should not be regarded as a subordinate part of the general conflict nor as one from whose direction Australia could be deprived of the fullest participation.

> Without inhibitions of any kind [Curtin said in a celebrated message to the Australian people], I make it quite clear that Australia looks to America, free of any pangs as to our traditional links with the United Kingdom. We know the problems that the United Kingdom faces. We know the constant threat of invasion. We know the dangers of dispersal of strength. But we know too that Australia can go and Britain can still hold on. We are therefore determined that Australia

THE SECOND WORLD WAR

shall not go, and we shall exert all our energies towards the shaping of a plan, with the United States as its keystone, which will give to our country some confidence of being able to hold out until the tide of battle swings against the enemy.

There was some sharp criticism of this statement, not least by Menzies, who described it as a blunder, but Curtin was in fact merely stating the logic of Australia's position. The Dominion lacked the means to defend itself and Britain was incapable of sparing adequate forces for the Far East even if it had wanted to (and it was suspected it did not), British strategy being concentrated on the European and Middle Eastern theatres of war. In effect, Australia had no choice but to turn to the United States, for it was with the United States that its interests in the Pacific more nearly coincided: a circumstance which thoughtful Australians had already accepted and which the Menzies government had recognised when, in 1940, it had appointed a minister to Washington. The lack of confidence in the mother country's ability to discharge its obligations in the Pacific was accentuated by the swift success of the Japanese, who took Hong Kong, Manila, Rabaul and, most significant of all, Singapore, which fell on February 15, 1942. An Australian division, under Major-General H. Gordon Bennett, fought well in Johore during the disastrous Malayan campaign, but, along with the British and Indian forces, had to capitulate at Singapore, where 15,000 Australian troops became prisoners of the Japanese. In the Netherlands East Indies an Australian infantry battalion reinforced the Dutch garrison on Amboina, but after a short resistance finally surrendered south of the town of Ambon on February 3, 1942. Over 1,100 Australians were captured by the enemy in Dutch Timor before the end of the month, and in March nearly 3,000 more were lost in Java. By the end of May the victorious Japanese were in the East Indies, Malaya and Burma, and were within striking distance of India to the west and Australia to the south. 'Our honeymoon is finished', said Curtin, 'now we must fight or work as never before.'

When the war with Japan began, all Australia's best troops were overseas: three divisions in Egypt and one in Malaya. To defend its own shores it had one armoured division greatly in need of tanks, seven ill-equipped and inexperienced divisions of militia, and a volunteer defence corps of 50,000 men. It was inevitable that in this national emergency the government should seek to recall its troops from the Middle East in order to help defend Australia. Churchill reluctantly agreed, and as soon as shipping became available two of the Australian divisions in North Africa embarked for home. On February 20, 1942, however, Churchill asked the Australian government to approve the diversion to Rangoon of one of the divisions then crossing the Indian Ocean. Without reinforcements the Allied forces in Burma could not stem the Japanese advance which threatened to cut off the Burma Road. Since American troops were already on their way to Australia ('with all possible speed' according to President Roosevelt), the Australian division was not essential to the defence of Australia and would be more use in Burma. Curtin returned a strong negative to this request, affirming pointedly that his government felt 'a primary obligation to save Australia not only for itself, but to preserve it as a base for the development of the war against Japan'. Consequently, the convoy carrying the Australian troops turned back from Rangoon, refuelled at Colombo, and proceeded to Australia as originally planned. Churchill, indeed, had already diverted the division towards Rangoon when the Australian answer arrived. This apparent assumption that a favourable response to his request was largely a matter of form annoyed the Australian cabinet, although it was obvious that if Churchill had waited for Australian consent the troops would probably have arrived in Burma too late or the ships would have lacked the fuel to get there. The British government evidently felt entitled to ask of Australia a decision similar to that which itself had taken in August 1940, when it had despatched reinforcements to the defence of Egypt even though England's own shores were threatened. 'We could not help feeling', wrote Churchill,* looking back on this unhappy episode, 'that when in 1940 we had been exposed to the same kind of fearful danger in a far closer and more probable form we had not lost our sense of proportion or hesitated to add to our risks for the sake of other vital needs.'

The British prime minister's outlook was conditioned by an

* *The Second World War*, Vol. IV: 'The Hinge of Fate', p. 138.

outmoded conception of a maternal England and a far-flung empire, while in contrast Curtin was possessed of a jealous regard for his country's dignity and perhaps also of an unduly narrow view of the world conflict. It is doubtful whether the return of the Australian troops to their home soil was as vital as Curtin insisted, and his fear that another failure in Burma 'would have the gravest consequences on the morale of the Australian people' probably underestimated the fibre of his own countrymen. The difference, essentially, lay between a British prime minister by now accustomed to the anxieties of extreme national peril and disposed to survey the gamut of Allied strategy with a calculated insensitivity to the fears of others, and an Australian prime minister leading his country through a new experience which he conceived to be a fight for national survival, and who was disposed, therefore, to see the war solely through Australian eyes and with Australian interests only in mind.

Curtin's government sought the complete mobilisation of the nation's manpower and material resources for defence. In February 1942 drastic measures were announced to prevent profiteering of any kind, especially that by owners of capital. In March the federal treasurer, J. B. Chifley, announced that the commonwealth would exercise priority powers in income tax collection, but a conference of state premiers the following month rejected a proposal to make income tax uniform throughout the country. The financial problem was now urgent: war expenditure had risen to over £500 million a year, but the commonwealth could not tax incomes to the limit, as it needed to, while the states were also taxing. The Menzies government had made several attempts to solve this problem, but each proposal had been rejected by the states. In order to circumvent state opposition, Chifley introduced legislation the effect of which was to exclude the states from the taxation field. The legislation enabled the commonwealth to impose an income tax at rates that brought in as much revenue as the former commonwealth and state taxes combined and to offer grants to states which did not collect income tax. Moreover, it gave commonwealth tax priority over state tax and entitled the federal government to take over the state income tax organisations. The opposition parties criticised some of the details of these measures but they approved the principle of uniform taxation and the new system was passed by Parliament and came into operation on August 1, 1942. Four state governments* applied to the High Court for a decree declaring the Acts unconstitutional, but the Court upheld the validity of the legislation, arguing that if state laws on taxation were inconsistent with a commonwealth law on taxation, then, in the words of section 109 of the constitution, 'the latter shall prevail, and the former shall, to the extent of the inconsistency, be invalid'. Nevertheless, whatever the practical merits of the legislation and whether or not it could be technically justified in law, the ejection of the states from the taxation field constituted a severe blow to the federal principle upon which the commonwealth of Australia had been founded. The power of taxation is a fundamental power and to deprive the states of their own means of securing the resources of government was to upset the constitutional balance for which the fathers of the federation believed they had made adequate provision.

The national danger in 1942 which necessitated the government's extending its authority over the economy also stirred it to seek a large voice in the direction of operations in the Pacific. The minister for External Affairs, H. V. Evatt, visited the United States and England and prevailed on the American and British governments to create two Pacific War Councils, one based in Washington and the other in London. Australia was represented on both these councils but neither fulfilled the hopes which the commonwealth government entertained of it. Evatt appears to have been under the delusion that because Australia was deeply involved in the struggle in the Pacific it would possess a major role in the direction of operations. In fact, Australia was a secondary power, and whatever courtesies the American and British governments might show it in the interest of Allied unity, they had no intention of permitting their conduct of a world war to be sidetracked by a small partner with a brazen minister of External Affairs. The war was in Europe as well as in the East and the onus of bringing it to a successful conclusion rested almost entirely on the United States and the United Kingdom. Australian hopes of an

* Queensland, Victoria, South Australia and Western Australia.

early large-scale counter offensive against the Japanese were dashed by the fundamental decision already taken by America and Britain that the defeat of Germany should have priority over that of Japan. The Pacific War Councils functioned not as arbiters of high Allied strategy—for that remained with the American and British governments—but as useful machinery enabling Australia and the small countries to be consulted on developments and have an opportunity to present their views.

The first half of 1942 was in many ways less distressing for the Allied cause in the Pacific than it was elsewhere. In May the German army under Rommel began an offensive in North Africa which flung the British forces out of Libya and by the end of June had pressed far towards the Nile delta, where the British 8th Army dug itself in at El Alamein only seventy miles from Alexandria. At the same time Germany declared war against Russia and its armies were soon heading rapidly for the Volga and the Caucasus.

In the Pacific, on the other hand, the Japanese suffered their first reverse, if not defeat, at the hands of the Americans in the naval and air battles of the Coral Sea on May 7 and of Midway Island in the first week of June. But, although the Coral Sea battle prevented the Japanese from making an attack from the sea on Port Moresby in Australian New Guinea, in July 1942 they landed unopposed west of Buna and occupied Kokoda along the jungle track that led over the Owen Stanley range to Port Moresby. During August and September the Japanese, many of whom were suffering from dysentery and food poisoning, drove the Australians southwards, but by the middle of September the reinforced Australian troops stopped them at Eoribaiwa Ridge, little more than thirty miles from Port Moresby.

On September 23, General Blamey arrived at Port Moresby to assume command of an offensive operation designed to recapture Buna. Despite appalling difficulties of terrain and climate, the enemy were pressed back across the Owen Stanley mountains to the north coast, Kokoda was reoccupied, and the last footholds of the Japanese in New Guinea gradually dislodged. By January 1943 the New Guinea offensive had achieved its objective at a cost of nearly 6,000 Australian and 3,000 American casualties.

The threat of a Japanese invasion of Australia had now passed. At the same time in the Middle East, troops of the 9th Australian Division contributed magnificently to the British offensive from El Alamein, which in October 1942 sent Rommel's army reeling back thousands of miles along the North African coast from Egypt right up to the border of Tunisia.

The events of 1942 increased the necessity for the Commonwealth Defence Act to be amended in order to provide for the use of the conscripted militia in areas outside Australia. As Curtin pointed out, Australian defence depended on the expulsion of the Japanese from Timor and the East Indies as well as from Papua and New Guinea. Conscription for overseas had always been a controversial issue in Australian politics. Curtin showed some courage in introducing it early in 1943, an election year, with a Bill proposing that the militia should be capable of being employed in an extended sphere of operations in the south-west Pacific defined as 'the area bounded on the west by the 110th meridian east longitude, on the north by the equator, and on the east by the 159th meridian east longitude'. This definition included New Guinea, New Britain, New Ireland, Timor and part of the Solomon Islands, but excluded Malaya, the Philippines, Sumatra, New Caledonia and parts of Java and Borneo. Its limited scope provoked strong criticism from the opposition and from sections of the public who wanted a more comprehensive amendment. The passage of the Bill was marked by diffuse and recriminatory debate that indicated a degree of political manoeuvring normally to be expected in an election year but hardly to be admired in a period commonly recognised as one of national emergency. The opposition adopted an equivocal attitude, befitting perhaps the somewhat equivocal character of the Bill, but eventually decided not to oppose it. The political acrimony, however, continued unabated right up to the election which took place in August 1943.

The Labour party naturally based its claims to be re-elected on its successful record as a wartime administration. The strength of the fighting services and the numbers working in war industry had been nearly doubled since it came into office in October 1941. The aircraft industry had developed, the production of machine tools had increased, and shipbuilding had revived. Australia was now firmly established on a war footing both domestically and militarily. The civilian population had become accustomed to restrictions on its liberties and standard of living; petrol, clothing and basic foodstuffs were all rationed, and people carried coupon books and identity cards as they did in England. The scarcity of certain materials led to curtailments in gas, electricity and transport services; the size of newspapers was pared down, unessential building was prohibited, and wages and rents were pegged. The farmers suffered severely, losing labour to the armed services and their supplies of superphosphate being reduced after the Japanese occupied Nauru. A series of mediocre seasons was to culminate in a devastating drought in 1944 and 1945. Wheat yields declined, mainly as a result of the shortage of fertiliser, but meat and vegetable production remained high, the acreage under potatoes having doubled since before the war, and the output of milk multiplying nearly five times. Australia's food exports in 1943 exceeded 1,000,000 tons and were only 7,000 tons below the highest pre-war figure.

Not all this was the Labour government's doing, but even so its record was impressive in that the whole nation had been successfully organised for the war effort and sacrifices demanded equally of all. The opposition reiterated charges that the Labour party was dominated by Communists, and proclaimed itself to be standing for individual freedom against complete socialisation, although Curtin had promised that his government would not socialise any industry during the war. The result was an overwhelming Labour majority and a defeat for the United Australia party from which it never recovered. The dispirited remnants of the defeated party were reorganised by Menzies late in 1944 to form a resurgent Liberal party, which, though new, was rapidly to resume most of the characteristics of its shattered predecessor.

Greatly strengthened by its electoral victory in 1943, the Labour government bent its energies in the closing years of the war to making Australia's influence felt in the international preparations for peace. An interesting advance was made at a conference in Canberra between representatives of the Australian and New

I

Zealand governments which, on January 21, 1944, signed what was known as the Anzac Agreement. This provided for 'fuller exchange of information regarding both the views of each government and the facts in the possession of either bearing on matters of common interest', arranged for the establishment of a permanent secretariat 'to ensure continuous collaboration', and contained mutual declarations on the prosecution of the war, future security for both countries, civil aviation, and the welfare of native peoples in the Pacific. The fundamental feature of the Anzac Agreement, as described by the Australian minister for External Affairs, was its expression of joint aims for the peaceful development of the Pacific regions in which the two countries were vitally concerned. 'It says, in effect', said Evatt, 'that Australia and New Zealand have taken to heart the bitter experiences resulting from the failure to achieve collective security and the international order which must be based on security. It says that Australia and New Zealand are resolved to establish in their part of the world a regional system of defence and security.' The Agreement was never to be as important as its signatories liked to pretend, but it did represent an ambitious attempt by the two countries to take the initiative in ensuring some sort of mutual assistance and consultation in the maintenance of their regional security.

The Anzac Agreement of 1944 was expressly related to the provisions of the United Nations Charter, in the formulation of which Evatt played a prominent part, championing the rights of small nations to exercise their influence on any new international machinery created to keep the peace after the war had ended. A meeting of British Commonwealth prime ministers in May 1944 discussed and approved the Moscow declaration of the previous October, when America, Britain, Russia and China had stated their intention of founding an international organisation open to all peace-loving states, large and small, and charged with the duty of maintaining peace and security.

The Commonwealth countries were not individually represented at the Dumbarton Oaks conference which met in August and September 1944, and the tendency now apparent for the major powers to arrogate to themselves a dominant role in the proposed organisation was resented by others. Criticism of these pretensions became the regular theme of Evatt's public pronouncements, particularly at the conference in San Francisco in 1945, when he was supported by the New Zealand delegation in seeking modification in the veto power on the Security Council. On June 12, 1945, however, his attempts to restrict the exercise of the veto were finally rejected and a fortnight later the delegates signed the Charter. In explaining Australia's policy to the House of Representatives, Evatt said he believed that the stand taken by Australia and New Zealand on the veto issue 'was largely responsible for clarifying the meaning of the voting formula' and also, he continued (with, as it proved, unwarranted optimism), 'for eliciting from the Great Powers the important undertaking that in cases of peaceful settlement the veto power would be used sparingly, and only in an emergency, and, further, that the veto would never be used to block preliminary consideration and discussion by the Council of any dispute'. Evatt made a forceful contribution to the debates on the United Nations Charter, but his notion of justice and equality between nations, though natural for the delegate of a secondary power, was inevitably quite unacceptable in practice to the Great Powers upon whom the preservation of international security would largely depend.

Nevertheless, when the war ended in 1945 Australia had reason to be satisfied with the role it had played both in the Allied victory and in the preparation for peace. Its army had fought in Africa against the Germans and in New Guinea and Malaya against the Japanese; the Australian navy had participated in engagements throughout the world, losing three cruisers and four destroyers as well as many smaller vessels; Australian airmen had flown with other members of the British Commonwealth in the day and night bombing of Germany and had joined the Americans in the air battles to defend Australia's own soil against the Japanese. The Australian people had proved themselves once again equal to the stress of war, and their government had given a purposeful direction to the war effort that answered Australia's needs if it did not always meet the broader requirements of Allied strategy. The changing order of the post-war world, in which buoyant nationalism would be rampant abroad and tentative socialism explored at home, would call for greater statesmanship.

9

Socialism at Home and Nationalism Abroad (1945-1949)

ONLY A few weeks before the end of the war with Japan, the main architect of Australia's contribution to the Allied victory died in his sleep at Canberra. The death of John Curtin on July 5, 1945, robbed the Labour party of a leader who in pre-war years had patiently worked to give it a unity and a purpose from which the whole country had benefited since it came into office in the tense days of 1941. Curtin was succeeded as Labour's leader by Joseph Benedict Chifley, the federal treasurer, a friendly, good-humoured and likeable person, more popular on all sides than his predecessor had been, but also perhaps less respected. Chifley had been born the son of a New South Wales blacksmith and had become an engine-driver on the state railways before entering politics. He had been minister for Defence in the Labour government of 1929 and had served in important honorary positions under non-Labour administrations when he became treasurer in the Labour cabinet of 1941. Chifley was not an impressive speaker and had few of the intellectual qualities of Curtin, but his tall, not too robust figure always commanded attention in the House, for his grasp of financial matters was generally acknowledged, and his lucidity, sincerity and parliamentary skill and tact were quietly effective in debate. He became prime minister at a time when Labour's reputation was high and it was expected that his government would take advantage of the return to peace to achieve some of the fundamental objectives in the party's program.

For a generation or more the Labour party had sought to

introduce a measure of socialism by a process of gradual reform. In 1908 the goal had been described modestly as 'the collective ownership of monopolies and extension of the economic functions of the state', but during the more revolutionary mood after the first world war the general objective had been altered by a federal conference in 1921 to 'the socialisation of industry, production, distribution and exchange'. The boldness of this resolution had alarmed some members, and the Blackburn declaration at the same conference explained that the party did not seek 'to abolish private ownership even of any of the instruments of production where such instrument is utilised by its owner in a socially useful manner and without exploitation'. Extremist influence in the party declined later in the 1920s, and by the second world war little had been done to implement the socialist ideal except by the Lang administration in New South Wales. Even in Queensland, where Labour had been in power for most of the period, the only evidence of a socialist motive was the abolition of the Legislative Council, some intensification of State control, and the introduction of uncontroversial social services. It was not, in fact, until after 1945 that a determined attempt was made on a national scale to fasten some of the rudiments of socialism on the Australian community.

The socialist objective was obscured by the Communist taint which Labour's opponents deliberately magnified for their own ends. The anti-Labour forces were given plenty of material upon which to work by the industrial unrest in the months immediately following the end of the war. The steelworkers at the Broken Hill Proprietary Company went on strike and were joined by the miners of the New South Wales coalfields and by the Seamen's Union, which in four states refused to man ships carrying coal or steel. The result in 1945 was severe transport and lighting restrictions in New South Wales and the greatest industrial stoppage in Australia since 1917. The strikes and the industrial disorder as a whole were generally attributed to the influence of Communists in the executives of some of the trade unions, especially the Miners' Federation, the Seamen's Union, the Waterside Workers, and the Metal Trades Federation. The Labour party's distaste for the disruptive tactics of Communist sympathisers was put on record at the annual conference of the New South Wales branch in June 1946, when a resolution was passed emphatically condemning the Communist party as 'a danger to Australian democracy and a permanent foe of the Australian Labor Party' and rejecting 'without hesitation or qualification' any association with it. The problem of Communist association stayed with the Labour party, however, and embarrassed the government, for Communist officials remained in control of several of the unions upon which it normally depended for electoral and political support.

Another difficulty with which the Chifley government had to wrestle was the inhibiting structure of the federal constitution, to which sectional interests were able to appeal in order to check attempts at introducing measures that smacked of socialism. The policy of extending social services had been started during the war, and it was the Menzies government which had introduced a commonwealth scheme of child endowment. A scheme for widows' pensions had been devised in 1942, and in 1944 more comprehensive legislation had provided for unemployment insurance and sickness and maternity benefits, while plans were laid both for pharmaceutical and hospital benefits. The challenge to the Pharmaceutical Benefits Act of 1944 in the High Court, which declared that for a social benefit to be valid it must be named in the constitution, as old-age and invalid pensions were, raised the possibility that all provision by the commonwealth for social services might be *ultra vires*.

In consequence the federal government decided to seek wider powers. In March 1946 Chifley announced that a referendum would be taken concurrently with the next general election to ratify constitutional amendments embodied in three Bills which were quickly passed through Parliament. The first Act was designed to continue existing social services such as maternity allowances, widows' pensions, child endowment, and unemployment, sickness, hospital, and students' benefits and to empower the government to pass further legislation leading to the establishment of a national health service. The second Act enabled the government to organise the marketing of primary products; and the third provided for commonwealth regulation of industrial conditions, including the basic wage and standard hours of work, and for commonwealth jurisdiction over intra-state disputes hitherto solely a matter for the state tribunals. Only the first of these proposals was accepted in the referendum, the other two being subjected to criticism by the opposition and rejected by the voters, but none of the amendments was given the attention at election meetings that might have been expected.

The opposition's campaign was opened by Menzies on August 20, 1946—three days after the dissolution of Parliament, and it at once became apparent that taxation reductions were the main issue. Menzies offered better conditions, greater individual freedom and ample security and promised a reduction of 20 per cent in income tax: a bid which Sir Arthur Fadden, his colleague at the head of the Country party, raised to 28 per cent. It was an inspiring prospect, but met with violent hostility from extremists, who organised demonstrations and on one occasion in Sydney disconnected the amplifiers which Menzies needed in order to be heard at all above the uproar, and threw small linen bags of pig-iron towards the platform to show they had not forgotten the treatment meted out by the speaker to the waterside workers' boycott of shipments to Japan before the war.

Chifley opened the Labour campaign two weeks later with a broadcast from Canberra that seemed drab and unimaginative beside the promises of his opponent. He reviewed the record of his government in the past and used it as a guarantee of sound administration in the future. The Labour party made no rash pledges and maintained that income tax, which had already been reduced by about 22 per cent from the level reached at the height of the war, could not prudently be cut much more in existing circumstances. Chifley also risked losing much of the rural vote by his refusal either to raise the minimum price guaranteed by his government's new plan to stabilise the wheat industry or to exclude from its operation the crop harvested in the current year. As things then stood, and had the new plan not become operative, the wheat-growers could have expected to command an overseas price nearly twice the proposed legislative minimum, which would have compensated them for the impoverishment they had recently suffered through several years of drought. The wool-growers were antagonised by the government's insistence that the £7 million accumulated from the wartime marketing of wool should be devoted to publicity and research instead of being distributed among the growers, who regarded the funds as legally and morally theirs.

Menzies supported these rural interests in their objections to government policy, and also charged Labour ministers with being lenient to strikers and failing to prevent stoppages in the coal mines which had slowed up the whole of industry. Nevertheless, the result of the election was a disappointment to the Liberals, who had striven to represent themselves in a new role as the party of progress and initiative, and a triumph to the Labour party, whose majority in the House of Representatives was not seriously impaired and whose position in the Senate was considerably improved.

The Labour government was re-elected on its record, which in 1946 was a good one. A great deal of legislation had been passed, social welfare had been enhanced, and export figures had risen. Perhaps the most important aspect of government policy at this time, however, was the extensive immigration program instituted by the vigorous minister for Immigration, A. A. Calwell. In April 1946 he announced agreements between the British and Australian governments providing for the free passage to Australia of British ex-servicemen and their dependants and for assisted passages to other British residents over the age of nineteen who were to contribute £10 towards their passage, the remainder of the cost, including the free passage of children under fourteen, being borne by the two governments equally. Australia was the first member of the British Commonwealth to decide on its immigration policy, setting a target for 1947 of 35,000 assisted immigrants which it was hoped to increase at least to 70,000 a year after 1948. These objectives were unduly optimistic in view of the world-wide shortage of shipping and an acute national housing problem, and at a conference in Canberra in January 1947 the minister for Immigration and representatives from the states concluded that plans for large-scale immigration would have to be abandoned for some years, despite the urgency of relieving the country's labour scarcity. The government wished to ensure that the intake was predominantly of British stock, but it boldly admitted large numbers of people from the continent of Europe. New migration offices were opened in Norway, the Netherlands, France, Germany and the United States. In July 1947 an agreement was signed with the International Refugee Organisation for the settlement of displaced persons in Australia.

The immigration program created, as well as solved, economic problems, and it emphasised the concentration of population in the coastal towns instead of contributing to the dispersal over rural areas that was widely recognised as being desirable. The government was aware of the difficulties that a sustained immigration program would cause, and Calwell declared that it must be associated with a 'social service program of creating economic security and higher standards of living as an inducement to young Australian couples to have larger families'. Nevertheless, if Australia was to obtain the additional population it needed, it was sound policy to seek immigrants in the immediate post-war years, when there were more displaced and rootless persons than ever before, and to deal with the economic and social consequences as best as possible as they arose. There were 7½ million people in Australia in 1947 and it was generally conceded that they were far too few.

Australia's fear that its empty spaces could become the prey of its over-populated Asian neighbours was not removed by the defeat of Japan. Indeed, the post-war world produced an upsurge of nationalism and independence movements abroad that posed new problems for the conduct of Australian external affairs. The rapid disappearance of European control intensified the danger to Australia's security, and the parliamentary debates of 1946 and 1947 revealed an obsession with the idea that the dark-skinned masses of the countries to the north would one day descend upon Australia. The government, under the guidance of its assiduous minister for External Affairs, Dr Evatt, adopted a sensibly pragmatic attitude towards the changing situation in the Pacific, conscious that the new nationalism was strong and that Australia would have to repress prejudices and learn to live alongside independent Asian peoples.

Evatt believed that, instead of being alarmed at the success of the freedom movements, Australia should work for a regional association of democratic states and place more confidence in the United Nations Organisation and the enforcement of its principles. The revolt against Dutch colonial rule in the Netherlands East Indies, therefore, was given qualified support by the commonwealth government which, at the end of July 1947, joined the Indian government in bringing the matter before the United Nations Security Council. This was a bold action in that it was inevitably interpreted as support for the Indonesians and it aligned Australia with India and other countries in the attack on European colonialism. It was, in fact, the best evidence of a new and positive policy by Australia towards its external problems, although it was bitterly denounced by the Liberal and Country party opposition.

The exception in this moderate and broad-minded approach was the defeated Japan, for whom Australians preserved a burning hostility born of old fears and the late war. In his review of Australian foreign policy in February 1947, Evatt stressed Australia's right to be a full party in any negotiations concerning Japan, and in July of that year he discussed with General MacArthur, Supreme Commander of Allied Powers in Japan, the principal features which a Japanese peace treaty should have. The Australian view of how Japan should be dealt with was harsher than that of the United States, and the two countries were not easy partners in Allied treatment of Japan in the post-war years. Australia's hatred of the Japanese died slowly, and its desire to obtain substantial retribution and eliminate the Japanese for ever as a danger in the Pacific conflicted with the more tolerant policy of the United States, which was unwilling completely to emasculate or unnecessarily humiliate a former enemy nation which policy-makers in Washington were coming to regard as a future American bastion in Asia. In these circumstances Australia was gratified at becoming spokesman for the British Commonwealth on the Allied Council in Tokyo and at an Australian soldier's being appointed commander-in-chief of the British Commonwealth occupation forces in Japan: positions which gave the government the opportunity to watch closely and critically the development of Allied policy in the north-west Pacific.

It was at home, however, that the Australian government was now to meet its sternest test. There were still industrial disturbances, and the defeat of the Labour government in Western Australia for the first time since 1933, the re-election of a non-Labour coalition in South Australia with an increased majority, and the return of Labour governments in New South Wales and Queensland with reduced majorities—all between March and May 1947 —suggested a weakening in Labour's hold on the electorate.

At this juncture, in an attempt to accelerate industrial arbitration in accordance with the philosophy of the trade unions, the commonwealth Parliament in April 1947 passed amendments to the Conciliation and Arbitration Act assigning the settlement of industrial disputes to fifteen conciliation commissioners. The Arbitration Court was entrusted only with making awards on basic wage rates, hours of work and annual leave. The changes were not revolutionary but were designed to remedy the difficulties that had arisen from a court whose procedure was generally admitted to be too slow and whose legal delays were exasperating unionists. As if to demonstrate its laboriousness, the Arbitration Court took twenty-two months to consider an application for a standard working week of forty hours, judgement on which it finally delivered in September 1947. The Court decided unanimously that the forty-hour working week should operate from the first pay period the following January, but added that there should be a transitional period. More than 900,000 workers were affected by the decision, which was based on the evidence that industry was booming and the economy was in a position to stand it.

One of the first consequences of the Court's order was a strike in Melbourne in January 1948 by the Tramway Employees Union which objected to the rearrangement of hours by the Tramways Board. Later in the month railway maintenance engineers in Queensland, impatient of waiting for their application to be heard, went on strike, were joined by the waterside workers, and were involved in street fighting with the police in Brisbane before they returned to work in April. Public dismay grew at what were regarded as Communist-inspired activities, and the opposition moved a resolution censuring the government's failure to deal with the problem adequately.

Of equal concern was the inflationary tendency in the economy as higher wages and higher prices followed each other rapidly. The average earnings of factory employees rose 16 per cent in the twelve months ending in June 1948 to reach a level 78 per cent higher than before the war. Retail prices in the same period rose 7 per cent to become 40 per cent higher, and export prices rose 50 per cent to become 300 per cent higher than pre-war. In his budget speech of September 1948, Chifley warned of the dangers inherent in these rises. 'Unless firmly restrained', he said, 'this movement must cause grave dislocation, provoke industrial unrest, and lose for us advantage in point of costs which we have had for some years in our trade with other countries.' Nevertheless, Australia continued to enjoy a favourable return for its exports of primary produce, especially of superior grade wool, whose price was particularly high, and there were no signs of any serious slackening in world demand. Whatever the strains in the industrial economy, for the rural population it was a period of exceptional prosperity.

Superimposed on these issues in 1947 and 1948 was the controversy generated by the government's offensive against the private trading banks. The Labour party had been convinced by the depression of the early 1930s that the banking system should be subject to central control and should not be in the hands of narrow and bureaucratic conservatives capable of frustrating the financial policy of the government as the Commonwealth Bank had done in 1931. Since its foundation in 1911, the Commonwealth Bank had conducted the federal government's banking business, and since 1924 it had controlled note issue. During the second world war it had strengthened its position by a legislative requirement for the trading banks to deposit their 'surplus investible funds' with it, thus restricting their facilities for gaining higher profits, and an Act of Parliament in 1945 improved its competitive position in ordinary banking business. In August 1947, however, the High Court ruled invalid that section of the 1945 Banking Act under which the federal treasurer could direct all state and local government bodies to conduct their business through the Commonwealth Bank. This High Court ruling convinced the government that further injury might be inflicted on the Banking

Act in this way, and only a few days later it was announced that legislation would be prepared for nationalising the private banks. Although the final decision to nationalise was precipitated by the High Court judgement, the idea had long been in Chifley's mind. He was known to be an inveterate opponent of the trading banks. It was recalled that, as a member of a royal commission on Australian banking in 1935, he had submitted a minority opinion criticising the private banking system as a whole on the grounds that it made the community 'the victim of every wave of optimism and pessimism that surges through the minds of financial speculators'.

Whatever its merits and faults financially, the Nationalisation Act passed in October 1947 was politically ill-advised in that it aroused intense public controversy and supplied the opposition with an excellent platform for its attacks on the government. Members of Parliament were inundated with petitions, letters and telegrams which clogged the postal services in Canberra. Rowdy public meetings and debates on bank nationalisation were held in an acrimonious atmosphere and church dignitaries pronounced against it, although in the end they admitted that it was a secular matter on which the individual must be allowed to form his own opinion. Outside the ranks of Labour there was widespread condemnation of nationalisation, and in the fierce argument there was much extravagant language on both sides. The critics spoke freely of totalitarianism and financial dictatorship. The *Sydney Morning Herald* described the legislation as politically and financially 'the most revolutionary in the country's history', and the Melbourne *Age* called it a 'revolutionary and extremely socialistic design'. Bank nationalisation inevitably became an issue in the Victoria state election early in November and contributed to the most resounding political defeat for Labour since the federal elections of 1931. Nevertheless, the Act was passed and received the governor-general's assent on November 27, 1947. It was taken to the High Court which, in August 1948, delivered a judgement that in effect made the Act inoperative. Chifley promptly announced that the government would appeal to the Privy Council, and the hearing was set to begin in March 1949: election year.

The pending general election dominated Australian politics throughout 1949. The year opened with the government under heavy criticism for its policy towards the fighting between the Dutch and the Indonesians in the Netherlands East Indies. In the Security Council discussions in December 1948, the Australian delegate, Colonel Hodgson, introduced amendments to an American resolution in order to stiffen the terms against the Netherlands, whose operations in the Indies he described as worse than Hitler's invasion of Holland in 1940, and he spoke of expelling the Dutch from the United Nations if they failed to obey the cease-fire order. The government incurred more criticism in January 1949 when Australia became the only fully participating western country among the nineteen Asian and Pacific nations which met at Delhi to devise a collective approach to the Indonesian problem. The resolutions of the conference were, in fact, moderate in tone, affirming support for the principles of the United Nations and declaring the Dutch resort to force to be a breach of the Charter and a menace to peace in south-east Asia. But the press and the opposition in Australia were none the less hostile to what they considered an extreme stand taken by the government in foreign policy. They castigated a policy which helped in the removal from Asia of white friends whom Australia might need later on, and in a debate in February 1949 Menzies, the leader of the opposition, questioned the whole purpose of the Delhi conference. 'In plain terms', he declared, 'we have been assisting to put the Dutch out of the East Indies. If we continue to do that the same process will, no doubt, eject the British from Malaya and the Australians from Papua and New Guinea.' The opposition suggested that Australia should dissociate itself from the anti-colonialism of the Delhi conference and negotiate a pact not only with the United States and Canada but also with India, Pakistan and the Philippines, which were evidently considered to be amenable to Australia's white allies.

The Labour government was unnecessarily vehement in its Indonesian policy in 1948 and 1949, though it could be argued that, when sovereignty was transferred from the Netherlands to an independent national republic in December 1949, Australia was in the excellent position of having the respect of its new Asian neighbour. The opposition, on the other hand, had shown itself to be possessed of outmoded concepts of external relations and to be apparently unwilling to adapt itself to the changing world order and Australia's new role in it.

The opposition's vigorous offensive against the government's management of external affairs did not exempt from its censure the sphere of British Commonwealth relations. In April 1949 Australia joined with the other countries of the British Commonwealth of Nations in accepting India as a republican state which would acknowledge the Crown merely as 'the symbol of the free association of its independent member nations and as such the Head of the Commonwealth'. Chifley and Evatt represented Australia at the Commonwealth Conference in London and were not happy with the compromise formula for Indian membership, declaring that the Australian government believed the personal relationship of the sovereign to the Commonwealth to be of supreme importance. When the text of the declaration issued at the conclusion of the conference was tabled in the federal Parliament in May, the prime minister stated emphatically that the government regretted India's decision to become a republic. 'However', continued Chifley, 'that decision having been made, the government believes the new relationship with India, which will come into force when the republic is proclaimed later this year, is in the best interests of the British Commonwealth.' Australia's allegiance to the Crown, he added, and its part in the British Commonwealth, would remain unaltered. The opposition also deplored India's decision to become a republic, and feared that at the London conference Australia had participated in moves that could lead to the disintegration of the British Commonwealth. Exaggerated and unconvincing as the opposition's apprehension and criticism were, the compromise solution permitting republican India to remain in the Commonwealth of Nations was regarded everywhere in Australia as a melancholy one and at best as a regrettable necessity.

A less esoteric development and one more likely to have serious practical consequences was the success of the Communists in the civil war in China. Hitherto the Chinese imbroglio had not attracted much attention in Australia, where the struggle had been viewed with passive detachment as a matter for American rather than Australian concern. But the misfortunes in 1948 and 1949 of Chiang Kai-shek and the Kuomintang, unflattering as their reputation was in Australia, raised the possibility of a strong Communist China's becoming the partner of the Soviet Union and the generating force behind Communist expansion throughout Asia and the Pacific. In commenting in June 1949 on the situation in Asia, Evatt told the House of Representatives it was not sufficient to assume that, because a country was Communist, it was impossible to work with, and something might be gained by establishing at least a commercial relationship with the *de facto* Chinese government. In October he announced that the United States, the United Kingdom and Australia were in complete accord in their attitude to China: they wished to maintain friendly relations, but in the absence of specific assurances that it would respect the territorial integrity of neighbouring countries and discharge all its international obligations, the new Communist government could neither be recognised nor admitted to the United Nations. This statement was publicised in the press in Hong Kong, where British officials and merchants regarded it as unfortunate and undiplomatic in that it gave the impression of speaking on behalf of Britain and America as well as of Australia and could only have an unfavourable reaction on the Chinese themselves. The Australian government in fact believed that the best and most logical policy would be to accept the existence of Communist China and grant its government diplomatic recognition, but it delayed action partly because it wished to act collectively with Britain and the United States, and partly because the Liberal and Country parties were opposed to recognition, and a premature move by the government at this time could result in the issue's becoming a contentious and unpredictable factor in the coming general election.

Although its policy had sometimes been thwarted, by 1949 the Labour government could fairly boast of a substantial record of achievement. The Snowy Mountains Hydro-Electric Bill was passed, despite sceptical comment from the opposition, and plans were put into effect for diverting the waters of the Snowy River in south-east New South Wales westward in order to extend the irrigation areas of the Murray and the Murrumbidgee and to generate power as the diverted waters dropped some 2,000 feet from the Snowy mountains. This combined irrigation and hydro-electric project—the most grandiose scheme undertaken by the commonwealth government—involved a vast expenditure on the construction of dams, power stations, tunnels and canals, which, it was estimated, would take at least twenty years to complete. It was inaugurated by the governor-general on October 17, 1949, in a ceremony which the opposition boycotted. A week later the foundation stone was laid in Canberra of the Australian National University designed to provide special facilities for postgraduate research: an aspect of tertiary education that the other universities in the various states were compelled to neglect under the growing demand for them to function as predominantly teaching bodies.

Of more direct significance so far as electoral prospects were concerned was the government's embarrassment two days later when the Privy Council dismissed the commonwealth's appeal on the bank nationalisation measures of 1947: a setback that was bound to affect the government's public reputation notwithstanding Evatt's statement that nationalisation could not now become an election issue. Banking interests were determined that no effort should be spared in the coming campaign to eject the Labour party from office, and a stream of propaganda vilified the government and classified Chifley variously with Hitler, Mussolini, Ned Kelly and Judas Iscariot.

The opposition's offensive against socialism, and its posture as the only real safeguard against communism in industry, were given added strength by strikes which paralysed the normal domestic and industrial life of the nation. The Miners' Federation submitted several claims to the arbitration tribunal. The claim for a wage increase was soon withdrawn; that for a thirty-five hours working week was being heard when the Federation requested an adjournment; and the tribunal draft award on the claim for long service leave was withdrawn when, on June 16, the miners voted to pursue their objectives by direct action. On June 27, 1949, a strike began in all states except Western Australia and developed into the last great challenge to the Labour government, which, with elections due before the end of the year, now had to prove that it

K

was capable of dealing firmly with Communist influence in the trade unions. It contested the validity of the ballot by which the strike had been ordered, and rushed emergency legislation through Parliament to freeze the funds of the Miners' Federation and prevent their use in prolonging the strike. Acting in close co-operation with the state governments, the commonwealth employed drastic measures to break the strike, and when the miners returned to work on August 15, several of their officials had been sentenced to terms of imprisonment, fines had been imposed on the Miners' Federation and supporting unions, and troops had been called in to work the open-cut mines.

The Liberal and Country parties adopted a responsible approach to the government's difficulties in these months and did not seriously attempt to embarrass it in its struggle to preserve authority and restore order. But when the election campaign started, they claimed that the only way to eliminate strikes against the arbitration system was to outlaw the Communist party and destroy Communist leadership in the trade unions. When Menzies opened the campaign on November 10, it was immediately evident that he intended to make socialism the central issue. His speech was a thorough-going indictment of the socialistic policy of the Chifley government, and he promised to introduce constitutional amendments to make the passage of legislation such as that on the banks impossible in the future without a referendum. The prime minister's speech a few days later was largely a description of his government's record and contained none of the promises being made by the opposition. Neither side devoted much attention to the fundamental problems of labour shortages, unarrested inflation, or foreign policy in the light of buoyant nationalism in Asia. The debate was on socialism, and in the polling of December 10, 1949, the electorate turned against the controls and integration associated with the Labour government and voted into the greatly enlarged House of Representatives a Liberal and Country party representation of seventy-four against Labour's forty-seven and one independent. After eight years in opposition the anti-Labour forces were returned to office committed to a policy of restraining the progress of socialisation and increasing the freedom for individual initiative.

10

The Communist Bogy (1949-1955)

THE NEW government that emerged from the elections of 1949 conformed to the now accepted pattern of anti-Labour coalitions in Australia, the Country party holding a minority of portfolios in an administration led by its predominantly metropolitan partner. The Liberal party had grown out of the disintegrating United Australia party at the end of the second world war, and it embraced the same social elements and fundamental political philosophy as its predecessor. Its appeal was to the business sections of the community, to the manufacturers, traders, commercial firms, financial institutions and the higher-paid professions, and it depended on business interests to supplement the revenue obtained from members' subscriptions. It operated as a federation of state organisations each of which possessed its local branches, executive, and annual conference, forming a structure similar to that of the other parties. Its parliamentary organisation and discipline were theoretically less rigid than those of the Labour party and its leader enjoyed more latitude in the exercise of his own discretion, including the selection of cabinet: a function which in the Labour party belonged to the caucus. The Liberal party's policy revolved around its distrust of collectivism and was directed to preserving the essentials of a free economy and the conditions necessary for the success of private enterprise. The wealthy classes looked to the Liberal party to protect their position, and it was therefore from the fashionable suburbs of the big cities that its most solid support came. But its appeal extended also to those who were repelled by trade union irresponsibility and by the doctrinaire and bureaucratic traits that sometimes came to the surface of the Labour party. The Liberals were the party of property and social order and cultivated a mien of respectability, refinement and the graces attaching to an overt loyalty to the British connection.

The arch-exponent of these virtues was the Liberal party leader, Robert Gordon Menzies, to whose genius largely belonged the credit for revitalising the anti-Labour forces and carrying them to electoral success. Menzies had been in public life for many years but had never won the respect in Australia that was accorded him overseas. Born in Victoria, he cut short a brilliant scholastic and legal career in order to enter politics. He had served with distinction in Victoria's state politics before transferring to the commonwealth Parliament, where he had become a prominent member of the Lyons ministry in the 1930s and ultimately prime minister for two years at the beginning of the second world war. His reorganisation of the United Australia party after its eclipse in 1943 was a remarkable achievement, and the fortunes of the new Liberal party that he created were necessarily related to his ability to restore his own reputation in the community. Menzies was respected for his undoubted legal ability and admired for his skill and quickness in debate. He possessed a dignified presence, an easy, courteous manner, and a command of lucid exposition and polished eloquence that were outstanding in a Parliament where the standards of public debate and speech were generally low. The inferior calibre of so many of those around him and opposed to him gave Menzies an exaggerated eminence that perhaps accounted both for the complacency and arrogance he occasionally exhibited, and for the fierce and angry emotions he aroused among people who instinctively recoiled from anyone with pretensions to superiority. In the polemics of debate at which he excelled, Menzies could seldom resist a patronising air, his admirably rounded phrases, wrapping an explanation or an argument of unrivalled clarity or logic, would be marred by a gibe at the expense of opponents less talented than himself. The opposition's criticism he would treat with condescension or scorn, and its views he would regard as odd or unhealthy when they differed from his own. Menzies was the paragon of those who revered fine speaking, but the suspicion lingered that he preferred to demonstrate his command of words rather than to take the positive action a situation might require. His propensity for assuming the mantle of a statesman in international affairs revealed limitations in his understanding of modern developments which, though of little consequence in an Australia normally unmoved by world problems, would have been a serious liability to the leader of any responsible greater power. Menzies was fortunate in the prosperity of the period during which he bestraddled the Australian parliamentary scene. But he was to prove himself a masterful and courageous prime minister, never afraid to court unpopularity if the occasion demanded it, and a skilful and ruthless political tactician, unblushingly British yet proudly and conspicuously Australian.

In fulfilment of its electoral promises, the new government abolished successively the rationing of petrol, butter and tea between February and July 1950. The abolition of petrol rationing was criticised both in England and Australia as a danger to the common resources of the sterling area, and was regarded with some concern by the British government which bore the responsibility for the sterling area's gold and dollar reserves. The consumption of petrol entailed expenditure of dollars at a time when there was an urgent need for economy, and this would be difficult if other countries followed Australia's example. Menzies believed the cessation of petrol rationing would not substantially affect Australia's dollar position and he emphasised that his government would maintain the program of stringent dollar economies agreed upon at a conference of British Commonwealth finance ministers in London in July 1949.

In March 1950 the government outlined a policy for developing the country's resources, and in August the prime minister returned from a tour overseas with a loan of $100 million from the International Bank for Reconstruction and Development intended for advancing plans for irrigation, land clearance and increased power supply. Nevertheless, when Parliament rose in June only two substantive Bills had been passed: one for creating a wool stabilisation fund, and the other extending the application of the child endowment scheme to all children of a marriage and not, as hitherto, excepting the first. The government was frustrated by its lack of a majority in the Senate, where the Labour opposition was able to thwart legislation it disliked. The Houses were deadlocked on three major Bills, the most significant of which was that to dissolve the Communist party, rejected by the Senate on its third reading.

The Communist Party Dissolution Bill recited allegations against the Communist party, declared it to be a menace to the security of Australia, dissolved it as an illegal association, and empowered the governor-general in Council to dissolve organisations dominated by Communists. The Bill prevented from holding office in a government department or a trade union covered by federal law any person named in a declaration as a Communist or member since May 1947 of an illegal organisation. Appeals against such a declaration were to be heard by a judge sitting without a jury, and the onus of proof would rest with the appellant unless he gave sworn evidence and exposed himself to cross-examination by the Crown, which, for its part, needed only to provide the written statement of the prosecutor without producing the witnesses from which its information derived or exposing them to cross-examination. The Labour opposition's criticism of the Bill was principally against those aspects of it which impinged on civil rights and were at variance with the traditions of English judicial practice, but the Labour party did not oppose the Bill outright, contenting itself with pressing for certain amendments. After prolonged discussion the Bill was eventually passed by the Senate in October 1950, but even in its amended form the Act was a grave infraction of English legal usage. It interfered with judicial procedure, and was repugnant to accepted principles of common law. The government was no doubt motivated by its view that communism was a criminal conspiracy insidiously undermining the fabric of the State, and believed that unusual methods were essential if the evil was to be countered. The government, indeed, was obsessed with the Communist bogy, and whether or not it would have been feasible, let alone morally or constitutionally defensible, to attempt to suppress a political movement by judicial means, the measure produced by the government in 1950 showed scant respect for the canons of a democracy to which it was proud to trace its lineage.

The unsettling passions to which the Act gave vent were demonstrated in the rowdy public meetings addressed by the prime minister: one in Sydney Town Hall in June 1950 required a hundred police to line the aisles and guard the door while another hundred waited in reserve outside. The difficulties inherent in the operation of the Act were illustrated by the prime minister's confession that five of the names he had read out in Parliament as alleged Communist trade union leaders had been included by mistake. The climax to the political turmoil came on March 9, 1951, when the High Court declared the Act invalid on the grounds that it attempted to interfere directly with civil liberties and property rights which were matters belonging to the states. Commonwealth interference in such matters was allowable only under its defence power and this could not be exercised except at a time of open war, and despite the conflict in Korea and extreme international tension the present was in fact a time of peace.

A week later the Senate referred to a select committee the Commonwealth Bank Bill which had been shuttled between the House of Representatives and the Labour-dominated Senate for twelve months, and the government, interpreting the Senate move as a refusal to pass the Bill, secured a dissolution of both Houses of Parliament. In the election campaign of April 1951, the government parties emphasised the dangers of communism and indicated that either a reference of powers from the states or a constitutional amendment would be sought to overcome the High Court's recent decision and to implement a program of economic controls and elimination of strikes in industry. The government parties were returned with a reduced margin in the House of Representatives, but their previous minority in the Senate was replaced by a working majority.

Fortified in its policy, the federal government ordered a raid on the offices of Communist-led trade unions in Sydney and Melbourne, and in July introduced a Bill to amend the constitution and give itself the power to legislate 'with respect to Communists or Communism as the Parliament considers to be necessary or expedient for the defence or security of the Commonwealth'. The government had good reason to believe the proposed amendment

151

would be accepted in the referendum in September 1951, but the Labour opposition embarked upon a vigorous nation-wide campaign to secure a negative vote. The campaign was assisted by liberal-minded people and intellectuals who protested against a measure they regarded as potentially a menace to the fundamental rights and liberties of a democratic community. The opponents of the amending Bill were given an initial advantage by the very complexity and ambiguity of its provisions, which were capable of having a sinister construction placed upon them disturbing to the layman who could not himself understand the document as it stood. Consequently, although in the early stages of the controversy a majority of the people was probably inclined to favour the suppression of communism, the doubts and difficulties attending the legislation in question were well ventilated and the result was its rejection, three states and a popular national majority of 52,000 voting in the negative. The main significance of the referendum, however, was not that the proposed amendment was rejected but that it was very nearly passed, and in the light of the traditional response of Australians in a referendum and the grave defects and dangers in the legislation itself, the people's decision on this occasion could not be construed as a victory for sanity or democracy over narrow and misguided zeal. The only reputation enhanced by the issue was that of Dr Evatt, who had succeeded to the leadership of the Labour party on the sudden death of Chifley in June 1951, and who devoted all his considerable talents and energy to the task of defeating a measure he deplored with evident conviction.

Herbert Vere Evatt was to become the most controversial and enigmatic figure in Australian politics during the next few years. His early legal career equalled that of Menzies in its brilliance and success, and at the age of thirty-six he had become a judge of the High Court. In the administrations of Curtin during the war and of Chifley after, he had taken a diligent part in the conduct of external affairs and served with distinction at the United Nations: an institution in which he placed what his critics regarded as a naïve and unjustifiable confidence. In intellect he was superior to the rest of the Labour party, and his academic attainments and scholarship outshone those of any member of either parliamentary chamber. In contrast to Menzies, however, he was lacking in platform graces; his clothes were often untidy, he had neither sense of humour nor gift of repartee, his voice was unpleasing, his material was sometimes desultory, and his standard of public speaking was unimpressive. He had a tremendous and unrelenting capacity for work, but was a difficult person with whom to be associated, and his unbridled personal ambition tended to cloud his judgement and tarnish an international outlook which made him of all Australian politicians at that time the country's nearest approximation to a statesman. Evatt's good qualities were never to make an impact on the Australian people, but the anti-Labour forces made sure that his bad ones were fully advertised, fostering calumnies that reflected on his private and public life and threw doubt on his mental stability. The government parties conceived an almost pathological antipathy for Evatt, perhaps actu-ated partly by a grudging respect for his courage and intellectual stature, partly by an instinctive assumption that a man of his legal ability and cultural interests was a traitor to his class in not belonging to the Liberal party, and partly by the suspicion that he was infected with Communist sympathies. Evatt, by his actions, foolishly laid himself open to the charge of Communist leanings, and his opponents sedulously propagated it among the public at large and made it their justification for the duty they allotted themselves of keeping him out of office at all costs.

In working for the defeat of communism at home, Menzies' government was not unmindful of the parallel necessity of helping to check its expansion abroad, particularly in the countries of south-east Asia and the Pacific from which the dangers to Aus-tralian security were most likely to come. Soon after the Liberal and Country parties had come to power at the end of 1949, the minister for External Affairs, P. C. Spender, had emphasised the need for Australia to assist the economic development of its neigh-bours and he had taken the initiative in seeking a concerted effort by the countries of the British Commonwealth in raising living standards in south-east Asia. The first meeting of the British Commonwealth Consultative Committee on Economic Aid, which had been set up at the Colombo Conference in January 1950, was held in Sydney in May 1950 and made recommendations. Soon Australia was contributing to the program of aid to Asian countries and its universities were receiving an increased flow of Asian students.

Three features of the scene to the north disturbed Australia: the first was the success of militant Chinese communism and the danger that its influence would spread; the second was the claim of the newly independent Indonesian Republic to the Dutch territory of West New Guinea, which bordered the Australian territories in Papua and East New Guinea; and the third was the American policy of building up defeated Japan as an ally of the democracies in any future war with the Communist powers in the Pacific.

Australia regarded the question of China as one primarily for the United States to answer, and the government contented itself with adhering to the American line of non-recognition and refusal to support the admission of the Peking régime to the United Nations. The Indonesian claim to West New Guinea constituted a closer and more alarming threat. Australian apprehension was roused in 1950 by speeches of the Indonesian president, Dr Sukarno, promising that the territory would be added to Indonesia before the end of the year, and by the statement of an official in the Indonesian Foreign Ministry that all New Guinea, British North Borneo and Portuguese Timor were essentially parts of Indonesia: a claim that was not endorsed by his superiors but nevertheless produced a sharp rebuke from the Australian minister for External Affairs. After a speech by Sukarno in May 1950 the Australian ambassador was recalled, and a debate in the federal Parliament in June confirmed that all parties were strongly opposed to Indonesian pretensions. On August 30, Sukarno announced that he would not be deflected from his objective by Australian opposition, and thenceforward the issue remained a subject for recurrent hostile comment in Australia.

The American decision to rearm Japan was not one that Australia could accept lightly, and the completion in September 1951 of the Japanese Peace Treaty on American terms was received without enthusiasm by the commonwealth government and was denounced by the opposition. The new minister for External

Affairs, R. G. Casey—an active and experienced successor to Spender and more profound than his parliamentary performances suggested—defended the treaty as 'the best compromise that could be achieved between a large number of countries with wide varieties of interests', but admitted that the government was not happy about Japan's unrestricted right of rearmament and facile restoration to the comity of nations. Evatt condemned the treaty as an 'open, unashamed abandonment of all the standards of international justice' and predicted that Japan would use its revived military power in its own interest and not necessarily in that of the democracies. In order to allay consternation in Australia and New Zealand over the Japanese Peace Treaty, the United States agreed to join them in a tripartite pact, which was signed in San Francisco in the same month as the peace treaty and committed each signatory to 'act to meet the common danger in accordance with its constitutional processes' if either of its partners were to be attacked. The ANZUS pact was the first treaty Australia had signed with a foreign country, and its omission of the United Kingdom, though severely criticised in some quarters, was a tacit acknowledgment by Australia and New Zealand that the mother country was no longer in a position to guarantee their security in the Pacific.

Australia's stake in the security of south-east Asia and the Pacific involved greater outlay on defence, for which the budget of September 1951 provided an estimate of nearly £182 million: an increase of £52 million over the expenditure of the previous year. This trend, dictated partly by contributions to the United Nations forces in Korea, helped quicken the inflation which in 1949 the Liberal party had pledged itself to check. A rise in imports was draining off overseas balances, and in the closing months of 1951 there was a substantial deficit in Australia's overseas trading accounts. Perplexed by the economic crisis at hand, the government procrastinated until March 1952 when it suddenly extended import licensing and reduced the volume of permitted imports. The prime minister pointed out that exports were running at the rate of £660 million a year against imports at the rate of £1,250 million; he called for increased agricultural output, especially of wheat, in order to restore Australia's purchasing power. Some unemployment appeared, but the government's measures were effective. Before the end of 1952 export earnings had risen while imports had declined, and by the middle of 1953 the balance of trade, excepting that with the dollar area, was a favourable one. Inflation slowed down, and the general improvement in the economic situation was reflected in the budget of September 1953, when income tax, company tax and sales tax were each reduced, and social service payments were increased.

In July 1953 a commonwealth scheme came into force providing a national anti-tuberculosis service, and hospital, medical and pharmaceutical benefits. The scheme was based on the principle of voluntary insurance and was largely a financial arrangement for assisting patients to pay their medical expenses. It was not a national health service in the true sense, for there was no positive control over hospital administration or the employment of doctors; it did not lead to demonstrable improvement in medical and hospital standards, and it made no provision for dental care because of the heavy expense it would have entailed. Any attempt to establish a national health service on the British model would not only have been contrary to the philosophy of the government parties but would have encountered the firm opposition of the whole medical profession. Such a scheme was eventually approved in principle at a conference of the federal Labour party in 1957, but there was never much real hope of a national health service's being accepted in Australia, for the expense was regarded as prohibitive and doubt was thrown on its value by criticism of the British system.

The Labour party, indeed, was trying to divest itself of its socialist incubus and its common portrayal as the party of centralisation and State control. The steady increase in wages and the achievement of the forty-hour working week, paid annual holidays and long-service leave, had blunted the force of a great part of Labour's original program, and it was recognised by the moderate section of the party that the policy of nationalisation set down in the party platform had become more of an embarrassment than a practicable objective. The constitutional barriers to nationalisation had been demonstrated in the Chifley government's banking legislation, which was generally assumed to have contributed significantly to the electoral defeat of 1949. Emotional appeals for social reform and State ownership made little impact on a community with a remarkably high standard of living. Labour leaders were now inclined to qualify the socialist element in the party's program and to explain away nationalisation as a weapon to be employed only in the last resort. Their dominant concern was not to risk halting the decline in the popularity of the Liberal and Country parties that had been revealed in various state elections. In December 1952 Labour won a resounding success in Victoria and displaced the Country party administration; in February 1953 Labour retained power in New South Wales with an increased majority and in Western Australia ousted a coalition of the Liberal party and the Country Democratic League; and in March 1953 the Labour government in Queensland was returned to office in greater strength. By the end of 1953 the Labour party was in office in five of the six states, the exception being South Australia where the repeated re-election of the Liberal Country League was assisted by an electoral system weighted in favour of the rural constituencies.

The federal Labour party, therefore, had reason to take a sanguine view of the general election of May 1954. In his policy speech Evatt virtually abandoned the socialist objective and promised large depreciation allowances to industry, a reconsideration of company taxation, and more generous social services. The government also dangled some promises but laid its emphasis on the successful maintenance of economic stability and congratulated itself on the nation's prosperity, which it attributed to its recent policies. This was an extravagant assumption, for high export prices had helped, but the government was entitled to credit for adopting measures in 1952 to reverse the unfavourable balance of trade and check the deterioration in Australia's overseas currency reserves. The election campaign was a materialist one, the debate revolving around the amount of money that would enter or leave the voters' pockets, and the result was a reduction of the government's majority in the House of Representatives from fifteen to seven.

The election was conducted in the shadow of an espionage

case, the handling of which became the subject of heated controversy and may have had an indeterminable influence on the poll. In the last two days of the parliamentary session before the election, Menzies announced that Vladimir Petrov, a third secretary in the Russian embassy, had admitted the existence in Australia of a Soviet espionage system and had sought political asylum. An Act appointing a royal commission of three state judges to investigate Petrov's disclosures was hurriedly passed with the full support of the Labour party at the final sitting of Parliament. The commission began its hearing in June, but in the meantime Petrov's wife was recalled by the Soviet government, and in dramatic scenes at Darwin on the way home Mrs Petrov's escort was disarmed by the Australian authorities and she was granted political asylum. On April 23, the Soviet Union broke off diplomatic relations with Australia. The Petrov case was not openly an issue in the federal elections in May 1954, but any effect it had could only have been in favour of the government and to the disadvantage of the opposition, for it revived the public's sensitiveness about communism upon which the Liberal and Country parties always played. The Country party leader, Sir Arthur Fadden, sensing the mood of the electorate, probed this question in his policy speech in which he suggested that Evatt had been indulgent towards Communists in the past.

That the Petrov case was deliberately timed and exploited by the government for political purposes is doubtful. But if, as was possible, the prime minister knew most of the details of the matter some months before he revealed them to Parliament, his failure to transmit the gist of them to the leader of the opposition savoured of calculated discourtesy, and his decision to make the announcement with solemn urgency on the eve of the election campaign inevitably laid him open to the charge of timing the affair in order to impress and influence the electorate. It would have been impossible, however, to have foreseen the antics of Evatt himself, consumed with the anguish of his party's election failure and the severe blow to his ambition. In August 1954 he appeared before the royal commission in order to defend two members of his own staff who had been named as possible contributors of information contained in one of the documents handed over by Petrov. Evatt objected to the commission's giving prominence to his staff members when other persons were similarly mentioned in the document, and he alleged that Petrov had conspired with others to forge papers and produce charges in order to injure the Labour party and influence the federal elections.

Evatt's enraged recklessness went further early in September when he championed the cause of Madame Ollier, a second secretary in the French embassy, who, Petrov asserted, had promised to supply him with information on arms being shipped to Indochina. The French embassy sent Madame Ollier to Noumea, where she was arrested and taken to France for trial, whereupon Evatt denounced the Petrov correspondence as 'deliberately falsified and fabricated' with the aim of wrecking Madame Ollier's career and reputation, and characterised the whole tenor of the royal commission's proceedings as worse than American McCarthyism. In its interim report shortly afterwards, the commission described Evatt's charges as 'fantastic and wholly unsupported by any credible evidence', and dismissed the theory he had conceived that he and the political party he led had been made the victims of a political conspiracy. An attitude which, in other circumstances might have had much in it to admire, in this instance served only to besmirch Evatt's reputation; he was too obviously motivated by pique and political frustration, and his eccentric behaviour undermined public confidence in him and gave yet more scope for those among his opponents who delighted in depicting him as a Communist sympathiser. Furthermore, he had alarmed many of his supporters, and before the end of 1954 an open rift had appeared in the ranks of the Labour party.

The revelation of the existence in Australia of an espionage system controlled by the secret service of the Soviet Union was a signal to look closer at the nation's defence and to feel increased anxiety at the success of Communist subversion in Asia, especially after the French withdrawal from northern Indochina. The Australian contribution to the fighting in Korea and Malaya had been efficient, if small, but it had proved difficult to keep the regular forces up to their planned establishment in a period of abounding prosperity when conditions of military service were less attractive. Compulsory military training for all young men over the age of eighteen had been introduced in March 1951 in legislation providing for a recruit's continuous training during a period of between fourteen and twenty-five weeks in the first year and twenty-six days in each of the subsequent three years before he was transferred to the reserve. In September 1953 the training period had been reduced to a maximum of twenty-two weeks in three years: a scale which was greeted with derision by the critics and tallied with the general inadequacy of the whole defence program. 'Would you have us leave it to the people of Great Britain', asked Menzies when speaking of defence in February 1953, 'whose material living standards are so much lower than ours? I hope not.' Nevertheless, the Australian defence budgets, though increasing, continued to compare very un-favourably with those of the United Kingdom.

Australia's defence depended largely on collective action with its allies and on helping to check the spread of communism in the unstable countries to its north in south-east Asia. For this reason the deterioration of the French position in Indochina was watched with particular uneasiness, and fears mounted that Communist pressure would spill out over most of Asia. 'For America and Britain the defence of south-east Asia may be seen as strategic-ally desirable', wrote the *Sydney Morning Herald* in April 1954; 'for France it is a matter of national prestige; but for Australia it is life or death.' The demand grew for a collective defence arrange-ment, and in August the prime minister announced in Parliament that events in south-east Asia made Australia's security problem more acute and that his government would accept military com-mitments as a member of any collective defence system that might be devised. The commonwealth government participated actively in promoting the South-East Asia Collective Defence Treaty which was signed by eight nations at Manila on September 9, 1954, and brought into being what became known as the South-East Asia Treaty Organisation (SEATO). The treaty was less specific in its military terms than the Australian government had wished; it contained no provision for a unified military com-mand, and it had obvious limitations as an effective instrument of military co-operation. Nevertheless, it signified the concentration of Australia's foreign policy on the problem of Asia. Together with the ANZUS pact, support of the United Nations in Korea, and the dispatch in 1955 of Australian troops to join a strategic reserve stationed in Malaya, SEATO was evidence of Australia's concern for the success of collective measures against Communist subversion and imperialism in Asia.

The government's approach to foreign policy was criticised by the Labour party, which opposed sending troops to Malaya, disagreed with the government's refusal to recognise Communist China or to support its admission to the United Nations, viewed the collective defence arrangements in south-east Asia with some scepticism, and laid greater emphasis on negotiating settlements with the Communist forces. The tendency of the opposition in 1954 and 1955 to gravitate towards the left in its political outlook combined with differences over Evatt's provocative leadership to produce a split in the Labour party that reduced still further its already depressed political fortunes.

On October 5, 1954, Evatt publicly denounced 'a small minority of Labour members located particularly in the state of Victoria', who, he said, since 1949 had become 'increasingly disloyal to the Labour movement and the Labour leadership'. He was referring to a predominantly Roman Catholic section which regarded communism rather than capitalism as the enemy and made its principal business the removal of Communist leadership from the trade unions. This movement was organised and recruited largely by the members of Catholic Action, which had been founded before the second world war to enlist the support of the laity in the pastoral work of the Roman Catholic Church and existed in all parts of the world under the patronage of the pope. The movement supported attempts by the Menzies government to proscribe communism, and, fearing socialism as potentially dangerous to the property and income of the Roman Catholic Church, was inclined to be hostile towards the more radical notions of the Labour party, preferring the vaguer and less doctrinaire concept of social justice. Chifley had been aware of this influence in the Labour party, and not long before he died he had admonished those supporters 'who', he remarked, 'feel they can

L

AUSTRALIA IN THE TWENTIETH CENTURY

best serve their own personal interests or expediency by trying to see how far they can get over to the right without actually becoming members of the Liberal party'. The right wing steadily extended its strength in the Labour ranks, causing sectarian bitterness and the likelihood of an outright split which Evatt strove industriously to avoid. By the middle of 1954, however, it had become evident that the threat must be countered openly and with determination if it was not to undermine the Labour leadership completely. After Evatt's public accusation in October, charges and counter-charges filled the closing months of the year.

The first clear indications of the magnitude of the differences occurred in Victoria in February 1955, when a new state executive of the Labour party was appointed excluding those who had been critical of Evatt's leadership and the party's policies. Seventeen members of the state parliament thereupon resigned from the party and formed their own group. In March a federal conference of the Labour party at Hobart was boycotted by nearly half the delegates on the grounds that they could not recognise the newly appointed state executive in Victoria, but the delegates who attended recorded their confidence in Evatt, confirmed the appointment of the new executive in Victoria, and declared their opposition to the use of Australian troops in Malaya and their support for the admission of the Chinese People's Republic to the United Nations. In April seven Victorian members of the Labour party in the federal House of Representatives were expelled by their state executive and formed themselves into what was referred to as the 'Anti-Communist Labor Party'. In the elections in Victoria in May, sectarian controversy was intensified, and the Labour party's dissident elements campaigned and voted independently and contributed to the defeat of the state's Labour government and to the victory of the Liberal-Country party coalition.

The federal government was content to watch the Labour opposition disintegrate and its own position became correspondingly stronger. The country's economic prosperity continued. It was a period of full employment and rising wages, and consumer spending and private investment increased, but export earnings declined, and in the first sales of the 1956 season wool prices

162

dropped by 5 per cent. A substantial deficit in overseas trade and a fall in Australia's overseas credits caused some misgivings. At a conference in September 1954 with the prime minister and the governor of the Commonwealth Bank, the trading banks and hire purchase companies agreed to exercise more caution in making credit advances, but Menzies indicated that the government would not hesitate to introduce measures to correct the adverse balance of payments if this voluntary restraint failed to produce the necessary effect. Industrial developments included large oil refineries in Victoria and Western Australia, the beginning of hydro-electric power deliveries from the Snowy Mountains project, the near-completion of the plant of the Australian Aluminium Production Commission at Bell Bay in Tasmania, and record production at the Broken Hill Proprietary Company's iron and steel plants in New South Wales. The shortage of manpower was being relieved somewhat by the immigration program, which in November boasted a total of 1,000,000 new arrivals in the country since 1945. The Menzies government had maintained the immigration policy of its Labour predecessor, and the inflow was now at a rate of well over 100,000 a year, although economic difficulties in 1952 and 1953 had necessitated a temporary reduction.

The government had no reason to be ashamed of the economic situation, and the budget of August 1955 showed a surplus on the year of £30 million, but there were signs of renewed inflationary tendencies which would eventually require unpopular restrictive measures. In the knowledge of this, the government began to consider the possibility of an early general election, notwithstanding the fact that the House of Representatives could legitimately have continued until May 1957. The decision to hold elections in the December of 1955 was almost certainly clinched by the irreconcilable divisions within the Labour party and the rash behaviour of Evatt when the report of the royal commission on espionage was debated in Parliament in October.

The commission's report affirmed that the documents Petrov had brought with him were genuine, that espionage had occurred before 1949 when the Australian Security Intelligence Organisation had been established, but that there was no evidence of successful espionage after that year. Evatt attacked the report and

163

the commission which had produced it, repeated his allegations that some of the documents had been fabricated in order to discredit both himself and the Labour party, and startled everyone by announcing that he had written to the Russian foreign minister, who had assured him that the Petrov documents were forgeries. This summoning of the Russian foreign minister to his aid damaged Evatt's reputation with the Australian public more than any other single act of his.

The government took advantage of the circumstances to hold a general election almost immediately: cynical tactics, but possessing some constitutional justification in the opportunity it offered to bring into line elections to the Senate and the House of Representatives which had been divergent since 1951. The campaign was uneventful except in Victoria, where Labour's divisions were most marked and its internal antagonisms most bitter. The official Labour party promised increases in social service payments to be financed by a tax on excessive company profits and by reductions in expenditure on defence. The Liberal and Country parties relied on the government's achievements, the disunity of the opposition, and the Communist bogy, the prime minister declaring that Evatt was 'on the side of the Communists in any issue between the Communists and the responsible civil authorities'. The result of the election in December 1955 was narrowly to deny the government a clear majority in the Senate but to increase its majority in the House of Representatives from seven to twenty-eight. At the end of 1955 Australian federal politics consisted of a divided and discouraged opposition, and a government firmly entrenched and complacent in the prospect of a lengthy future in office.

11

Problems in the Territories (1940-1962)

IN 1955 the population of Australia was more than 9,000,000 and still overwhelmingly of Anglo-Saxon stock. Immigrants of several other European nationalities had been admitted into the country in large numbers since 1945, but Australia remained by design essentially a British nation, and racial homogeneity was preserved by the policy of excluding coloured peoples. Whether the White Australia policy was based purely on the need to protect the community from the economic and social problems experienced by countries with mixed populations, or whether it was based also on an innate Anglo-Saxon racial prejudice, accentuated by Australia's geographical context and rationalised ethnographically and economically in order to satisfy the Australian conscience, it was likely to become an embarrassment to the good relations with Asia which it was Australia's interest to cultivate. The government rejected suggestions that fixed quotas of coloured people be allowed to enter the country in order to deflect the charge of racial discrimination, but in June 1958 it replaced the hypocritical dictation test required by the original Commonwealth Immigration Restriction Act of 1901 by a system of entry permits. Australia was deliberately a white man's country, but being situated on the edge of Asia, where there was marked sensitivity to racial discrimination, the policy of accepting only those immigrants who were readily assimilable into the existing society had to be administered with tact as well as determination. Equally, it was incumbent upon Australia to demonstrate to the world its appreciation of the responsibilities the policy of racial isolationism imposed upon it, and the manner in which the nation discharged its obligations towards the Aborigines and Papuans, the dark-skinned peoples already within its frontiers, became a gauge by which the sincerity of Australia's racial policies might be measured.

The attitude towards the Aborigines had been liberalised since the end of the nineteenth century, but the records of the federal and state governments remained poor until after the second world war. The military activity in northern Australia during the war brought many servicemen into contact with Aborigines, who provided casual labour for army and air force units and responded well to the routine of labour units and camp life, with the result that after the war there was less reluctance on the part of many Aborigines in these areas to co-operate in any positive native policies devised by the government. Indicative of the concern now being shown by some organisations and individuals for aboriginal welfare was the lively public controversy in November 1946 over the dangers to which the tribes of central Australia might be exposed by the rocket-firing tests then being planned. Official assurances were made that the governments of the commonwealth and the states concerned (South Australia and Western Australia) would take full responsibility for safeguarding the interests of the inhabitants. How many were likely to be affected was difficult to determine, for although the aboriginal population had been much reduced from the 300,000 estimated to have inhabited the continent in the eighteenth century, it was still impossible to take a reliable census among those who lived on the remote edge of settlements and were scattered over an area exceeding 1,000,000 square miles. In 1946 there were probably about 70,000 full-blood and half-caste Aborigines in Australia, located chiefly in Queensland, the Northern Territory and Western Australia, to a lesser extent in New South Wales and South Australia, and negligibly in Victoria and Tasmania.

The various governments were all dedicated in principle to raising the Aborigines to a standard that would enable them to assume the full rights and privileges of citizenship. It was with this end in view that, in October 1946, the commonwealth announced new plans for the Northern Territory. Training establishments were to be erected to educate the Aborigines in crafts and industries so that they could take a larger part in industrial life; the missions were to be assisted in founding appropriate agricultural and industrial enterprises; and specialist officers were to be appointed to collaborate with them in the education and general direction of the welfare of the aboriginal population. Hitherto, in New South Wales, Victoria, South Australia and Tasmania, Aborigines were entitled to vote in state elections; in Western Australia those who had served in the defence forces or obtained a certificate of citizenship under state legislation could vote; while in the Northern Territory, apart from members and former members of the forces, only those Aborigines declared by ordinance to be fitted to vote were entitled to do so. In 1949 the right to vote in federal elections was extended to all Aborigines who had been members of the defence forces or possessed the franchise under state law.

The policy of preparing the Aborigines for gradual assimilation into the white community necessitated a new appreciation of their importance as individuals, and this could be detected in the welfare legislation passed by the Northern Territory Legislative Council in June 1953 giving the commonwealth power to declare any needy Aboriginal a ward of the State. This Act repealed the ordinance that had controlled the lives of the Northern Territory Aborigines for a generation, and although the commonwealth government retained authority to protect and restrict the movement of those not ready for full citizenship, henceforth all Aborigines were to have freedom of movement until taken under the wardship of the State, which would relinquish its control as they proved ready to assume citizenship rights.

In the post-war years, greater attention was paid to the commonwealth's other native problem in the Territories of Papua and New Guinea, which had been neglected hitherto, but which now assumed a new significance as a vulnerable target for criticism of Australia from those independent countries of Asia with which it wished to maintain cordial relations. The parsimony heretofore exhibited by the commonwealth in its budgeting for the Territories was now replaced by a willingness to make substantial grants towards economic reconstruction and development. The government was probably influenced by the example set by Britain's program of colonial development and welfare, but unfortunately it failed to imitate the extensive planning, research and preparation of new administrative machinery that Britain undertook. Nevertheless, the war had witnessed some progress in government thinking on New Guinea. As early as August 1943, the minister for External Affairs had proclaimed the welfare of the New Guinea natives to be one of Australia's imperative duties when peace came, and in February 1944 two anthropologists were appointed at the request of General Blamey to ensure that anthropological knowledge would be applied to the problem of protecting native society from the disruptive effects of military operations. The war also made New Guinea familiar to thousands of Australians who had formerly known little of it except as an island of gold, head-hunters and rare orchids. Moreover, military operations there had necessitated the construction of good roads, bridges and well-appointed airfields; these made accessible districts which might otherwise have been left indefinitely isolated. The business of government was then in the charge of the Australian New Guinea Administrative Unit: a military authority which had been hastily established after the Japanese invasion in order to supervise native affairs and prevent disaffection. It was commanded by a major-general answerable to the department of the Army; it controlled the Royal Papuan Constabulary of 2,000 native police, and it served its purpose well in enforcing order and ensuring the availability of native pack trains to carry supplies and wounded across difficult terrain. The Unit's senior officers were recruited mainly from the staffs of the earlier civil authorities in the territories, but in 1945 a School of Civil Affairs was founded in Canberra to train administrative officers, initially for the Unit and ultimately for the post-war administration that succeeded it. The School was later transferred to Sydney and established permanently as the Australian School of Pacific Administration, which became not only a training centre but also an institute for the study of colonial problems in general.

Civil administration was restored to the Territories in an Act passed by the commonwealth Parliament in July 1945. In explaining the Act to the House of Representatives, the minister for External Territories, E. J. Ward, announced that the indenture system of labour would be abolished within five years and that henceforth natives would be engaged by employers under licence for a maximum of twelve months and would not be eligible for re-engagement until after they had spent three months in their home villages. The weekly hours of labour were reduced from fifty-five in New Guinea and fifty in Papua to forty-four in both cases; the minimum age of employment was fixed at sixteen; and the old monthly minimum wage rates of five shillings in New Guinea and ten shillings in Papua were raised in both Territories to a rate of fifteen shillings plus rations, housing and medical care: a modest enough increase in view of the fact that the five shillings minimum had been introduced by the German administration before the first world war, remaining unchanged despite the decline in money values since 1914.

It was clear from the measures taken in the months immediately after the second world war that the Australian government entertained no idea of the New Guinea Territories' passing out of its control, and this was solemnly affirmed in April 1946 by Evatt in the House of Representatives and by the Australian delegate at the United Nations Assembly. Australia declared that it did not regard the dissolution of the League as lessening its responsibility for advancing the inhabitants of the Mandates in New Guinea and Nauru, which it would continue to administer in accordance with the provisions of the Mandate until they were brought without any interruption in control under the trusteeship of the United Nations. In August 1946 the then prime minister, Chifley, announced the terms of an agreement by which New Guinea would become a United Nations trusteeship territory, and this was approved by the General Assembly of UNO in the following December. The new agreement admitted Australia's right to ally the Trust Territory with the Territory of Papua in an administrative union to be known as the Territory of Papua and New Guinea, which would possess a single administrator, supreme court and public service. The process of effecting the administrative union was carried further in the Papua and New Guinea Bill introduced into the House of Representatives in June 1948.

The Bill was revised in the light of suggestions made by the Trusteeship Council and not passed until the following year.

The Papua and New Guinea Act came into force on July 1, 1949 and dismantled the provisional administration established in 1945. It provided for an executive council to be appointed by the governor-general and to consist of at least nine officers of the Territory, and for a legislative council to consist of the administrator and twenty-eight other members, sixteen of whom were to be official members from the administrative departments; of the remainder, three were to represent the interests of the christian missions, three were to be natives, and three were to be elected by voters of the Territory. The commonwealth retained controlling powers and the right to approve or disallow the council's ordinances, but the new legislative council which was inaugurated under the provisions of the 1949 Act on November 26, 1951, was significant in that it contained three native members: the first to sit in any Australian legislature. Their membership was criticised on the ground that they would be incapable of properly understanding the issues discussed or of participating fully in the technical work of the legislative council, but so far as the commonwealth government was concerned their presence fulfilled a purpose in meeting the requests of the United Nations for the natives to be given a role in political life. The large official majority on the council ensured that only those ordinances supported by the administration would be passed.

The attention given to New Guinea by the United Nations and Trusteeship Council was both a spur to the commonwealth to improve its administration and a source of resentment and irritation on the part of the government, which grew impatient of what it regarded as often misinformed and prejudiced criticism. Some of the censure was undoubtedly exaggerated and failed to appreciate the difficulties involved or the real progress achieved, but there was a tendency for the commonwealth government to give the impression that it regarded New Guinea, as well as Papua, as Australia's private property. In 1950 the minister for External Affairs, P. C. Spender, declared that Australia must remain in New Guinea 'in all circumstances' and that it was its duty to administer the Territory 'in a way best calculated to protect the welfare of the native inhabitants and at the same time to serve Australia's security interests'. It was, perhaps, the fear that the Territory would be removed from its control and the country's northern defences laid bare that made Australia peculiarly sensitive to United Nations judgements on its administration and quick to take offence.

The Trusteeship Mission which visited New Guinea in 1953 produced a sober report commending much that had been done there, but indignant exception was taken in Australia to its recommendation that pidgin English should be discarded. Pidgin, according to the report, was not a suitable language for instruction, for the characteristics it had derived from the circumstances in which it was invented reflected 'outmoded concepts of the relationship between indigenous inhabitants and immigrant groups'. This recommendation was described by the Australian minister for Territories, P. M. Hasluck, as ridiculous and unrealistic, pidgin having been used for generations as the only common tongue between peoples with scores of different languages. The minister's retort was in some ways justified, especially as the mission may on this point have been inspired by the anti-colonialist emotions of one or two members; but to dismiss the criticism was unfair to a mission that had taken considerable care to understand the difficulties confronting the Territory's administrators. It was government policy to introduce standard English as soon as possible, but until then the use of pidgin was regarded as an indispensable minimum linguistic basis for understanding between the people and the administrators. Pidgin employed a restricted vocabulary and a different grammatical system from that of standard English; it represented a simplified language derived largely from the natives' faulty imitations of the sounds they heard from English speakers, who on their side consciously imitated the accent and style of the natives, so that the language of both parties converged into a mutually comprehensible hybrid. Useful as pidgin was, however, disapproval of it by the United Nations did raise the important question of whether it was wise to perpetuate a tongue which possessed no status and reflected a master and servant relationship.

Among the developments praised by the United Nations mission of 1953 was the institution of native village councils. Each of these exercised authority over several villages and was elected every two years by taxpayers, who recorded their vote by verbally notifying the returning officer in confidence. A village council could levy taxes, assist in maintaining law and order, and organise any enterprise that would benefit the community; in many cases it gave important help towards the provision of schools, roads, medical aid posts and houses. On land policy the report was cautious and uncritical; on economic policy it urged that a long-term plan of development should be devised; and on public health it expressed satisfaction that the administration was aware of the improvements needed. The Trusteeship Council was not always so restrained, however, and its resolutions in later years calling upon Australia to set a date for the grant of independence or self-government were disagreeably received by the commonwealth government. In August 1956 the minister for External Affairs, R. G. Casey, stated that it was impracticable to draw up an advance timetable for the various stages of political development, and in the following February he denounced the idea as an example of the irresponsibility with which certain members of the United Nations approached trusteeship and colonial questions.

The pivot of Australia's whole attitude towards New Guinea was the common recognition that the Territory represented a vital factor in the nation's security. This was amply demonstrated by the reaction to Indonesia's persistent and bellicose claim to the western portion of the island which the Dutch had retained out of their old East Indies empire. The commonwealth government, backed by the parliamentary opposition, supported the Dutch rejection of the Indonesian claim and, in consequence, became associated with the remnants of colonialism in Asia, occupying a position on this issue diametrically opposed to that of the neighbours with which it was its policy to remain friendly. The decision to support Dutch retention of West New Guinea was due partly to ethnological reasons, the inhabitants having no racial, linguistic or cultural affinity to the varied inhabitants of Indonesia, and partly to concern for the West New Guinea peoples. Their

welfare, it was argued, would not be furthered by their transference to an Indonesian government already grappling with intractable economic and political problems.

But the principal factor shaping Australian opinion was the
fear that Indonesia would be a difficult and undependable neighbour, liable to fall under Communist influence and threaten the
Australian hold on eastern New Guinea. 'If the claim of Indonesia
to Dutch New Guinea were conceded to any degree at all', stated
Spender at the Hague in August 1950, 'it would be but a matter of
time, no matter how genuine may be assurances to the contrary,
when the claim would be pushed further so as to include the
Trust Territory of Australian New Guinea and its people.' Behind
this concern was the traditional assumption that a New Guinea
in Australian or reliable hands was necessary for the protection of
Australia's vulnerable north. 'If we allowed the Indonesians into
Dutch New Guinea', said the deputy leader of the federal Labour
party, A. A. Calwell, in January 1958, 'there would be no hope
of holding the northern portion of Australia and the fate of this
country would be sealed and certain.' It was debatable whether
this conception of New Guinea as integral to the defence of
Australia was still valid in an age of long-range weapons and
highly scientific military techniques, but there was at least a
reasonable argument for denying a potential aggressor the advantage of a strategically well-placed base from which to plan
an attack.

The complications in Australia's approach to the West New
Guinea issue came from the interaction of two elements in its
policy of safeguarding national security: the strategic and the
diplomatic—two elements which in this case were largely incompatible. Assuming that the New Guinea islands were, as
Spender declared in 1950, Australia's 'last ring of defence against
aggression', then strategic considerations required that they should
be in the possession of a peaceful power of proven stability.
So far as West New Guinea was concerned, the Netherlands met
this requirement better than did Indonesia. On the other hand,
if it was Australia's policy to accept the realities of its geographical position and strive for a permanent amicable relationship with the countries of south-east Asia, then diplomatic

173

considerations dictated that the Netherlands should not be so firmly supported as to antagonise Indonesia and all the Asian countries.

A good case could be made out for giving either the strategic or the diplomatic element priority, but whatever course was pursued should have allowed for the likely effects of the dispute on the Dutch, who no doubt wished to uphold their national prestige over West New Guinea but could not be expected to remain there indefinitely, incurring heavy expenditure and a good deal of international odium in developing and defending it. Moreover, if at any time the Dutch decided to cut their costs, relent to the unabating Indonesian pressure, and evacuate West New Guinea, it was doubtful whether Australia would be able to prevent the Indonesians from achieving their purpose. In these circumstances, Australian policy on the West New Guinea dispute was short-sighted and mismanaged; it lacked even the merit of consistency. The government demonstrated its solidarity with the Dutch with such effect that in January 1958 the Australian embassy in Djakarta was constrained officially to rebut allegations that Australian forces were being sent to the defence of West New Guinea. If Australia had really been prepared to give military backing to its encouragement of the Dutch stand, there might have been some justification for the attitude adopted throughout the 1950s, but Australia was not in a position to do so and the ultimate result was, predictably, that not only was its good name with Asian countries put in jeopardy but also Australia's policy failed to prevent West New Guinea from passing into Indonesian possession.

Australian doubts about the régime in Indonesia were intensified at the beginning of 1957 by evidence of its acute economic difficulties, by a political crisis in which provinces in Sumatra defied the authority of the central government, and by proposals announced in February by President Sukarno for the organisation of an all-party administration in which the Communists would be represented. This may have strengthened the commonwealth government's determination to press ahead with its policy of denying West New Guinea to Indonesia by cementing links between the Australian and Dutch authorities in the island, by calling for restraint from the two disputants, and by working for the principle of self-determination for the Papuan peoples in accordance with the terms of the United Nations Charter. On November 6, 1957, the Australian and Dutch governments issued a joint statement expressing their agreement to establish liaison offices in each other's territory in New Guinea, to co-operate in certain administrative matters, and to co-ordinate policy towards political, economic, social and educational development: the whole process to be evolved, continued the statement, 'until such time as the inhabitants of the territories concerned will be in a position to determine their own future'. The statement was followed by talks in Canberra between Dutch and Australian ministers, and in October 1958 by a conference between Dutch and Australian administrative officials on technical field problems of native administration in New Guinea.

This collaboration between the Netherlands and Australia provoked a sharp reaction in Indonesia, whose spokesmen suggested that it was a preliminary to a military alliance: an interpretation which the Australian minister for External Affairs hotly refuted as 'a deliberate campaign of falsification from the mouths of responsible ministers of the government of Indonesia'. Australia also continued to align itself with the Netherlands in the United Nations debates on the issue, reiterating its belief in the legal correctness of the Dutch position and urging a settlement that would be peaceful, consistent with the Charter, provide for self-determination, and promote the welfare of the New Guinea people. This was the essence of the Australian case at the United Nations debate in the later months of 1961, but the militant intransigence of the Indonesians, and indications that in any military operations the Dutch would not have the support of either the Americans or the British, brought about a modification in the Australian approach.

In January 1962 reports circulated in the Australian press that the government was about to change its attitude on the West New Guinea issue, and although the minister for External Affairs, Sir Garfield Barwick, said that no alteration was contemplated, it became clear that the probability of the disputed territory's passing soon to Indonesia had been accepted in the federal cabinet. On August 15, 1962, after several months of negotiations, the Netherlands and Indonesia signed a formal agreement at United Nations headquarters transferring West New Guinea from Dutch to United Nations supervision in the following October and from the United Nations to Indonesia in May 1963. The agreement was received without enthusiasm in Australia, where, despite ministerial claims that Australia had joined with the United States and other countries in helping to prevent war over West New Guinea, it was felt that Australian policy had not shown up to good effect and that its results were far from satisfactory.

In the last few years of their rule in West New Guinea, the Dutch had feverishly accelerated political and economic development, and it was inevitable that their activity should infuse new energy into the Australians in the eastern half of the island. With international interest focusing on a dwindling number of colonial and trust territories, a laggard administration was likely to attract increasingly severe criticism. It was becoming belatedly clear to the government that its adherence to the concept of uniform and gradual development in New Guinea, admirable as it may have been earlier in the twentieth century, would not suit the temper of the 1960s and that Australia would have to readjust its policy and reassess its responsibilities towards the Territory. The Territory's cost to the commonwealth was not large but had been steadily growing; by 1959 annual public expenditure on it had risen to over £18 million, of which less than a third was raised within the Territory itself. In August 1959 the federal government abolished all export duties in the Territory, reduced import duties, and for the first time imposed an income tax at about half the Australian mainland rate. This was strongly opposed by planters, miners and traders in the Territory, and three elected members resigned from the local legislative council in protest when the Bill was introduced. Their criticisms were taken up in Canberra by government backbenchers who demanded the resignation of Hasluck, the minister for Territories, but he was supported in his policy by the prime minister, most of the government party, and by the Labour opposition.

The change in government thinking was confirmed when Menzies and Hasluck discussed colonial problems with the

British Commonwealth prime ministers in London in May 1960 and returned to Australia convinced that to be premature in granting self-government to areas such as New Guinea was preferable to risking the bitterness that could arise from undue delays. 'At one time', said Menzies, on June 20, 1960, 'it was thought better to move slowly towards independence. The school of thought now is that it is better to go sooner than later. I belong to that school of thought, although I did not always.' This suggested a realisation that Australian control over New Guinea would eventually come to an end. Whereas the government had always circumspectly avoided mentioning a time limit for self-government in New Guinea, Hasluck now intimated that thirty years was a possible minimum.

An important political advance quickly followed in September 1960, when legislation was introduced into the House of Representatives amending the Papua and New Guinea Act of 1949 to increase the membership of the Territory's legislative council from twenty-nine to thirty-seven, of whom fifteen would be officials, including the administrator, and might be either European or native; ten would be nominated members and include five natives; twelve would be elected and include six elected by the natives. This meant that the Papuans, whose political experience had hitherto been confined to village government, were for the first time given elective representation in a central legislature, from which the administration's former official majority had been eliminated. In presenting the proposed changes to the House of Representatives, Hasluck declared that the reconstituted legislative council, while subordinate to the commonwealth, would possess 'full legislative powers and the complete structure of a Parliament'. Elections were held on March 18, 1961, and the new council, inaugurated on April 12, included twelve Papuans.

This political advance had its critics, Russia deprecating the legislative council as anti-democratic; but as a measure it manifested a greater willingness on the part of the Australian government to modify its somewhat staid policy on the Territory in order to meet demands in the Trusteeship Council for more rapid progress towards independence. It did not mean, however, that Australia was prepared to move as fast as others wished, and in June 1962 the minister for Territories questioned the sense and realism of the suggestion made by the Trusteeship Council mission earlier in the year that a general election should take place in the Territory not later than April 1964 for a truly representative parliament of a hundred members. The Australian government maintained its view that progress must necessarily be gradual and geared to the capacity of the Papuan people themselves. It still felt that criticism was often misinformed and took inadequate account of the difficulties with which the administration had to deal: the exceedingly backward society; the abundance of languages; the dissimilarity of racial types; the absence of a widespread common religious belief; the interior dominated by jungle, mountains, swamps and torrential rivers. In his statement to the House of Representatives in August 1960, Hasluck declared that the unusually intricate circumstances in New Guinea were not presented by the Australian government as reasons for delaying the advance of the indigenous inhabitants, but: 'The world would be acting in ignorance if it did not appreciate the primitive and unique character of the conditions in the Territories and the size of the basic civilising tasks to be completed. The administering power and the advanced native peoples with whom it is working need time for the job.'

Nevertheless, further advances quickly followed. In October 1962 the Australian government approved proposals for an enlarged legislative council of sixty-five members, including forty-four elected Papuans, and in November of that year the ban on natives' purchasing or drinking alcoholic liquor was relaxed in response to criticism by the United Nations mission, which had described the restrictions as a survival of racial discrimination. The government assured the people of Papua and New Guinea that their right of self-determination would be respected, notwithstanding the change in control of the western half of the island, and it now professedly looked forward to a time when the population of both parts of New Guinea—the Indonesian and the Australian—would be given the opportunity of uniting into one independent country.*

* Developments in the Territories since 1962 are described in Chapter 13, pages 205-6.

The slow, reluctant, but visible mutation in the government's attitude towards its native communities applied also to the Aborigines of the mainland. In 1957 the first Aborigine to matriculate passed the school-leaving examination in Western Australia; in both Queensland and Western Australia a university scholarship was awarded to an Aboriginal for the first time.* And in 1962 Aboriginal women were sworn in as justices of the peace at Taree on the north coast of New South Wales. The federal budget of August 1959 removed the restriction of pensions and maternity allowances to those Aborigines who had been granted citizenship by the states in which they lived, and made provision for all except the nomadic and most primitive to receive the payments. Surveys by welfare officers in Western Australia three years later showed that the Aborigines who accepted the pension generally made prudent use of it and as a result were better fed, clothed and housed than ever before. In 1960 a conference of commonwealth and state ministers resolved that the practice of segregating Aborigines in reservations should be abandoned as soon as possible and measures taken to assist the Aborigines to be assimilated into the main stream of contemporary Australian life. The federal government was now spending £1 million a year on the welfare of the Aborigines in the Northern Territory, and in May 1960 it issued new regulations which awarded them two weeks' annual holiday on full pay, sick leave, regular wages and a right to notice of dismissal, provided for minimum standards of housing, and required employers of aboriginal labour to have a licence, which might be cancelled if correct conditions of work were not observed.

In October 1961 a select committee of the commonwealth Parliament unanimously recommended that the right to vote in federal elections should be conferred on all adult Aborigines. Those in Victoria, New South Wales and South Australia already possessed the vote in state elections and therefore in federal elections, but the majority in Queensland, Western Australia and

* Several Aborigines have benefited from a fund established by the National Union of Australian University Students which provides scholarships for Aborigines at any Australian university. In 1963, Monash University in Victoria established two scholarships for students of aboriginal descent.

the Northern Territory were still denied it and these the committee wished to be enfranchised, although it recommended also that they should not be compelled either to enrol on the electoral register or to vote while they were still only just emerging from the tribal stage. The Bill giving effect to the committee's recommendations passed the House of Representatives in May 1962 and acted as a spur to encourage Queensland and Western Australia—the only states in which Aborigines were debarred from voting—to bring their franchise into line with the rest of the commonwealth.

The practical effect of these measures was small, but they signified an awareness that the aboriginal population could no longer be ignored. As with the trusteeship in New Guinea, the Australian government was beginning to recognise that its obligations towards the native peoples within its territories were not capable of indefinite postponement or disregard, that it was no longer possible to hope that its policies would pass unnoticed in the world at large, and that if Australia pretended to the status of a mature and civilised power, it must accept fully the responsibilities involved.

12

The Menzies Hegemony (1955-1962)

AUSTRALIAN POLITICS in the 1950s, as always, were concerned primarily with economic affairs. Foreign policy, defence and native welfare were important, but they were subjects of occasional interest, and although there was heated controversy over New Guinea and particular international issues as they arose, it was upon the state of the economy that the fortunes of the political parties were balanced. It was portentous, therefore, that the Liberal and Country party coalition, which had been re-elected in December 1955 with an increased majority in the House of Representatives, was obliged almost at once to check inflationary pressures and the deterioration in Australia's overseas trading position. Import licences had been reduced in September 1955 with the object of cutting the value of imports by £80 million, but it was futile to limit imports unless internal purchasing power was correspondingly restricted, and in the early months of 1956 measures to this end were adopted. The interest rate on bank overdrafts was increased, and in March the federal treasurer introduced a supplementary budget raising the tax on company profits and on sales of consumer goods.

This emergency budget was strongly criticised by the Labour opposition and the business interests affected, and it contributed to the unexpected return in April of a Labour government in Western Australia with a handsome majority in a chamber that before had been equally divided. The impositions were considerable but not unduly severe, and the revised sales taxes were still not high by prevailing standards in many western countries;

but there was understandable resentment at the failure to curb growing governmental expenditure. At the end of June new restrictions cut the value of imports by about 6 per cent, and in his August budget the treasurer retained the tax level imposed earlier in the year, raised postal charges, and presaged no relaxation in the controls over imports and credit. Nevertheless, some relaxation was soon made possible by a rise in the size and price of the wool clip, which helped to eliminate the unfavourable trade balance more rapidly than had been anticipated, and by the initialling in November of a new five-year trade agreement with the United Kingdom. The advantages to Australia of the Ottawa Agreement, revised in 1938, had been decreasing with monetary inflation, and the scope for restoring its place in the British and European markets had been narrowed since 1948 by the General Agreement on Tariffs and Trade (GATT). The United Kingdom now undertook to purchase more Australian wheat and flour and consented to a reduction in the tariff preferences on many British goods imported into Australia, which consequently would be in a better position to negotiate trading agreements with other countries.

The economic debate was temporarily overshadowed by an international crisis in which the Australian prime minister played a prominent role. On July 26, 1956, President Nasser of Egypt suddenly proclaimed the nationalisation of the Suez Canal and defied Britain and France, the two countries whose interests were most directly affected. The minister for External Affairs, R. G. Casey, issued cautious statements condemning the Egyptian action in moderate terms, but Menzies, who was visiting England and America, took a stronger line, denounced the nationalisation in forthright language, and associated himself closely with the British prime minister, Sir Anthony Eden, in his uncompromising animosity towards Nasser. The Labour opposition in Australia echoed the less indignant disapprobation voiced by the Labour and Liberal opposition in the United Kingdom and suggested that the United Nations was the only body competent to deal with the matter. But the Australian press, with a few exceptions, notably the Adelaide *News* and the *Newcastle Morning*

Herald, assumed a belligerent tone towards Egypt and supported British military preparations in the Mediterranean. In August Menzies led an abortive mission to Cairo to secure acceptance of proposals which had been devised at a conference in London by twenty-two nations using the canal; afterwards the dispute was referred to the United Nations. A fortnight later, on September 25, Menzies made a statement to the federal Parliament reiterating his view that the nationalisation of the Suez Canal was contrary to international law, and adding that if the United Nations failed to produce a satisfactory settlement it might be necessary to impose economic sanctions against Egypt or even to use armed force.

Force was, in fact, used at the end of October, when Israel attacked Egypt and the British and French governments sent an ultimatum demanding that the Israeli and Egyptian armies each withdraw from an area of ten miles on either side of the Suez Canal. Egypt rejected the ultimatum, and in the first week of November British and French troops landed at Port Said. The Australian press now became more critical of British and French policy, and with one or two bellicose exceptions, such as the *Sun* and the *Daily Telegraph* in Sydney, condemned the employment of military forces or at least expressed concern at the lack of consultation between Britain and its Commonwealth partners. Within Britain itself, criticism of the government's moves intensified; the Labour and Liberal opposition and all but the most conservative and imperialist of the newspapers evinced their misgivings. The United States and Canada were against an action about which they had not been consulted and of the propriety and wisdom of which they were sceptical, while India and all the Asian countries were firmly and, in many cases, bitterly opposed to it.

The Labour party in Australia, like its counterpart in England, objected to the use of force, and Evatt inveighed against an ultimatum which, under a veneer of impartiality, was really directed against Egypt and designed as an excuse for reoccupying the canal zone. 'Was there ever', he asked, 'such a transparent device employed previously in international affairs?' The British and French attack, said Evatt, was 'a naked exercise of military power' and could not succeed. He remarked upon the lack of consultation between Britain and the governments of the Commonwealth and the United States, which, he suggested, were not informed of the proposed attack because the British and French governments did not want them to know of it until it had been irrevocably launched.

Menzies, on the other hand, never faltered in his unequivocal support for the British and French policy, and he completely identified the Australian government with the attitude of the British government. British prestige and British traditions had always been dear to him, and the unity and power of the British Commonwealth was, to him, something real and binding and not something to be trimmed to the winds of mere self-interest or world popularity. Any doubts that Casey or other members of the government may have felt over the policy adopted by Australia were over-ridden by the prime minister, who made himself the spokesman for a divided Australia, fashioning for the nation an international outlook distinguished by an admirable and un-wavering loyalty to the mother country and a deplorable contempt for the United Nations and the opinions of Australia's neigh-bours in Asia. Menzies admitted that his government had not been consulted before Britain issued the ultimatum to Egypt and Israel, but declared that the British government had not acted im-properly because effective consultation would have been not only useless but a waste of time in an emergency when speed was essential. In the opinion of the Australian government, he told the House of Representatives, 'Great Britain, whose canal and other Middle East economic interests are so vast, was correct in pro-ceeding upon her own judgment and accepting her own responsi-bility. We are not living in an academic world. The normal pro-cess of consultation should always be followed wherever feasible, but there are instances like the present one in which events move too fast for normal processes.' When Russian threats, United Nations pressure, and American anger compelled Britain and France to order a cease-fire in Egypt on November 6 and to give way to a United Nations emergency force in December, the Australian prime minister was unrepentant. On the contrary, he justified the British and French attack on the grounds that it had, in effect, been the means of galvanising the United Nations into action. But his cynical strictures on the United Nations Organisation continued, and the exclusion of British and French troops from its emergency force he derided as 'sheer bedlam nonsense'.

Menzies' outspoken stand on the Suez Canal crisis was virtually a reaffirmation of old-style British imperialism, but it was not necessarily an unfaithful reflection of the mood of a large, and probably major, section of the Australian people. The historic and emotional links with the mother country were strong, disdain for the Egyptians was rife (especially among ex-servicemen who recalled wartime days in the Middle East), and disgust with the prevarication and seemingly faithless reaction of the United States was apparent. All these feelings helped to strengthen Australian sympathy with the now almost isolated British government. In spite of these popular emotions, Evatt might have acquired the moderate and sensible image that he deserved by his disavowal of a policy that flouted the principles of the United Nations. Instead, he further impaired his already crumbling reputation by a marked reluctance to be more specific in his advocacy than a general and, so his opponents alleged, naïve respect for the machinery of the United Nations, and also by his equation of the British and French invasion of Egypt with Russia's ruthless suppression of the national uprising in Hungary.

It was Evatt's propensity for allowing himself to be aligned with communism that led to doubts about the value of his leadership to the Labour party. The 'Democratic Labor Party', founded at a conference in March 1957 of those groups which had left official Labour in 1955 and 1956, adopted a policy emphasising the importance of combating communism and censuring the existing leadership and methods of the Australian Labor Party. Democratic Labour derived its strength principally from Labour's Roman Catholic dissidents in Victoria and New South Wales, but in April its influence extended to Queensland, where the Labour premier and twenty-five of his parliamentary following, on being expelled from the official Labour party, formed themselves into the 'Queensland Labor Party' which, though emerging the weaker of the two opposition Labour parties after the state elections in August, remained a political force closely, if not formally, allied to Democratic Labour in other states.

By the middle of 1957, therefore, the Labour party's electoral prospects appeared little better than they had been at the end of 1955 and they were receiving no assistance from conditions in the economy. The favourable balance of trade which had been established with unexpected rapidity in late 1956 continued through most of 1957 as the market for wool was held and even improved. Inflation slowed down, manufacturing progressed, general prosperity was maintained and economic anxiety was lessened, at least until the last few months of the year. The most ominous trading development, as it was to prove, was the signature in March 1957 by France, Germany, Italy, Belgium, Holland and Luxembourg of the Treaty of Rome, which envisaged the creation in 1958 of a European Common Market involving the eventual elimination of their internal tariffs and the establishment of a customs union with a uniform external tariff. The Australian government was particularly concerned at the likelihood of tariff barriers' being raised by the Common Market against the agricultural products of countries outside it. It was evident that traditional markets in the United Kingdom and Europe might not always in the future provide a fully satisfying outlet for Australian exports and that Australia might be obliged to find itself a substitute in the Americas or in the emergent countries of Asia and the Pacific. In fact, the old patterns of trade were already changing; in 1957 Japan, which as a customer of Australia was now second only to England, became the largest purchaser of Australian wool. In July Australia and Japan signed a trade agreement by which Australia abandoned its discriminatory policy against Japanese goods and Japan provided reciprocal advantages for Australian products.

In November 1957 the prime minister announced with great pride and with the support of the whole House that the government accepted the recommendations of a committee appointed by him to investigate university education in Australia. The committee, under the chairmanship of Sir Keith Murray, had produced a report in September which was to become the charter of future university development. The Australian universities varied greatly in size, from the large in Sydney and Melbourne to the comparatively small at Hobart in Tasmania and at New England in northern New South Wales. All universities outside the Australian Capital Territory at Canberra were state, not federal, institutions depending much on state grants. In the years immediately following the second world war, returned servicemen had increased the numbers attending university, and these levels were maintained in the 1950s as a result of the immigration program, a rising birth-rate and a generous scheme of commonwealth scholarships. The expansion in the student population had not been accompanied by a corresponding increase in staff or accommodation and most of the universities suffered from overcrowded classes, inadequate library facilities, and obsolete laboratory equipment.

The Murray Report recommended emergency grants by the commonwealth over the next three years and the creation of an advisory body on the model of the University Grants Committee in Britain. In 1959 the Australian Universities Commission was established with the duty of advising the prime minister on the financial requirements and the balanced development of tertiary education. The report estimated that the university student population would grow from 36,000 in 1957 to 71,000 in 1965 and to 80,000 by 1967: increases with which the universities were not equipped to cope. The implementation of the Murray Committee's recommendations, therefore, was in many respects a rescue operation to ensure production of the graduates in science and technology required by industry and Colombo Plan commitments, and of the graduates in arts required by the teaching profession and governmental and administrative services.

Whether the fundamental problems of Australian universities would be solved was open to question. The high rate of failure among students in their first year at university was described in the report as 'a national extravagance' which could ill be afforded. But in an educational system which enabled students to enter university at the age of barely seventeen (more than a year younger than in the United Kingdom), and to begin a degree course without the background or experience in undirected study provided by the sixth form of English schools, a high failure rate was inevitable unless standards were to be permitted to fall. The most dangerous feature of Australian tertiary education was not the ready admission and financial assistance to all who reached a minimum examination level at school, for this could be justified on many grounds, scholastic and democratic; the weakness lay in the emphasis on the general pass degree as the normal pinnacle of academic achievement and in the consequent debilitation of honours and postgraduate studies. To this extent the university system mirrored the Australian preference for the average over the outstanding.

Neither intellect nor creativity was at a premium in Australia. The suspicion of intellectualism and the scattering of cultural life between small minorities in widely separated capital cities made it difficult for the tiny groups of arts lovers to influence a people, who, if not altogether the philistines upon whom visitors customarily remarked, were indisputably more inclined to the pleasures of the beach and sun than to those of the mind. The introduction of television in time for the Olympic Games in Melbourne at the end of 1956, for example, brought excellent productions from overseas but confirmed that Australia lacked the population to support local television programs of comparable standards. The emigration from Australia of talented local artists continued, denuding still further its already slender resources at home. Nevertheless, there were a few signs that creative activity was increasing, improving, and securing wider public recognition and encouragement. In 1957 the New South Wales government decided to build in Sydney an opera house of an unconventional but arresting design. In 1958 the paucity of serious newspapers and journals was alleviated by the appearance of the *Observer* and the *Nation*—two fortnightly journals of political and cultural criticism similar to the English weeklies, though at the end of the decade the *Observer* was to be incorporated into the conservative and nationalistic *Bulletin*.* The Elizabethan Theatre Trust, though poorly subsidised and wary of staging Australian plays, was developing what promised to become a national theatre, while the Australian Broadcasting Commission had become one of the largest organisers of musical concerts in the

---

* The tone of the *Bulletin* has mellowed since its amalgamation with the *Observer* and it is now markedly less conservative and nationalist than it used to be.

world, arranging tours of Australia by the most distinguished overseas artists. The Australian people thrilled to the operatic success of their own Joan Sutherland, and the success overseas of Ray Lawler's *Summer of the Seventeenth Doll* was regarded as evidence of Australia's ability to create its own distinctive drama, especially when it was followed in 1958 by another Australian play, Richard Beynon's *The Shifting Heart*. Australian poetry still failed to make any impact abroad, but the artist Sidney Nolan was well received in Europe and America, and Patrick White's novels *Voss* and *Riders in the Chariot*, which emphasised the movement of Australian fictional themes from the bush to the city, won acclaim from foreign critics. These were considerable achievements in a nation whose interests were predominantly materialist and whose politicians and governing authorities, local, state and federal, had generally been indifferent to cultural attainment.

The parliamentary debate on the Murray Report in November 1957 was notable for the absence of party rancour. Federal politics remained quiet, and the government had little reason to be anxious about the elections that would be due before the end of 1958. Although the Liberal and Country party coalition had now been in office for nearly eight years, its position was stronger than ever before. Industrial relations were smooth, whereas the opposition was demoralised and harassed by sectarian dissension. The economy was affected late in 1957 and throughout 1958 by a decline in export prices, especially of wool, and some unemployment appeared, but the adverse balance of payments was not as serious as it had been on several occasions in recent years.

When the election campaign opened in October 1958, it was generally predicted that the government would be re-elected with a comfortable majority. The Labour vote in many constituencies was bound to be divided by Democratic Labour which, determined to keep the Australian Labor Party out of office, recommended its supporters to give their second preferences to the government parties. The Communist bogy was resurrected, and in the last days of the campaign the Roman Catholic archbishop of Melbourne, the aged but still outspoken Daniel Mannix, made a statement which must have resolved the doubts of any Roman Catholics unsure of whether or not to vote for Labour. 'Every Communist and Communist sympathiser in Australia', said Mannix, 'wants a victory for the Evatt party. That is alarming. It should be a significant warning for every Catholic and every decent Australian.' No one expected the government to be defeated, but the energetic electioneering of the ailing Evatt and the negative complacency of the Liberal and Country parties had made some reduction in their majority probable when sectarian and anti-Communist emotions were thrown so demonstratively into the scales on the eve of the polling. The result of a divided and maligned Labour opposition was that the government was returned to power in November 1958 for another term and flattered with an increased majority.

No longer frustrated by an obstructive Senate, the government was able to pass in 1959 its previously rejected legislation on banking reform. Under a series of Acts, the commonwealth banking system was divided from January 14, 1960, into three main sections: first, a Reserve Bank which assumed the functions of a central bank, controlled note issue, and acted as banker to the commonwealth and some of the states; secondly, a Development Bank to assist the development of enterprises in primary and secondary industries which would otherwise be unable to secure the necessary finance on reasonable terms; and thirdly, the Trading and Savings Banks which conducted general banking business. The Trading Bank, Savings Bank and Development Bank were under the control of the Commonwealth Banking Corporation—a body entirely separate from the Reserve Bank and with functions stated in the Act as ensuring 'that the policy of the Trading Bank, of the Savings Bank, and of the Development Bank are directed to the greatest advantage of the people of Australia and have due regard to the stability and balanced development of the Australian economy'. The legislation was an attempt to satisfy demands which the private banks and many members of the Liberal party had been making since 1949, especially for the separation of central banking from trading banking functions, and it was passed against the continued opposition of the Labour party.

Effective political debate had been compromised, however, by the reduced condition of federal Labour, which had been out of office a long time and had little hope of achieving it in the foreseeable future. Evatt was not the man to bring Labour victory; his unpredictability and the Communist sympathies which Democratic Labour and the government parties attributed to him had made him an embarrassment to his party, notwithstanding his acknowledged distinction and ability. In the closing months of 1959, his appointment as Chief Justice of the New South Wales Supreme Court was freely mooted and took place in February 1960. Evatt resigned from the federal Parliament, where he was succeeded as leader of the Labour opposition by A. A. Calwell, a craggy Roman Catholic from Victoria but an inveterate enemy of the Catholic political movement there.

Calwell was sixty-three when he succeeded Evatt, had been a member of Parliament since 1940, and deputy leader of his party since 1951. Possessed of a rough wit, a strained, raucous voice and a taste for stormy debate, Calwell had mellowed from the ebullient politician he had once been, and he came to the leadership with a widely, if not deeply, respected reputation that he was to enhance rapidly. His deputy was E. G. Whitlam, a young non-Catholic lawyer from New South Wales, a big man who prepared his speeches carefully and was perhaps the most effective debater on the opposition benches. The change in Labour's leadership did not produce any immediate alteration in policy or prospects, but the depression within the party began slowly to lift as the government showed signs of foundering.

The prosperity of 1959, when the price of wool and primary exports recovered and the capital inflow from overseas was substantial, enabled the government in August to remove many import controls and simplify the remainder in preparation for their virtual abolition, which was announced in February 1960. The abandonment of import licensing was directed partly at curbing renewed inflationary trends, the hope being that the competition from imported goods would inspire Australian manufacturers to greater efficiency and help to prevent rises in the price level. Nevertheless, retail prices of consumer goods continued to rise, speculation on the stock exchange and in real estate flourished and imports increased. By the middle of 1960 the government was confronted with unmistakable inflation, an unfavourable balance of trade, and a serious decline in overseas reserves. The budget of

August 1960 increased taxes, but soon proved inadequate as a move against inflation or the deteriorating balance of trade. Only three months later, on November 15, the federal treasurer, H. E. Holt, announced increases in the interest on bank overdrafts and in the sales tax on motor vehicles (the industry most associated with the boom in hire purchase), and authorised the Reserve Bank to enforce a reduction in the advances made by trading banks 'for land and share speculation, for consumer credit, and for purely financial dealings'. The effect of these measures was a decline in stock exchange and real estate activity, a substantial rise in unemployment, and also a hostile public reaction against the government and a fillip to the spirits of the Labour opposition, which was at least given material for sustained criticism in a vein that would endear it to the electorate.

Growing doubts about the government's economic policy were accompanied by some concern at the course it was pursuing in foreign affairs under the personal guidance of the prime minister. In October 1960 occurred the first clear indication since the Suez crisis of 1956 that Australia's cultivation of good neighbourly and commercial relations with Asia had not affected the congenital philosophy upon which Menzies based his international statesmanship. His attendance at the session of the United Nations General Assembly which opened in September 1960 was motivated by the desirability for Australia to be represented by its head of government when so many other nations at this particular session were represented by theirs. At the end of September, five neutralist countries presented a joint resolution to the Assembly requesting the leaders of the United States and the Soviet Union to recall the summit meeting recently abandoned on account of Russia's anger at the flight of an American U-2 spy-plane over its territory. Menzies objected to this resolution because it omitted Britain and France from the proposed meeting, and he offered an amendment changing the resolution to a recommendation that there should be a meeting of the four major powers at 'the earliest practicable date'. Only Britain, France, the United States and Canada supported the Australian amendment in a vote from which even New Zealand and South Africa abstained. Nehru, the Indian prime minister, commented acridly on the Australian prime minister for putting the amendment forward, describing it as absurd and Menzies' whole approach as trivial.

Nehru's strictures were both unfair and uncivil from a leader of one Commonwealth country airing his views of the leader of another in a public forum, and Menzies was understandably incensed. Nevertheless, the Australian prime minister's performance at the United Nations displeased his countrymen, although he could claim that Nehru soon afterwards withdrew the original five-nation resolution. In many Asian countries it was inferred from Menzies' action that, whether or not the amendment was his own idea, its purpose was to preserve British status and avoid for President Eisenhower of the United States the inconvenience of a meeting which for personal reasons he had no wish to attend. The amendment was bound to be interpreted as evidence that Australian foreign policy was at the behest of Britain and America. The Labour opposition moved in Parliament on the prime minister's return that he had 'failed to serve the interests of Australia and the cause of world peace, provoked a public disagreement among Commonwealth countries, and compromised Australia with the new members of the United Nations'. This was an unduly pessimistic assessment of the consequences of an episode, the significance of which appeared greater to observers in Australia than it did elsewhere, and the idea inherent in the argument of the critics that the government should always seek to please the African and Asian countries rather than the western powers was unrealistic and untenable as a consistent line of policy. Even so, it was obvious that Menzies, by his tactlessness and inelastic notion of international relations, had needlessly mishandled the Australian contribution.

As if to emphasise his loyalty to the old order of things, the prime minister took an isolated and individual stand at the British Commonwealth conference in London in March 1961, when the South African government's application to become a republican member of the Commonwealth was withdrawn after general antipathy had been expressed towards its racial policy of apartheid. Menzies regarded South Africa's racial policies as an internal matter upon which the remainder of the Commonwealth

N

was not competent to adjudicate, and he tried to stem the pressure to refuse South Africa admission. Addressing a press conference after South Africa's withdrawal, he reiterated his opinion that South Africa should have been retained within the Commonwealth and that apartheid was an issue of South African domestic policy. 'It is as much a matter of domestic policy to South Africa as Australia's immigration policy is a matter for us', he stated. 'To have a member of the Commonwealth virtually excluded from the Commonwealth on a matter of domestic policy presents, in my opinion, a rather disagreeable vista of possibilities for the future.' To the prime minister's legalistic mind the situation was clear, and the apprehension he sincerely felt about the future of the British Commonwealth may well have been justified. But his public statements on this subject, and notably his association of apartheid with Australia's immigration policy, were unwise, unnecessary, and served only to exclude Australia from whatever credit or goodwill flowed from the rest of the Commonwealth's dramatic refusal to accept a régime dedicated to the perpetuation of racial prejudice.

By the middle of 1961, the government was open to cogent criticism both of its management of the economy and of its conduct of external affairs. The measures taken in late 1960 against inflation and the adverse balance of trade achieved the desired effect in that, after May 1961, the balance of payments position began to improve and the rise in domestic prices was halted. In February 1961 the government abandoned the increased sales tax on motor vehicles, which the prime minister declared had served its purpose, and between June and October the restrictions on bank overdrafts were removed. But resentment continued against a policy which, critics insisted, could have been less drastic if it had been implemented sooner. Full employment had been replaced by unemployment which mounted to over 100,000, and the building, textile and automobile industries all suffered and had difficulty in returning to their former capacity.

The state of the economy inevitably became the central issue in the federal election at the end of 1961, and the Labour party devised a detailed program for reducing unemployment and reinvigorating business and industrial activity that was well received by sections of the community normally disposed to be critical of Labour's promises. The *Sydney Morning Herald*, which, though sometimes disapproving of Liberal policy, was regarded as an anti-Labour paper, unexpectedly urged a change of government and supported Labour's program as 'more in accordance with the country's immediate needs'. By December 9, when the elections were held, it was recognised that Labour had greatly improved its position, but the extent of the reduction in the government's majority surprised everyone. Whereas in the previous Parliament, the Liberal and Country parties had enjoyed a handsome majority of thirty-two, they were now returned with a majority of one after electing the Speaker, the depletion in its ranks including three former ministers.

The result was interpreted as a protest against the government's recent economic measures and a public rebuke to the complacency it had exhibited in seeking a renewed mandate almost entirely on the basis of its record and proficiency, in which it sported an inordinate pride. Menzies accepted the implications of the electors' verdict and immediately promised that the government would modify its recent policies. 'It is clear', he admitted, 'we have been opposed by many people normally our supporters. They appear to have felt that our economic measures of last year were too severe and that we were not sufficiently conscious of unemployment.' In January 1962 the cabinet held a series of meetings with business and industrial interests, and early in February new steps to stimulate the economy were announced, including a rebate in income tax, a reduction in sales tax on motor vehicles, and special grants to the states for public works with the aim of relieving unemployment. These measures were confirmed in August by a budget which provided for a deficit of £118 million: the largest since the Liberal and Country parties first took office in 1949. Though plagued by its dangerously narrow majority, the government had no intention of permitting Labour to retain the initiative, and it set itself to employ the slender margin by which it had been preserved to rehabilitate itself in the electorate before the next dissolution fell due or was provoked.

One of the claims made by the government parties during the election was that their experience would be needed to protect Australian interests in the negotiations which had begun in November 1961 for Britain's entry into the European Common Market. Early in 1962 the prime minister and his minister for Trade, John McEwen, the Country party leader, demonstrated their intention of seeking suitable provisions for the preservation of Australian trading interests if Britain joined the Common Market, and both made visits to London to publicise their concern. The government's immediate reaction to Britain's decision in 1961 to negotiate with the European Economic Community had been indignantly critical, for the United Kingdom absorbed about one fifth of Australia's export trade and to lose this preferential outlet would, it was assumed, damage the Australian economy. In a statement to the House in August 1961, Menzies had expressed his solicitude for exports of meat, dairy produce, wheat, sugar and fruits should adequate safeguards not be urged upon the British and European negotiators. Along with the British Commonwealth's other temperate zone members—Canada, New Zealand and Cyprus—Australia could lose substantially in export earnings unless Britain obtained suitable terms from the Common Market. The Australian government's approach was outlined by McEwen, the minister for Trade, in a parliamentary statement in May 1962:

> No one could validly challenge Britain's right to join. Our attitude is to accept her application as real, to take in good faith her assurances that she would not join if the price was serious damage to Commonwealth trade, and, with these points constantly as the background of our thoughts, to proceed to propose constructively the kind of solution which would protect our trade.

McEwen represented the party of farming interests, which were those most likely to be hurt by the ending of Britain's preferential tariffs, and his party's presence in a coalition government clinging precariously to office with a majority of one intensified the reproachful and economically self-centred distrust of the Common Market negotiations in Brussels.

The zeal with which McEwen and Menzies expounded the Australian case raised suspicions that they were using the issue as a springboard to re-establish their administration in the affections of the electorate, and by the middle of 1962 the impression was growing that the potential dangers to the Australian economy had been greatly, and perhaps deliberately, exaggerated. The margin of preference for Australian products in the United Kingdom had been declining, and the proportion of Australia's total exports entering Britain and Western Europe had fallen from 71 per cent before the second world war to 38 per cent, while the proportion entering Japan, North America, mainland China and the countries of Asia and the Pacific had increased from 24 per cent to 53 per cent. The threat to Australia's economic welfare was not denied, but the disastrous consequences which the overseas visits and initial alarming statements of the prime minister and minister for Trade had tended to imply as possible, seemed to have derived partly from the calculated histrionics of party leaders. There was something to be said for presenting a tough and vocal front on the Common Market problem in order to ensure that Australia's interests were known and attention given to measures for their protection, but whether in fact the immoderacy of Australia's earlier tone assisted its case with the European countries was open to question. Certainly by the time a conference of British Commonwealth prime ministers met in London in September 1962, Menzies and McEwen had adopted a more conciliatory posture.

The political implications of Britain's adhesion to the European Economic Community were of genuine concern to Menzies, an avowed protagonist of the traditional British Commonwealth association. 'For us', said Menzies in London in June 1962, 'the Commonwealth is more than a compromise or form of words. It is not expendable. It has deep roots which have drawn sustenance from the rich soil of common loyalty and affection.' He feared that the mother country would be absorbed into a European federation to which it would necessarily surrender some of its sovereignty and that in consequence the special relationships within the British Commonwealth would be loosened and perhaps forfeited. Nevertheless, it was reluctantly conceded by the

Australian government that for the United Kingdom to remain strong, as it must if the Commonwealth were to mean anything tangible, it might be necessary for it to associate with the potentially more satisfactory market in Western Europe. A commonwealth and empire created in a period of British hegemony and sustained by British naval power could not remain unaffected by the disappearance of the conditions by whose favour it developed. Although President de Gaulle of France was able to bar British entry into the Common Market in January 1963, geography and economic and political self-interest drew Britain towards Europe, and similar factors were altering the traditional patterns elsewhere in the Commonwealth. Australia had already become dependent on the United States for defence, had made its own regional security arrangements with America and New Zealand, and had expanded its sales of wool and wheat to Japan, mainland China and the American continent. The links with Britain would always remain, but the paramountcy of the Commonwealth association was waning. Australia had to discard any lingering regrets for days past and brace itself for the problems and responsibilities of a new and challenging future.

13

New Horizons

ALTHOUGH THE negotiations for Britain's admission to the European Economic Community foundered on French opposition, they nevertheless spelt for Australia the end of an era. Britain's probable withdrawal from distant commitments intensified the problems for Australian defence and foreign policy. There was nothing new or dramatic in the necessity for Australia's triangular relationship with the mother country and the United States to be slanted markedly towards the American angle, for it had long been recognised in Australia that in the final analysis the nation's security depended on the United States. The events of 1962, however, in their demonstration that the United Kingdom intended in future to associate itself more closely with Europe, indicated that a process which had been going on steadily since the second world war was now nearing its completion.

The indispensability of the American alliance was generally recognised in Australia, but there was disagreement on the extent to which the country should be committed to it. Despite their sentimental attachment to the old idea of the British Commonwealth and all that it had stood for earlier in the century, the Liberals were the more ready in the 1960s to accept the full implications of dependence upon the United States. The Labour party, on the other hand, was sensitive about Australia's getting entangled in Great Power nuclear strategy: a contingency that seemed inevitable when, early in 1963, the government announced proposals for the establishment of an American naval radio communications station at North-West Cape in Western Australia. The station's whole cost was to be borne by the United States, which alone would control it for a minimum period of twenty-five years, though Australian armed forces were to enjoy the right to use its communications services and the commonwealth government might at any time consult the United States about its effect on Australia's national and international interests. At a special federal conference in March 1963, the Labour party decided by a narrow majority not to oppose construction of the station provided that it was under the joint control of the Australian and American governments. The Labour party held that the base should not be permitted to stockpile nuclear arms in peacetime and that, in the event of the United States' being at war, Australian territory and facilities should not be employed in any way which would involve Australia without the prior knowledge and consent of its government.

The anomalies inherent in Labour's standpoint were obvious, and the government parties, conscious of their narrow majority and seeing electoral advantage in publicising the issue, decided to submit the proposed agreement to Parliament, notwithstanding the fact that the government possessed the constitutional capacity to sign it without parliamentary authority. The prime minister, in particular, ridiculed Labour's criticism of the Bill approving the establishment of the base, scoffed at suggestions that American control should be hedged with restrictions, and tried to exploit the differences within the opposition's ranks. The Labour party did not oppose the second and third readings of the Bill, but promised that when it gained office it would renegotiate the agreement in order to ensure that the station was jointly controlled.

The signing of the agreement meant that for the first time Australian territory was to be directly involved in the operation of American nuclear strategy, and that hopes of keeping Australia free from the tensions of nuclear confrontation were dimmed, if not entirely destroyed. For at least the next quarter of a century Australia would be in danger of what Calwell termed 'annihilation without representation', of becoming involved in the retaliatory consequences of orders transmitted from the American base. The crucial question was whether the disadvantages of exposure to the hazards of nuclear warfare were outweighed by the advantages of having the United States physically concerned in the security of

Australia and also, though this was doubtful, more amenable to Australian influence in its policy in the south Pacific.

Australia's greatest fear was of Indonesia, whose absorption of West New Guinea carried it to the frontier of Australian territory in the island. The new proximity of the menace from Indonesian expansionism brought added urgency to the need for taking precautions against it. There was relief in Australia, therefore, when at a meeting of the ANZUS Council in New Zealand in June 1963, the United States' under-secretary for Political Affairs, Averell Harriman, pledged American support for the defence of Papua and New Guinea. Comforting as was this promise, however, it was debatable what it would in fact mean for Australia in the sort of emergency most likely to arise. Asian aggression against Australian territory was improbable except in circumstances which involved the United States in serious hostilities in other areas and which consequently made assistance to its ANZUS partner problematical. From another angle, in a world dominated by the supreme strategy of the rivalry between the major powers of East and West, it was doubtful whether the United Kingdom or the United States would wish to become embroiled in action that might antagonise neutral countries merely in order to protect Australian external territorial interests. (It had been the realisation that its western allies were not prepared to defy Indonesian claims to Dutch New Guinea that had ultimately compelled the Australian government to accept the extension of Indonesian territory which for a decade or more it had sought to prevent.) Moreover, the traditional American sympathy for anti-colonial movements might make the United States unwilling to countenance strong measures against any nationalist uprising in the Australian territories, even if the agitation were to be incited from across the border, as in the case of the self-styled nationalists in the British-protected sultanate of Brunei in North Borneo whose campaign against the formation of Malaysia was encouraged by Indonesia at the beginning of 1963. It could be argued, therefore, that ANZUS and SEATO, though integral to Australian defence and foreign policy, were not a sufficient safeguard for Australian territorial interests, even when reinforced by statements from American officials. Something more was required, and this Australia had to contribute itself.

The commonwealth government's response to this challenge began on October 24, 1962, when the minister for Defence, Athol Townley, announced a three-year program for defence. Its inadequacy was immediately apparent, for it envisaged an outlay little higher than in the previous three years, and in view of probable rising costs and a growing population it meant in terms of expenditure per head virtually no advance whatever. In January and May 1963 further increases were announced in defence expenditure for the five years commencing 1963–4, the revised estimate being the more significant because it did not include the cost of replacing the Royal Australian Air Force's Canberra bombers with new strike reconnaissance aircraft. The considerations behind the government's defence reassessment were outlined by the prime minister in the House of Representatives on May 22, when he referred to uncertainties in Laos and South Vietnam, to the possibility of trouble over the Malaysian federation between Malaya, Singapore and the British North Borneo territories, and, especially, to the insecurity of Papua and New Guinea. 'We will defend these territories as if they were part of our mainland', Menzies said; 'there must be no mistaken ideas about that.' The new program was designed not only to fulfil Australia's obligations to its allies in south-east Asia but also to provide Australia with the capacity for independent action to meet any emergency that might directly affect its own national interest.

The government's new defence effort was a considerable advance on its massive complacency of the 1950s, when it had maintained defence expenditure around the figure of £200 million a year. In real terms this had meant spending increasingly less as time went by, the percentage of the gross national product devoted to defence falling by 1963 from 5 per cent to under 3 per cent, as compared with the 6 per cent in Britain and the 11 per cent in the United States. The disparity could be explained by the Australian government's assumption that Australia would never be required to fight alone for its interests but would be able to rely upon its British and American allies. That these carefree years of defence expenditure might soon be over was implied by the American secretary of State, Dean Rusk, who, while on a visit to Canberra in May 1962, made it clear that Australia was not contributing as much as the United States' government thought it should to regional security in Asia and the Pacific. Dean Rusk's warning could be interpreted as meaning, in effect, that the degree of American support for Australia might in future be related to the sort of contribution Australia chose to make to regional defence against communism, and it was perhaps no coincidence that twelve months later the commonwealth government's announcement of increased defence expenditure occurred only a fortnight before the meeting with its American and New Zealand partners in the ANZUS Council.

The real significance of the new defence program, however, was not that it yet represented an adequate contribution to Australian security—for the Australian people remained comparatively unburdened with defence costs by British and American (or Indonesian) standards—but that it was devised by a government in political difficulties and naturally interested in contriving tax concessions if possible. The government, indeed, was at last consciously moving towards a greater measure of military self-sufficiency and was no longer content to rest comfortably on the assumption that Australia's battles would be fought by powerful friends. There was no attempt to disguise the fact that Indonesia was regarded as the most likely potential enemy; a pointer to where Australia's allies in a local conflict might be found lay in the Malayan government's request from its Parliament, also in May 1963, for an additional defence allocation.

Another modification in Australia's outlook on Asia was brought about by improved relations with India. A closer understanding with India had long been valued by a few thoughtful Australians but had been made difficult by differences between the Indian and Australian prime ministers. They held disparate, though not necessarily opposing, views on international tensions, and had disagreed on the Suez crisis in 1956 and on the question of South Africa's membership of the British Commonwealth. The Australian committal to western alliances and unalloyed opposition to communism contrasted with the Indian policy of non-alignment and preoccupation with Asian independence. India's composure was shaken, however, by the Chinese attack on its frontier in 1962 which threw in doubt the validity of its leadership of Asia and revealed India's ultimate dependence upon support from the West. Australia's immediate response to India's needs in the emergency laid the foundations of a closer association which might mean little in military terms but which could give their joint counsel great influence in an area of common concern. The visit to Canberra in April 1963 of the Indian minister for Economic Defence Co-ordination, following the visit to Delhi four months previously of the Australian minister for External Affairs, demonstrated the new awareness in both countries of the usefulness of fostering mutual contact.

Australia's potential affinities with India and Malaya were of intrinsic importance to a British Commonwealth in danger of becoming a concentric organisation with an inner circle of Anglo-Saxon members and an outer circle of Afro-Asian countries. For Australia to begin bridge-building between the old and the new sections of the British Commonwealth would have been a radical departure for a government which had hitherto left the task to Canada, and it would be an exaggeration to regard Australian-Indian relations in this light. Nevertheless, the conduct of Australia's external affairs in 1962 and 1963 suggested a reappraisal for which the new minister, Sir Garfield Barwick, was perhaps responsible. Foreign affairs had never been a prominent subject for discussion or debate in Australia, and editorial and academic comment was usually confined to explanatory syntheses from air-mail editions of English newspapers and journals. For a long time such discussion as there was of Australian external policies had been bedevilled by common-place generalisations about the diverse influences of geography and history and of the role Australia might fill as mediator between east and west in the Pacific. Intellectual criticism had been concerned with the idea of strengthening Australian national security by befriending the countries of Asia: a vague concept that in practice seemed to amount to little more than distributing economic aid and not opposing Asians when they wanted something. The Liberal and Country party government, on the other hand, prided itself upon its realism, and preferred to place its confidence more in powerful allies than in the notion of wealthy, underpopulated, white Australia's gaining the trust and respect of needy, over-populated Asia. By 1963, however, Australian policy-makers were beginning to recognise that their realism was no longer so sound as they had at one time supposed, that they may have underestimated the power of the Asian countries and been too sanguine about the willingness and ability of Britain and the United States to commit themselves to Australian interests. It seemed possible that Australian foreign policy was moving towards a sensible combination of cultivating dependable relations in Asia and of ensuring that Australia could, in certain circumstances, act to defend itself whether or not its western allies were involved.

A critical issue in Australia's future relations with Asia was its administration of the Territories in Papua and Eastern New Guinea. The federal government's anxiety over New Guinea was illustrated by its refusal to continue with the Indonesians the plans for joint enterprise in the island that had earlier been envisaged with the Dutch. Only a week after Indonesia's assumption of administrative control of West New Guinea in May 1963, the Australian minister for Territories, Paul Hasluck, introduced the Bill providing for an elective native majority in the House of Assembly in Papua and New Guinea.* He reaffirmed that the Australian government was 'moving with steady purpose and without hesitation or delay to bring self-government to the people of Papua and New Guinea. It is our firm intention', he said, 'to defend the freedom of choice and respect the wishes of those dependent on us.' International pressure was compelling Australia to reconsider urgently its approach to responsibilities in the Territories. Measures which earlier had been thought impracticable for a long time to come were being implemented with a speed remarkable for an administration previously distinguished for its dilatory complacency.

The nearly 2,000,000 indigenous inhabitants of Papua and New Guinea were now allowed alcohol; they could vote; an increasing proportion of the children attended school and a very few even reached university; and legislation attempted to eliminate the most glaring manifestations of racial discrimination. The principal danger was not that the pace towards self-government

* Elections to the new House of Assembly took place between February 15 and March 19, 1964.

would be too fast for primitive peoples unversed in the art of administration, but that an Australian government so long addicted to outdated thinking on its colonial or trustee responsibilities would regard the advances as anything other than provisional. Australian leaders would have to revise their whole approach to the problem, accept the fact that Australia's time in Papua and New Guinea would be shorter than they had expected, and shed the presupposition that the Territories would ultimately develop into component parts or self-governing dependent extensions of the Australian commonwealth.

Whatever changes were effected in Australia's attitude towards its Territories and its Asian neighbours, there was no likelihood of any alteration in its immigration policy, for on this all parties were agreed and adamant. The White Australia policy had been vigorously justified in emotional prose by Australians since the beginning of the century. The immigration restrictions did not exclude non-Europeans absolutely but were discretionary, and certain non-Europeans were admitted for educational, humanitarian, or diplomatic reasons. In 1963, for example, over 11,000 Asian students were attending Australian institutions of advanced learning. Nevertheless, the fact could not be disguised that the immigration laws were severely discriminatory in their operation and that non-Europeans found it virtually impossible to secure permanent entry. The White Australia enthusiasts justified this by the need to preserve the homogeneity of the population. They rejected the charge of racial prejudice, but insisted that the essentially western civilisation established in Australia should not be jeopardised by the influx of large numbers of people who were ethnically and culturally alien. In this sense, Australia was merely exercising the right to determine the composition of its society; a right exercised by other nations in every quarter of the globe. Most Australians accepted the restrictive immigration policy as indispensable to their economic and social well-being, but it appeared in the 1960s that the numbers of politicians, journalists, students and university teachers who questioned the policy were growing, or at least becoming more vocal, and an Association for Immigration Reform propagated suggestions for modifying it.

The White Australia policy was such a complex matter that neither its proponents nor the reformers were convincing in their arguments. It was true, for instance, that other countries had their immigration controls, but it was also true that the Australian policy was enforced more strictly than that of other nations and was motivated far more by pigmentation than was that of the Asian countries. However sincerely Australians believed that their policy was not founded on racial intolerance, it certainly gave that impression to all but the most charitable outside observers. The policy was embarrassing internationally because it was implemented by a nation energetically seeking immigrants and was invoked, unfairly, by the purveyors of *apartheid* in South Africa to justify some of their repressive and blatantly racial measures.

It was easier to criticise the White Australia policy, however, than to suggest a workable alternative. Even the most ardent reformers recoiled from the consequences of unfettered immigration, and no one seriously advocated it. A measured inflow of unskilled peoples from Asia might still undermine living standards, and the probable concentration of non-European elements at the bottom of the economic and social scale was more likely to foster prejudice than to subdue it. Perhaps the most practicable suggestion was for the negotiation with foreign governments of bilateral agreements, regulating the number of their nationals permitted to enter Australia and specifying the occupational skills the migrants must possess in order to qualify for admission. It was obviously essential that this procedure should allow for considerable flexibility in Australian requirements and conditions, and it was not difficult to foresee the problems to which it would give rise. Fixing the permitted ratios for different countries might touch on Asian susceptibilities as much as wholesale exclusion did; repeated excess of applicants over places might result in a growing backlog of disgruntled people whose hopes of a new life had been raised and then disappointed. The problem had so many ramifications, and any attempt to change the existing policy would be so enmeshed in complications and unpredictable consequences, that the Australian government and all political parties preferred to leave the issue alone.

Australian immigration policy was based on a preference for

migrants of British extraction, and the greatest recruiting drives were in the United Kingdom, but the net intake of British-born declined during the 1950s to about one third of the total. Reasons for this could be found in improved conditions in England and in the greater ease with which people could return there. Consequently, even though between 1945 and 1963 some 900,000 migrants entered Australia from Britain—nearly half of them by means of assisted passages—the commonwealth government was compelled to look to continental Europe if it was to maintain the target set in the early post-war years of one per cent net annual increase by immigration. Agreements with the International Refugee Organisation and with continental countries resulted in a vast increase in non-British European immigration. By 1963 Australia had absorbed 300,000 refugees—proportionately a larger number than by any other country—and unassisted continental immigrants, especially from southern Europe, added to the non-British element. By the 1960s the proportion of continental Europeans in the Australian population was approaching 20 per cent, compared with an estimated 8 per cent at the beginning of the century, while the proportion of the population of British origin had declined from about 90 per cent to about 80 per cent. These modifications in the composition of the population perhaps meant less in social terms than the figures might at first suggest, but in the long run, after the intermarriage of later generations and their blending of a variety of western cultures, they were liable to become of considerable significance.

Nevertheless, British migration could still be revived in certain circumstances, as was shown by the increase after 1955 (though it was Canada which benefited most from the exodus following the Suez crisis of 1956), and by the unprecedented spate of applications to leave England in 1963, following a disagreeable winter and the breakdown in the Common Market negotiations. That it was Australia, rather than Canada, which benefited most in 1963 was attributable not only to the publicity from a royal tour, Test cricket and the British Commonwealth games in Perth, but also to the impression that, although the political situation in both countries was finely balanced, Australia appeared to be the more successful in overcoming its economic difficulties.

After its electoral setback at the end of 1961, the Liberal-Country party government with its minimal majority tried to display its reinvigoration and to resuscitate the economy from the effects of the deflationary measures of 1960. Throughout 1962 there was evidence of a slow recovery, and by 1963 the economy was in better health; the cost of living was steady, and, with stable import prices and rising export prices, the balance of payments remained favourable. Primary industries benefited from favourable weather conditions and had a record year in 1962–3, the wheat harvest exceeding 300 million bushels for the first time, and the gross national product rose by 8 per cent. Successful testing in the Moonie oil-field in Queensland boosted hopes of commercial oil production: an important prospect for a nation whose imports of oil made up a tenth of its total imports bill. Capital continued to come in from overseas, and for the first time British investment in Australian companies was exceeded by American and Canadian. There was a distinct possibility that Japan would replace the United Kingdom as Australia's principal trading partner, for in a decade the proportion of Australia's total exports going to Japan had increased from 7 to 17 per cent. Japan was Australia's best customer for wool, and Australia was Japan's biggest market for cotton fabrics. Australian manufacturers were becoming less sensitive to the menace from Japanese imports, especially as Japan carefully avoided giving offence in this respect, and if the balance of trade was heavily in Australia's favour, both countries recognised the mutual advantage of expanding commercial contacts between them. Here again, Australia was having to forsake old prejudices to meet the requirements of altered international conditions.

The immediate economic task of the federal government was to restore business confidence. The numbers of registered unemployed were reduced, and by September 1963 represented 1.4 per cent of the estimated work force compared with over 2 per cent a year earlier. Even so, the fall in the level of unemployment was not as fast as governmental pledges had given cause to expect, and unemployment remained the central issue for opposition criticism. However, the Liberal-Country party coalition revealed a tenacious capacity for survival. Menzies continued with

o

an easy assurance to dominate the political scene as he had dominated it for thirteen years, and Queen Elizabeth's conferment upon him in March 1963 of the Order of the Thistle seemed to add to his already massive, if not unshakeable, pre-eminence. Sir Robert Menzies (as he was henceforth called) continued to hold his coalition ministry together, determined to defy a Labour party balked on the edge of victory. The Common Market episode had helped the government little, especially since ministerial statements on the matter had failed to make much impression in Britain or Europe and were refuted by one minister, Leslie Bury, who was obliged to resign for his audacity. Nevertheless, by coolly appropriating some of the Labour party's election platform, by consulting with industrial and trade union leaders about the condition of the economy, and by paying particular attention to Queensland—the state where it had lost most ground—in the allocation of federal funds, the government began to retrieve some of the support it had forfeited by the credit squeeze of November 1960.

In October 1963 the prime minister decided to dissolve Parliament and hold a general election on November 30—over twelve months earlier than he was obliged to. From the point of view of a government with a narrow majority, the time seemed opportune. The immediate economic outlook was encouraging, with overseas reserves rising, the employment position improved, and prices and costs stable, whereas it was possible that by the following year the government might be called upon to impose some restraint on the economy. Menzies, however, sought to fight the election not on domestic issues but on foreign policy and defence: subjects not normally significant in Australian peacetime politics. In the House of Representatives on October 15, the prime minister indicated the foreign policy questions upon which the parties differed. First, Labour would renegotiate the treaty establishing an American naval communications station in Western Australia; since the station was about to be constructed at great expense to the United States, it was important that this disagreement in Australia should be resolved. Second, the other countries concerned should know whether the Australian people supported the government's unilateral declaration on September 25 of military assistance for Malaysia in defence of its territorial integrity and political independence, for Labour had expressed a preference for a mutual treaty covering the presence and use of Australian troops in Malaysia. And third, Labour wished Australia to participate in a nuclear-free zone south of the equator, a policy which the government regarded as 'suicidal'.

The Labour party, while emphasising the domestic content of its program, accepted the challenge on foreign policy and sought to make electoral capital out of the government's recent decision to purchase for the Royal Australian Air Force the American TFX two-man bomber instead of the British TSR-2, a new tactical strike and reconnaissance aircraft. It was known that the United Kingdom had made a determined effort to sell the TSR-2 to the Australian government, which had been looking for an aircraft with a good performance at low altitudes to counter improvements in Indonesia's radar detection system and with a long range in case bases were lost in Malaya. The TSR-2 satisfied these requirements, but the government insisted that the American TFX was the more suitable for Australian conditions: its cost was less, and the terms attaching to its delivery and maintenance were more attractive than those offered with the British aircraft. Labour, however, was critical of the government's decision, and promised to reconsider the transaction if it won the election.

Both sides sought to exploit the TSR-2 issue for political purposes, but economic issues soon dominated the election campaign. It became clear that the government parties were gaining ground, and the assassination of President Kennedy in the United States may have won or ensured for Menzies the support of those who feared that the international temperature might rise in consequence. The result was the seventh consecutive electoral victory for the Liberal-Country party coalition, which gained a majority of twenty-two in the House of Representatives. The Australian voters had once again revealed their cautious, conservative approach to politics in a period of affluence, when an opposition's election promises can be made to seem prodigal and a threat to rising living standards.

The most perplexing question for the Liberal and Country party administration after its re-election was who would be its next leader. Menzies reached the age of sixty-nine in December 1963, and the knighthood bestowed upon him earlier in the year could be regarded as an augury of impending retirement, for the last knight to head the federal government had been the federation's first prime minister, Sir Edmund Barton, at the beginning of the century. On the other hand, his love of Parliament, his resolve to keep Labour out of office, his sense of history, and his predilection for the role of international statesman, might clearly encourage Menzies to stay, as he implied that he would. Certainly, the world for which he had expended much of his oratory and influence was disappearing, and the recent conferences of Commonwealth prime ministers had undermined his faith in the idea of a British, English-speaking and democratic family of nations united under the Crown. 'For most of its members', Menzies told Parliament regretfully in October 1962, 'the association is, in a sense, functional and occasional.' His devotion to the earlier Commonwealth was ingrained in him, and though he was still inclined to talk as if he and his followers monopolised patriotic virtues in Australia, his loyalty to the British connection and the concept of the Commonwealth of Nations would probably be the quality for which he would be most remembered.

No obvious successor to Sir Robert Menzies had yet been evolved by the Liberal party, but the choice seemed to lie between Harold Holt, the federal treasurer, and Sir Garfield Barwick, the minister for External Affairs. Holt, as deputy leader of the Liberal party since 1956 and chairman of the party's standing committee on policy, was the better placed to succeed. Suave and immaculate, a lawyer by training and a politician of great experience, having held a Melbourne seat in the federal Parliament since 1935, Holt's prospects may have been damaged by his unpopular fiscal measures in 1960. Sir Garfield Barwick had been a knowledgeable attorney-general and, as the new minister for External Affairs, had given a more constructive character to Australian diplomacy in Asia, but he was a comparative newcomer to Parliament and not the personality that impressed as a potential prime minister.* Another possible candidate was John McEwen, an experienced and

* Barwick left politics in April 1964 to become Chief Justice of the High Courts; Hasluck became the new minister for External Affairs.

hard-working minister for Trade and Industry, but he was handi-capped by his membership of the Country party—the minority partner in the coalition—and his chances were impaired at the end of 1962 by disagreement with the Liberal party over proposals for electoral redistribution.

The Country party's strength was 20 in a House of Representatives of 124 and 6 in a government of 25. Its importance was greater than these numbers implied, but it was likely to decline, if only gradually, for as population moved from the country to the towns and as the federal Parliament grew in membership, so the relative influence of the County party would diminish. Its coalition with the Liberals was becoming less harmonious, and in the 1963 election there were bitter contests between Liberal and Country party candidates for seats which it appeared Labour could not win. In one Western Australian constituency the sitting Liberal member was defeated by his Country party rival. The Country party was the major party in the Queensland government and it was strong in the New England district of northern New South Wales, but it was not in any real sense a national party. Its support was based within a few special areas, and it was doubtful whether it would ever be able to stretch itself over a wider foundation.

The Liberal party was not the same buoyant organisation that had come to power in 1949. Then, and for some time in the 1950s, it had found ideological inspiration in fighting socialism: a term it had been inclined to interpret as synonymous with communism. It identified itself with the virtues of capitalism and committed itself to a program of national development that included the maintenance of immigration and full employment and the curbing of inflation: objectives that were not easily compatible. For ten years the Liberal party took credit for the prosperity of the nation, but it became increasingly clear that the party was losing contact with its original principles. Free enterprise was difficult to maintain absolutely when governmental influence in the economy was necessary in order to ensure full employment or flatten out inflationary spirals. Its inflaming of public fears of communism distorted political values, and some of its decisions on the entry of certain overseas scholars and television programs trespassed

213

upon those liberties which it is the purpose of the true liberal to uphold. Its lengthy stay in office encouraged self-righteousness within the party; it became bankrupt of positive ideas with which to frame a policy, and it looked more to its record and administrative experience as argument enough for its retention of electoral confidence.

The future of the major parties hinged partly on that of the Democratic Labor Party (DLP), which consistently gave its second preferences to the Liberals: an electoral factor which in the 1963 elections provoked Labour into threatening to abolish the preferential system of voting when it came to power. Whether the DLP developed into a permanent Roman Catholic centre party or crumbled to pieces under the impact of successive election failures, it was important for the Australian Labor Party to win back followers from the DLP. There was little hope, however, of any reconciliation with the extremist Roman Catholic section of the DLP which was still under the influence of B. A. Santamaria, founder of the Catholic Social Movement in Australia, formerly director of the National Secretariat of Catholic Action, and one of the most controversial figures in the national life, whose devotees remained convinced that Labour in office would be a mere front for indirect Communist control. The aim of the DLP, indeed, was not to gain power—even its most zealous supporters knew that was impossible—but to prevent Labour from doing so; and in this it could claim to have been successful. It had caused the fall of state Labour governments in Victoria, Western Australia and Queensland, and had helped to sustain a Liberal and Country party administration in Canberra.

Nevertheless, the DLP was in a parlous condition in every state except Victoria, where it boasted 250 branches and some 12,000 members, where since 1955 it had increased its proportion of the total vote by 4 per cent to over 16 per cent, and where in 1963 it contested all thirty-three seats. Its strength in Victoria was due partly to vigorous support from most of the Roman Catholic bishops and from the archbishop of Melbourne, Daniel Mannix, who died in November 1963 at the age of ninety-nine. It had ecclesiastical support also in South Australia, Western Australia, Tasmania and Queensland, but in New South Wales it suffered from the hostility of Cardinal Gilroy, who used his influence to keep Roman Catholics within the Australian Labor Party. By 1963 the DLP in New South Wales was almost defunct, though it intervened effectively in some seats in the election of that year. It had scarcely 2,000 members; most of its branches were dead; it had little money; it had difficulty in persuading candidates to stand; and only the diligence of its general secretary kept it in existence. The DLP had one representative in the federal Parliament—a Senator from Tasmania—and it was doubtful whether its representation would increase in the future; but as long as it continued to draw even a small percentage of votes, the second preferences of its supporters would be an important, and sometimes decisive, factor in election results.

The formation of the DLP and the activities of the Catholic Social Movement in the Australian Labor Party in the 1950s led to a long and acrimonious debate about the role of Roman Catholics in politics. Irish Catholicism had always been influential in Australian radical politics, but its function was complicated in a period when radicalism might be associated more readily with the Soviet Union than with the Papacy or Ireland. The prevalence of Roman Catholics in both government and public service, not least in New South Wales, made plausible the fears of a section of the Australian population prone to believe in insidious Catholic conspiracies in high places. There was speculation on whether Santamaria's Catholic Social Movement, renamed the National Civic Council, had been intent not merely on replacing Communist officials in trade unions and denying Communists the benefit of Labour governments, but had also consciously planned the ultimate creation of a Roman Catholic Australia. It was argued that the beliefs of a good Catholic were incompatible with loyal citizenship of an essentially secular and democratic society, and non-Catholics found cause for concern in the ability of the Vatican to sway political controversy within an important segment of the Australian population.

Sectarianism was a huge and complex issue in Australian history and politics; it defied brief comment, and the unwary layman who touched on it was liable to be deluged with textual analysis, doctrinal dissertations, and quotations from papal encyclicals and centuries-old philosophical documents. Nevertheless, though Roman Catholics formed over 20 per cent of the Australian population, it was possible that their significance might gradually diminish. A church which used to be a social outlet for underprivileged working classes might lose its attraction in a more prosperous, welfare State, especially when it sullied its reputation by intervention in national politics. The Roman Catholic campaign in the states in 1962 to acquire aid for denominational schools was a failure, particularly in New South Wales. Neither the Labour government nor the Liberal and Country party opposition in the New South Wales Parliament was affected by the clamour of church leaders in 1963 against the legislation allowing poker machines and the proposed liberalisation of the drinking laws. It was clear, however, that the debate on the question of Roman Catholics and the free society would continue for a long time in the future and become, perhaps, more thoughtful and less impassioned than in the past.

The allegation that the federal Labour party was under Communist influence was less convincing by 1963. The Communist party was weaker than ever, barely 6,000 strong, and though the Petrov Commission and the struggle with Santamaria's National Civic Council had for a period kept the party united against its enemies and insulated from revelations among overseas Communists, many defections eventually took place, notably by intellectuals in Sydney and Melbourne. The Communist party continued to exert pressure through the trade unions and the Peace Movement, especially in Victoria, where the Labour party permitted its trade union members to join Communists in unity tickets for contesting ballots for union office. Labour's federal executive had laid a ban on unity tickets but it was not enforced, the Victorian executive insisting that unity tickets were essential in order to prevent certain unions from being dominated by Communists or Democratic Labour. It was a thorny problem for Labour's leadership, but until it was tackled ruthlessly and solved federal Labour would find it difficult to win office.

The Labour party was also reluctant to dilute its traditional deference to socialism, and in 1960 Calwell, the federal leader, rebuked those academics who advocated the abandonment of socialisation as the principal objective of the Labour movement. Nevertheless, modifications in Labour doctrine were taking place. In 1951 the Labour party had defined its objective as 'socialisation or social control of industry and the means of production, distribution, and exchange to the extent necessary to eliminate exploitation and other anti-social features of industry'. In 1957 it became the 'democratic socialisation of industry, production, distribution and exchange, to the extent necessary to eliminate exploitation and other anti-social features in these fields'. Whatever these phrases meant, it was questionable whether periodic refinement of terminology served any useful purpose, and it was at least arguable that it merely confused some supporters and estranged younger ones to whom such pious declarations were antiquated and unreal.

However much the political parties might cultivate the notion that they represented conflicting ideologies, it was difficult to discern much practical difference between their policies. Government regulation in economic and social affairs had been increasing from the middle of the nineteenth century onwards irrespective of the political grouping in power. Even the Liberal party, the avowed protector of private enterprise, had been obliged to accept the necessity for governmental supervision in certain utilities and had not hesitated to experiment in other forms of State action. The class basis of Australian politics had also become blurred, and although Labour still found the core of its support and its parliamentary representation among the working people and the trade unions, while the Liberal party looked to the business and wealthy sections for its votes and leaned heavily on the legal profession for its candidates, loyalties were becoming more fluid and there was greater flexibility in the selection of parliamentary candidates. Unlike the United Kingdom, Australia was not burdened with a highly educated and wealthy class which regarded itself as singularly fitted for the privilege of governing; but the corollary was less public respect in Australia for governments and the men who sat in Parliament.

It was commonly felt that Australian politicians were second-rate: an impression confirmed by the daily broadcast of federal debates and by the televised presentation of candidates at election times. The low esteem in which politicians were held found its fiercest expression in the denigration in press correspondence and editorial columns whenever Parliament lifted the salaries of its members, which it did periodically with cynical unanimity. Whether standards would improve was not yet a question that vexed many Australian electors, but it was probable that as the power of the central government grew in relation to that of the states, the federal Parliament would come closer to the national standards of other Anglo-Saxon countries. The integrity of federal ministers had risen since the second world war, and former ministerial laxity—as in the matter of holding directorships in firms carrying on business with the government—was being eliminated, or perhaps left to the peccadilloes of state administrations.

The elaboration of commonwealth authority in the federal system implied a relative decline in the status of the individual states. The premiers' conferences in March and June 1959, for example, agreed on a new formula for the commonwealth's annual financial grants which were to be linked with wage levels and population increases rather than to tax collections in the individual states. The grants were no longer considered as tax reimbursements or as compensation to the states for surrendering their taxation powers, but were now referred to as 'financial assistance grants'. The significance of the revised language lay in the inference that the states were subordinate units, at least so far as financial arrangements in the federal system were concerned, and although this did not necessarily mean political subordination it seemed that the state governments were becoming little more than the administrative agencies of the commonwealth. The states retained some freedom of action in deciding how their money was spent, but the commonwealth could impose conditions, and, after the election of December 1961, it distributed special non-repayable grants for particular projects without any regard to the normal formulas upon which finance for the states was decided. It was evident that soon the commonwealth Parliament might, in effect, have it within its power to destroy the political independence of the states. This was not an immediate danger, for the political repercussion of any such move precluded the attempt's being made, but as a contingency in the distant future it disturbed those dedicated to the idea of a truly federal organism.

The states themselves were still the main focus for popular loyalties, and their keen rivalry, particularly between the capital cities, remained undiminished. New South Wales, with over four million of Australia's eleven million people, was the wealthiest and most urbanised of any of the states, and the capital, Sydney (so the critics maintained), the most vulgarly materialist of any city in the commonwealth. Victoria was the main rival to New South Wales; its three million people included a high proportion of the European migrants who had come to Australia, and its capital, Melbourne, was perhaps the most sophisticated of Australian cities. In contrast, the island of Tasmania had a population of little more than 250,000 and despite remarkable hydro-electric development, was very much the vacation state for mainland Australians seeking the soft and varied beauties of the countryside denied them at home. Western Australia's population was double that of Tasmania but small for what was territorially the largest state, stretching across a third of the continent. South Australia was the most anglophile of Australian states, although there were large numbers of people of continental European origin among its one million people, and its capital, Adelaide, was the most consciously respectable of the nation's cities. Less exciting than New South Wales or Victoria, particularly in its politics, South Australia was engrossed in the slow industrialisation of its economy, while its deserts provided a rocket range and an atomic testing ground for western nuclear weapons research. Queensland, with one-and-a-half million people, was the most promising state, as it had been for half a century, its resources including wool, sugar, tobacco, fruit, bauxite, coal, metals and oil.* The Northern Territory, commonly regarded as a vast unprofitable desert, despite the importance of Darwin and Alice Springs, was the most intractable problem

---

* The first commercial production of crude oil in Australia began effectively on April 1, 1964, at the Moonie field in Southern Queensland. It was expected to supply two per cent of Australia's total annual oil requirements.

for Australian developmental programs. Politically, it lacked representation in the Australian Senate and possessed only non-voting representation in the House of Representatives, and its Territorial Legislative Council had little effective power independent of the responsible minister in Canberra. The Northern Territory called for imaginative action by a commonwealth government which had been inclined to recoil from the immense difficulties involved and to neglect both its responsibilities and its opportunities in an area recognised as being of possible future significance to national security.

Australians have a sensitive regard for their country that takes exception to patronising criticism. They have to suffer overseas visitors who, often on the evidence of a fleeting acquaintance with a few centres, readily disparage a society and way of life for which they have no sympathy. Most of this criticism comes from cultivated people who inevitably notice in Australia the astringency of intellectual life, the poor libraries, the struggling theatres, and the general absence of interest in cultural activities. Even among those to whom a community might legitimately look for an intellectual lead, there is a scarcity of independent thinking, and if the prevalence of mediocrity has been exaggerated by people who should know better, there is more parochialism, authoritarianism, and preoccupation with salary scales than is healthy. Paradoxically, the Australian patriotism which resents foreign criticism and solicits foreign compliments is accompanied by an extraordinary veneration for foreign scholarship, even though Australian contributions to the arts, science and technology are sometimes comparable with any in the world.

Those who deplore the absence from Australian life of anything more elevating than hedonistic materialism misunderstand the essence of Australian society. The cultural deity to which the critics pay homage is a European idol with a long western heritage, and it is a mistake to expect to find it resurrected on a similar pedestal in Australia. Australia does not pretend to be a land for aesthetes, but it has succeeded, where older nations have failed, in providing a full and self-respecting life for the working man in a society relatively untrammelled by rigid class barriers. Although its wholesome egalitarianism has its fallacies and disadvantages it is, nevertheless, a quality from which the so-called more cultured nations could profitably learn.

There are dangers, no doubt, in a society which gravitates around the beach and draws its inspiration from the sun and surf, as moralistic pessimists never tire of pointing out. Certainly, there is reason to wonder how long imports of foreign capital will continue to support such comfortable materialism, the forty-hour week and generous public holidays, and to wonder whether a people devoted to pleasure will in the long term preserve the moral fibre to withstand a real national emergency. Doubts and misgivings there must be, and with some cause, but Australians themselves are supremely confident that their country is a great nation of the future, and there is good reason to believe and hope they may be right.

FEDERAL MINISTRIES IN AUSTRALIA

Jan. 1901—Sept. 1903	Edmund Barton	Liberal (moderate protectionist)
Sept. 1903—April 1904	Alfred Deakin	Liberal (with Labour support)
April 1904—Aug. 1904	J. C. Watson	Labour
Aug. 1904—July 1905	George Reid	Free Trade—Liberal (anti-Labour) coalition
July 1905—Nov. 1908	Alfred Deakin	Liberal (protectionist with Labour support)
Nov. 1908—June 1909	Andrew Fisher	Labour
June 1909—April 1910	Alfred Deakin	Liberal (fusion of anti-Labour parties)
April 1910—June 1913	Andrew Fisher	Labour
June 1913—Sept. 1914	Joseph Cook	Liberal
Sept. 1914—Oct. 1915	Andrew Fisher	Labour
Oct. 1915—Nov. 1916	W. M. Hughes	Labour
Nov. 1916—Feb. 1917	W. M. Hughes	Conscriptionist Labour (with Liberal support)
Feb. 1917—Jan. 1918	W. M. Hughes	Nationalist (anti-Labour)
Jan. 1918—Feb. 1923	W. M. Hughes	Nationalist
Feb. 1923—Oct. 1929	S. M. Bruce (with Earle Page)	Nationalist and Country Party coalition
Oct. 1929—Jan. 1932	J. H. Scullin	Labour
Jan. 1932—Sept. 1934	J. A. Lyons	United Australia Party
Sept. 1934—Oct. 1937	J. A. Lyons	United Australia Party (coalition with Country Party in Nov. 1934)
Oct. 1937—April 1939 (Reconstructed, Nov. 1938)	J. A. Lyons	United Australia and Country Party coalition
April 1939—March 1940	R. G. Menzies	United Australia Party
March 1940—Oct. 1940	R. G. Menzies	United Australia and Country Party coalition
Oct. 1940—Aug. 1941	R. G. Menzies	United Australia and Country Party coalition
Aug. 1941—Oct. 1941	A. W. Fadden	United Australia and Country Party coalition
Oct. 1941—Sept. 1943	John Curtin	Labour
Sept. 1943—July 1945	John Curtin	Labour
6 July—13 July 1945	F. M. Forde	Labour
July 1945—Nov. 1946	J. B. Chifley	Labour
Nov. 1946—Dec. 1949	J. B. Chifley	Labour
Dec. 1949—May 1951	R. G. Menzies	Liberal and Country Party coalition

FEDERAL MINISTRIES IN AUSTRALIA

May 1951—May 1954	R. G. Menzies	Liberal and Country Party coalition
May 1954—Dec. 1955	R. G. Menzies	Liberal and Country Party coalition
Dec. 1955—Nov. 1958	R. G. Menzies	Liberal and Country Party coalition
Nov. 1958—Dec. 1961	R. G. Menzies	Liberal and Country Party coalition
Dec. 1961—Nov. 1963	R. G. Menzies (knighted March 1963)	Liberal and Country Party coalition
Nov. 1963—	Sir Robert Menzies	Liberal and Country Party coalition

READING LIST

JOURNALS

Royal Australian Historical Society Journal and Proceedings (1901–).
Australian Quarterly (Australian Institute of Political Science, 1910–).
Round Table (A quarterly review of British Commonwealth affairs, London, 1910–).
Economic Record (Journal of the Economic Society of Australia and New Zealand, 1925–).
Historical Studies: Australia and New Zealand (Melbourne University Press, 1940–).
Australian Outlook (Australian Institute of International Affairs, 1947–).
Australian Journal of Politics and History (University of Queensland, 1955–).

GENERAL WORKS

The Australian Encyclopaedia, ed. A. H. Chisholm (10 vols., 1958) and P. Serle, *Dictionary of Australian Biography* (2 vols., 1949) are good for reference purposes. W. K. Hancock, *Australia* (1930) and R. M. Crawford, *An Australian Perspective* (1960) are stimulating introductory essays. See also C. Hartley Grattan, *Introducing Australia* (2nd edn., 1949); Crawford, *Australia* (rev. edn., 1960); and Grattan (ed.), *Australia* (1947). *The Cambridge History of the British Empire*, Vol. VII, Part One (1933) is the major history of Australia, though a little dated. The following are the more recent histories, the best of which are those by Shaw, Greenwood (ed.), and Pike: Marjorie Barnard, *A History of Australia* (1962); F. K. Crowley, *Australia's Western Third: A History of Western Australia* (1960); B. Fitzpatrick, *The Australian Commonwealth* (1956); G. Greenwood (ed.), *Australia: A Social and Political History* (1955); D. Pike, *Australia: The Quiet Continent* (1962); and A. G. L. Shaw, *The Story of Australia* (2nd edn., 1961). A stimulating new interpretation is C. M. H. Clark, *Short History of Australia* (1963).

GENERAL WORKS (POLITICAL)

A. Brady, *Democracy in the Dominions* (1947); B. C. Fitzpatrick, *A Short History of the Australian Labour Movement* (1940); J. D. B. Miller, *Australian Government and Politics* (2nd edn., 1959); Louise Overacker, *The Australian Party System* (1952). S. Encel, *Cabinet Government in Australia* (1962) is the most important recent contribution to the study of political institutions.

GENERAL WORKS (CONSTITUTIONAL)

L. F. Crisp, *The Parliamentary Government of the Commonwealth of Australia* (3rd edn., 1961); G. Greenwood, *The Future of Australian Federalism* (1946); G. V. Portus (ed.), *Studies in the Australian Constitution* (1933); E. Sweetman, *Australian Constitutional Development* (1925); F. L. Wood, *The Constitutional Development of Australia* (1933).

P

READING LIST

GENERAL WORKS (SOCIAL)
The outstanding work is Russel Ward, *The Australian Legend* (1958). There is also some excellent material in two books by B. C. Fitzpatrick, *The Australian People* (1946) and *The Australian Commonwealth* (1956). A perceptive approach to one aspect is contained in R. Boyd, *Australia's Home* (1952); see also by the same author, *The Australian Ugliness* (1960). A general introduction can be obtained from G. Caiger (ed.), *The Australian Way of Life* (1953), but a more stimulating symposium is P. Coleman (ed.), *Australian Civilization* (1962). J. D. Pringle, *Australian Accent* (1958) is a brilliant, thought-provoking essay.

GENERAL WORKS (ECONOMIC)
Fitzpatrick and Shann are the leaders in this field, though writing from rather different points of view; Shaw adopts a moderate line between them: B. C. Fitzpatrick, *The British Empire in Australia: An Economic History, 1834–1939* (1941); E. Shann, *An Economic History of Australia* (1948); A. G. L. Shaw, *The Economic Development of Australia* (1955). Among books dealing with particular aspects are: E. Dunsdorfs, *The Australian Wheat Growing Industry, 1788–1948* (1956); F. E. Hitchins, *Tangled Skeins: A Historic Survey of Australian Wool Marketing* (1956); H. Munz, *The Australian Wool Industry* (1950); D. F. Nicholson, *Australia's Trade Relations: An Outline History of Australia's Overseas Trading Agreements* (1955); A. G. L. Shaw and G. B. Bruns, *The Australian Coal Industry* (1948).

GENERAL WORKS (CULTURAL)
H. M. Green, *A History of Australian Literature* (2 vols., 1961). See also the same author's *An Outline of Australian Literature* (1930) and *Australian Literature* (1959). E. M. Miller, *Australian Literature from its Beginning to 1935* (2 vols., 1940); W. Moore, *The Story of Australian Art* (2 vols., 1934); S. U. Smith (ed.), *Art of Australia* (1941); W. A. Orchard, *Music in Australia* (1952).

Amongst periodicals, two in particular merit attention: *Art in Australia* (fl. 1916–42), and *Art and Australia* (started in 1963).

HISTORICAL STUDIES ON AUSTRALIA BEFORE FEDERATION
On the English discovery of the continent: J. C. Beaglehole, *Exploration in the Pacific* (1934); E. Scott, *Australian Discovery* (2 vols., 1929); G. A. Wood, *Discovery of Australia* (1922); J. C. Beaglehole (ed.), *Journals of Captain James Cook on his Voyages of Discovery* (4 vols., 1955–   ), and *The Endeavour Journal of Joseph Banks* (2 vols., 1961).

On the foundation of New South Wales the best works are: E. O'Brien, *The Foundation of Australia, 1786–1800* (2nd edn., 1950); and C. M. H. Clark, *A History of Australia*, Vol. I, *From the Earliest Times to the Age of Macquarie* (1962); B. C. Fitzpatrick, *British Imperialism and Australia: An Economic History, 1783–1833* (1939). A worthwhile contemporary account is Watkin Tench, *Sydney's*

READING LIST

First Four Years, ed. L. F. Fitzhardinge (1961). Bill Beatty, *Early Australia with Shame Remembered* (1963) is a racy account of how the convicts fared. J. Cobley (ed.), *Sydney Cove, 1788* (1962) is an interesting collection of contemporary material.

On the early years of the nineteenth century see especially: M. H. Ellis, *Lachlan Macquarie: His Life, Adventures, and Times* (rev. edn., 1952), *Francis Greenway* (2nd edn., 1953), and *John Macarthur* (1955); and H. V. Evatt, *Rum Rebellion* (1939). Marjorie Barnard, *Macquarie's World* (1941) is a refreshing description. On Van Diemen's Land: R. W. Giblin, *The Early History of Tasmania, 1804-28* (1939); J. West, *History of Tasmania* (2 vols., 1852). R. M. Hartwell, *The Economic Development of Van Diemen's Land, 1820-50* (1954) is a particularly useful study. On the establishment of Western Australia: J. S. Battye, *History of Western Australia* (1924); Crowley, *Australia's Western Third*; M. J. L. Uren, *Land Looking West* (1948). On South Australia by far the best authority is D. Pike, *Paradise of Dissent: South Australia, 1829-57* (1957). On Victoria see F. P. Labillière, *Early History of Victoria* (2 vols., 1878-9); and H. G. Turner, *A History of the Colony of Victoria* (2 vols., 1904).

On the pastoral economies: S. H. Roberts, *History of Australian Land Settlement* (1924) and *The Squatting Age in Australia, 1835-47* (1935) are standard works. A. Barnard, *The Australian Wool Market, 1840-1900* (1958); R. V. Billis and A. S. Kenyon, *Pastures New* (1930); C. T. Burfitt, *The History of the Founding of the Wool Industry of Australia* (1913); J. Collier, *The Pastoral Age in Australia* (1911); Alexander Harris, *Settlers and Convicts, or, Recollections of Sixteen Years Labour in the Australian Backwoods* (1847; with a foreword by C. M. H. Clark, 1953).

On the acquisition of responsible government: the basic work is still A. C. V. Melbourne, *Early Constitutional Development in Australia, 1788-1856* (1934). A background to British policy is provided by K. N. Bell and W. P. Morrell (editors), *Select Documents on British Colonial Policy, 1830-60* (1928); and by W. P. Morrell, *The Colonial Policy of Peel and Russell* (1930). W. A. Townsley, *The Struggle for Self-Government in Tasmania, 1842-56* (1951); J. M. Ward, *Earl Grey and the Australian Colonies, 1846-57* (1958). Also of interest is G. Nadel, *Australia's Colonial Culture* (1957).

On the gold rushes there are several accounts of the Eureka episode and the circumstances surrounding it, notably by H. G. Turner (1913), J. Lynch (1949), R. Carboni (1953), C. Turnbull (1946) and C. H. Currey (1954), but of particular importance is the 'Eureka Centenary Supplement' in *Historical Studies* (Dec., 1954), and G. Serle, *The Golden Age: A History of the Colony of Victoria, 1851-61* (1963). Invaluable for the social history of the period are: Margaret Kiddle, *Men of Yesterday: A Social History of the Western District of Victoria, 1834-90* (1961); and G. F. James (ed.), *A Homestead History: Being the Reminiscences and Letters of Alfred Joyce of Plaistow and Norwood, Port Phillip, 1834-64* (1942).

RECOMMENDED READING FOR INDIVIDUAL CHAPTERS

CHAPTER ONE: A FEDERAL COMMONWEALTH (1901)

On the rise of the Labour Party: *The Australian Labour Movement, 1850–1907*, extracts from contemporary documents selected by R. N. Ebbels (1960); R. Gollan, *Radical and Working Class Politics* (1960); L. M. Ross, *William Lane and the Australian Labour Movement* (1938); E. W. Campbell, *History of the Australian Labour Movement* (1945).

On the coming of federation: Alfred Deakin, *The Federal Story*, ed. H. Brookes (1944); T. Bavin, *Sir Henry Parkes* (1941); V. Palmer, *The Legend of the Nineties* (1954); J. Reynolds, *Edmund Barton* (1948). The best account of the federation is J. Quick and R. R. Garran, *Annotated Constitution of the Australian Commonwealth* (1901). Other works on the constitution and federation include: B. R. Wise, *The Making of the Australian Commonwealth* (1913); and H. S. Nicholas, *The Australian Constitution* (1948).

CHAPTER TWO: THE ABORIGINES (1788–1940)

The most authoritative description is by A. P. Elkin, *The Australian Aborigines* (1938). Also illuminating are: H. Basedow, *The Australian Aboriginal* (1925); A. O. Neville, *Australia's Coloured Minority* (1948); and A. G. Price, *White Settlers and Native Peoples* (1949). Specific historical studies include: E. J. B. Foxcroft, *Australian Native Policy* (1941); P. Hasluck, *Black Australians: A Survey of Native Policy in Western Australia, 1829–97* (1942); C. Turnbull, *Black War: The Extermination of the Tasmanian Aborigines* (1948).

S. C. McCulloch, 'Sir George Gipps and Eastern Australia's Policy toward the Aborigines, 1838–46', *Journal of Modern History*, XXXIII (Sept., 1961), 261–9; and D. J. Mulvaney, 'The Australian Aborigines, 1606–1929', *Historical Studies*, VIII (May, 1958), 131–58 (Nov., 1958), 297–314.

CHAPTER THREE: THE FEDERATION AT WORK (1901–14)

H. G. Turner, *The First Decade of the Australian Commonwealth* (1911) is prejudiced but informative. Of the biographies the most useful are: H. V. Evatt, *Australian Labour Leader: The Story of W. A. Holman and The Labour Movement* (1940), a study of New South Wales politics; W. Murdoch, *Alfred Deakin* (1923); Nettie Palmer, *Henry Bournes Higgins* (1931); and Reynolds, *Edmund Barton* (1948). See also: J. A. La Nauze, *Alfred Deakin: Two Lectures* (1960); and A. N. Smith, *Thirty Years: The Commonwealth of Australia, 1901–31* (1933). Myra Willard, *History of the White Australia Policy* (1923) is a detailed account of one aspect of commonwealth policy.

C. Grimshaw, 'Australian Nationalism and the Imperial Connection, 1900–14', *Aust. Journal of Pol. and Hist.*, III (May, 1958), 161–82; A. T. Yarwood, 'The White Australia Policy: Some Administrative Problems, 1901–20', ibid., VII (Nov., 1961), 245–60, and 'The White Australia Policy; A Reinterpretation of its Development in the Late Colonial Period', *Historical Studies*, X Nov., 1962), 257–69.

CHAPTER FOUR: THE FIRST WORLD WAR (1914–19)

The standard authority is the *Official History of Australia in the War of 1914–18*, ed. C. E. W. Bean (12 vols., 1921–42). A valuable shorter narrative is C. E. W. Bean, *Anzac to Amiens* (1946). Of the memoirs the most important is by Sir John Monash, *The Australian Victories in France in 1918* (1920). An insight into the early years is provided by Bean, *Two Men I knew: William Bridges and Brudenell White* (1957). On the Navy: F. M. McGuire, *The Royal Australian Navy: Its Origin, Development, and Organisation* (1948). On the political side: Evatt, *Australian Labour Leader* (1940); L. C. Jauncey, *The Story of Conscription in Australia* (1935); and F. Murphy, *Daniel Mannix, Archbishop of Melbourne* (1948).

CHAPTER FIVE: A COLONIAL POWER (1888–1940)

The most responsible accounts are: J. D. Legge, *Australian Colonial Policy* (1956); Lucy P. Mair, *Australia in New Guinea* (1948); W. P. Morrell, *Britain in the Pacific Islands* (1960); S. W. Reed, *The Making of Modern New Guinea* (1943); and C. D. Rowley, *The Australians in German New Guinea, 1914–21* (1958). First-hand accounts include: J. H. P. Murray, *Papua or British New Guinea* (1912) and *Papua Today* (1925); J. Chalmers, *Pioneering Life and Work in New Guinea* (1895). L. Lett, *The Papuan Achievement* (1945) and *Sir Hubert Murray of Papua* (1949) are interesting but uncritical.

F. J. West, 'The Beginnings of Australian Rule in Papua', *Political Science*, IX (1957), 38–50, and 'Toward a Biography of Sir Hubert Murray', *Pacific Historical Review*, XXXI (May, 1962), 151–68. The same author makes a scholarly attempt to remove the tarnish from Murray's reputation in 'Sir Hubert Murray: The Australian Pro-Consul', *Journal of Commonwealth Political Studies*, I (May, 1963), 282–95.

CHAPTER SIX: INTER-WAR PROBLEMS (1919–32)

On the depression years: D. B. Copland, *Australia in the World Crisis 1929–33* (1934); W. R. McLaurin, *Economic Planning in Australia, 1929–36* (1937); E. R. Walker, *Australia in the World Depression* (1933); J. T. Lang, *The Great Bust* (1962). See also L. F. Giblin, *The Growth of a Central Bank: The Development of the Commonwealth Bank of Australia, 1924–45* (1951). For a discussion of Lang's dismissal see H. V. Evatt, *The King and his Dominion Governors* (1936). On the politics of the period: C. A. Bernays, *Queensland: Our Seventh Political Decade, 1920–30* (1931); D. Carboch, 'The Fall of the Bruce-Page Government', and A. Wildavsky, 'The 1926 Referendum', *Studies in Australian Politics* (1958); W. Denning, *Caucus Crisis: The Rise and Fall of the Scullin Government* (1937); U. R. Ellis, *The Country Party* (1958); L. L. Sharkey, *Outline History of the Australian Communist Party* (1944); and Sir Earle Page, *Truant Surgeon* (1963).

K. R. Cramp, 'The Story of Australia's Handling of the Financial Crisis in and after 1929', *Roy. Aust. Hist. Soc. Journal*, XXIII (1938), 81–121; L. F. Crisp, 'New Light on the Trials and Tribulations of W. M. Hughes, 1920–22', *Historical Studies*, X (Nov., 1961), 86–91; B. D. Graham, 'The Country Party and the Formation of the Bruce-Page Ministry', ibid., 71–85; C. Joyner, 'W. M. Hughes and the Powers Referendum of 1919', *Aust. Journal of Pol. and Hist.*, V (May, 1959), 15–23; and J. C. Vinson, 'The Problem of Australian Representation at the Washington Conference for the Limitation of Naval Armament', ibid., IV (Nov., 1958), 155–64.

CHAPTER SEVEN: THE BREAKDOWN OF INTERNATIONAL SECURITY (1932–9)

The best account of Australian foreign policy is contained in N. Mansergh, *Survey of British Commonwealth Affairs, Vol. III, Problems of External Policy, 1931–9* (1952), supplemented by *Documents and Speeches on British Commonwealth Affairs, 1931–52*, ed. Mansergh (2 vols., 1953). Of special value is P. Hasluck, *The Government and the People, 1939–41* (1952). Also helpful are: Gwendolen Carter, *The British Commonwealth and International Security: The Role of the Dominions, 1919–39* (1947); W. Levi, *American-Australian Relations* (1947); J. Shepherd, *Australia's Interests and Policies in the Far East* (1940); and Earle Page, *Truant Surgeon* (1963).

Sir Alan Watt, 'Australia and the Munich Agreement', *Australian Outlook*, XVII (April, 1963), 21–41.

CHAPTER EIGHT: THE SECOND WORLD WAR (1939–45)

The official history is *Australia in the War of 1939–45*, Series One (Army), Series Two (Navy), Series Three (Air), Series Four (Civil), Series Five (Medical). Particularly valuable on the political side of the early years is Hasluck, *The Government and the People* (1952). A broader picture is provided by N. Mansergh, *Survey of British Commonwealth Affairs: Problems of Wartime Co-operation and Post-war Change, 1939–52* (1958). Also useful are: H. V. Evatt, *Foreign Policy of Australia* (1945) and *Australia in World Affairs* (1946); J. Hetherington, *Blamey* (1954); W. Levi, *American-Australian Relations* (1947); and E. R. Walker, *The Australian Economy in War and Reconstruction* (1947).

CHAPTER NINE: SOCIALISM AT HOME AND NATIONALISM ABROAD (1945–9)

On politics: L. F. Crisp, *The Australian Federal Labour Party, 1901–51* (1955) and *Ben Chifley* (1961); A. W. Stargardt (ed.), *Things Worth Fighting For: Speeches by J. B. Chifley* (1952). See also W. D. Borrie, *Immigration* (1949). On external relations: W. M. Ball, *Nationalism and Communism in East Asia* (1952); F. W. Eggleston, *Reflections on Australian Foreign Policy* (1957); W. Levi, *Australia's Outlook on Asia* (1958); and Mansergh, *Survey of British Commonwealth Affairs: Problems of Wartime Co-operation and Postwar Change*. R. N. Rosecrance, *Australian Diplomacy and Japan, 1945–51* (1962) is a pedestrian but useful study.

G. Greenwood, 'Australia's Foreign Policy', *Australian Outlook*, I (March, 1947), 53–62; N. Harper, 'Australian Policy towards Japan', ibid. (Dec., 1947),

14–24; and D. W. Rawson, 'Labour, Socialism, and the Working Class', *Aust. Journal of Pol. and Hist.*, VII (May, 1961), 75–94.

CHAPTER TEN: THE COMMUNIST BOGY (1949–55)

S. R. Davis (ed.), *The Australian Political Party System* (1954); and L. Webb, *Communism and Democracy in Australia: A Survey of the 1951 Referendum* (1954). On the Roman Catholic factor: H. Mayer (ed.), *Catholics and the Free Society* (1961); J. G. Murtagh, *Catholics and the Commonwealth* (1951) and *Australia: The Catholic Chapter* (rev. edn., 1959); and T. Truman, *Catholic Action and Politics* (rev. edn., 1960). On external relations: G. Greenwood and N. Harper (editors), *Australia in World Affairs, 1950–55* (1957); W. Levi, *Australia's Outlook on Asia* (1958); and G. Modelski (ed.), *Seato: Six Studies* (1962).

H. W. Arndt and B. A. Santamaria, 'The Catholic Social Movement', *Aust. Journal of Pol. and Hist.*, II (May, 1957), 181–95; I. Campbell, 'A. L. P. Industrial Groups—A Reassessment', ibid., VIII (Nov., 1962), 182–99; W. M. Ball, 'The Peace Treaty with Japan', *Australian Outlook*, V (Sept., 1951), 129–139; J. Jupp, 'Socialist Re-thinking in Britain and Australia', *Aust. Journal of Pol. and Hist.*, IV (Nov., 1958), 193–207; M. Lindsay, 'Australia, the United States, and Asia', ibid., III (Nov., 1957), 33–45; J. A. Modelski, 'The South-East Asia Treaty Organisation', ibid., V (May, 1959), 24–40; D. W. Rawson, 'Politics and Responsibility in Australian Trade Unions', ibid., IV (Nov., 1958), 224–43; and *Current Notes on International Affairs* (Department of External Affairs monthly).

CHAPTER ELEVEN: PROBLEMS IN THE TERRITORIES (1940–62)

On policy towards the Aborigines see especially P. Hasluck, *Native Welfare in Australia: Speeches and Addresses* (1953); A. O. Neville, *Australia's Coloured Minority: Its Place in the Community* (1948); and C. Duguid, *No Dying Race* (1963). There are several good books on Papua and New Guinea: B. Essai, *Papua and New Guinea* (1961); I. Hogbin, *Transformation Scene: The Changing Culture of a New Guinea Village* (1951); J. D. Legge, *Australian Colonial Policy* (1956); Lucy P. Mair, *Australia in New Guinea* (1948); W. E. H. Stanner, *The South Seas in Transition* (1953); and J. Wilkes (ed.), *New Guinea and Australia* (1958).

A. P. Elkin, 'Australian Aboriginal and White Relations', *Roy. Aust. Hist. Soc. Journal*, XLVIII (July, 1962), 208–30; C. S. Belshaw, 'Native Administration in South-Eastern Papua', *Australian Outlook*, V (June, 1951), 106–15; see also ibid., VI (March, 1952), 50–9; C. J. Lynch, 'Constitutional Developments in Papua and New Guinea', ibid., XV (Aug., 1961), 117–40; J. P. Sinclair, 'Patrolling in the Restricted Areas of Papua and New Guinea', ibid., VII (Sept., 1954), 129–45; W. E. H. Stanner, 'New Guinea under War Conditions', *International Affairs*, XX (Oct., 1944), 481–94; C. D. Cowan, 'Indonesia and the Commonwealth in South-East Asia: Reappraisal', ibid., XXXIV (Oct., 1958), 454–68; N. Harper, 'West New Guinea: An Australian View', *International Studies*, III (New Delhi, Oct., 1961), 109–32; and J. A. C. Mackie,

'The West New Guinea Argument', *Australian Outlook*, XVI (April, 1962), 26–46.

CHAPTER TWELVE: THE MENZIES HEGEMONY (1955–62)

G. Greenwood and N. Harper (eds.), *Australia in World Affairs 1956–60* (1963); R. G. Casey, *Friends and Neighbours: Australia and the World* (1958); N. Harper and D. C. Sissons, *Australia and the United Nations* (1959); C. Clark, *Australian Hopes and Fears* (1958); and J. O. N. Perkins, *Britain and Australia: Economic Relationships in the Nineteen-Fifties* (1962). D. W. Rawson, *Australia Votes* (1962) is an examination of the 1958 federal election.

Current Notes on International Affairs; 'Australian Political Chronicle', *Aust. Journal of Pol. and Hist.*, series; 'Problems of Australian Foreign Policy', ibid., series; J. Mohan, 'Parliamentary Opinions on the Suez Crisis in Australia and New Zealand', *International Studies*, II (July, 1960), 60–79; R. S. Milne, 'The Australian 1958 General Election', *Parliamentary Affairs*, XII (1959), 230–9, 417–27; Joan Rydon, 'Some Aspects of Voting in the 1961 Elections', *Aust. Journal of Pol. and Hist.*, VIII (May, 1962), 98–101; F. Holmes, 'The Commonwealth and a Free Trade Area in Europe', *International Affairs*, XXXIV (Jan., 1958), 49–56; and J. G. Crawford, 'Britain, Australia, and the Common Market', *Australian Outlook*, XV (Dec., 1961), 221–39.

CHAPTER THIRTEEN: NEW HORIZONS

A. A. Calwell, *Labour's Role in Modern Society* (1963); Sir Garfield Barwick, *Australian Foreign Policy, 1962* (Thirteenth Roy Milne Memorial Lecture); Creighton Burns, *Parties and People: A Survey based on the La Trobe Electorate* (1961); A. F. Davies, *Private Politics: A Study of Five Political Outlooks* (1962); P. Coleman (ed.), *Australian Civilization* (1962); and A. L. McLeod (ed.), *The Pattern of Australian Culture* (1963).

Current Notes on International Affairs; 'Australian Political Chronicle' and 'Problems of Australian Foreign Policy', *Aust. Journal of Pol. and Hist.*, series; and A. F. Davies, 'Politics in the New Suburb', ibid., VIII (Nov., 1962), 214–23.

Index

ABORIGINES: description of, and policy towards, Chapter 3 *passim*; at federation, 23, 38; in recent times, 107, 166–7; progress of assimilation policy for, 179–80. *See also under names of states*

Adelaide, 219

Adelaide *News*, 182

Advisory War Council, 115, 116

Ainsworth, Colonel John: report on New Guinea, 73

Air Force, Australian, 100; in 1st world war, 63; in 2nd world war, 113

Air services, 106, 107

American bases, 199–201, 210–11

Anglo-Japanese alliance (1902), 41, 78

ANZAC Pact, 129–30

ANZUS Pact, 155, 161, 201, 203

Appeasement policy, 100–1, 103, 107–8

Arbitration Court, 139; established, 46–7; Bill for abolition of, 92. *See* Industrial arbitration

Army, Australian: organisation of in 1st world war, 50–1; at Gallipoli, 51–4; in Middle East, 54; in France, 54–5, 60–1, 62, 63–4; organisation of in 2nd world war, 113; in North Africa, 116; in Greece, 117; in Crete, 118; at Tobruk, 119; in Malaya and East Indies, 123; in New Guinea, 127–8

Arnhem Land, 34, 35

Art, 12, 88, 189

Austral, Florence, 88

Australia: geographical description of, 11; colonisation of, 11–12

Australian Academy of Science, 89

Australian Broadcasting Commission, 188–9

Australian Capital Territory. *See* Canberra

Australian Council of Trade Unions, 90–1

Australian Imperial Force. *See* Army

Australian Labor Party. *See* Labour party

Australian New Guinea Administrative Unit, 168

Australian School of Pacific Administration, 168

BALFOUR Report, 86

Banking: Commonwealth Bank established, 45; nationalisation controversy, 140–1, 145; legislative reform of, 151, 190

Barton, Sir Edmund: as prime minister, 22; and the tariff issue, 40; moves to High Court, 41; at Imperial Conference, 42

Barwick, Sir Garfield, 175, 212 and n.

Basic wage, 46

Beasley, J. A., 101

Bennett, Major-General H. Gordon, 123

Beynon, Richard, 189

Blackburn declaration, 133

Blamey, Lt-General Sir Thomas, 113, 117–8, 119, 127

Boldrewood, Rolf, 12–13

Brennan, Christopher, 88

Bridges, Major-General W. T., 51

British Commonwealth and Empire: naval defence before 1st world war, 41–4; at peace conference, 65; and the Turkish crisis, 79; co-operative migration policy, 84–5; relations defined, 86; trade relations in, 96; sanctions against Italy, 101; defence co-operation, 103–4; relations in

British Commonwealth—*Cont.*
2nd world war, 117–18, 123–5; India's republican status in, 143

British Commonwealth prime ministers' conferences; (1944), 130; (1961), 193–4. *See also* Imperial Conferences

Broken Hill Proprietary Company, 56, 114, 133, 163

Bruce, S. M. (Viscount): on Commonwealth consultation, 79–80; character of, 80–1; combats industrial discontent, 83, 90–2; immigration policy, 83–5; government of, 89, 90; defeated, 92; at Ottawa Conference, 96

Budgets, federal: (1928), 89, 107; (1933), 98; (1951), 155; (1955), 163; (1956), 181, 182; (1960), 192; (1962), 195

Bulletin, 13, 14, 58, 188

Burns, Philp and Company, 74

Bury, Leslie, 210

CALWELL, A. A.: as Immigration minister, 136–7; on importance of New Guinea, 173; as Labour leader, 191; on American bases, 200

Canada, 17, 18, 44, 57, 60, 63–4, 65, 78, 87n, 192

Canberra, 87–9, 114

Canberra Agreement, 129–30

Casey, R. G. (Baron); candidate for party leader, 109; minister to Washington, 114; minister for External Affairs, 154–5; on New Guinea trusteeship, 172; on Indonesian complaints, 175; and Suez crisis, 182, 184

Catholic Action, 161–2. *See also* Roman Catholic Church; Sectarianism

Chifley, J. B., 169; character of, 132; government of, 132–46 *passim*; on

Catholic influence in Labour party, 161; death, 152

China. *See* Communist China

Christian missions: among Aborigines, 32–3, 34; in New Guinea, 67–8

Churchill, Sir Winston: and Gallipoli, 51; on defence against Japan, 115–16; attitude to Dominions, 118–19; Australian disagreement with, 119, 124–5

Collier, Frederic, 88

Colombo Plan, 153–4

Commonwealth Grants Commission, 99

Commonwealth Scientific and Industrial Research Organisation, 88

Commonwealth Shipping Line, 90

Communist China, 143–4, 154, 162

Communist party: and Labour party, 129; and industrial discontent, 83, 133–4, 139; position of, 216

Communist Party Dissolution Bill, 150–2

Compulsory military training, 43, 113, 160

Conscription issue, 57–9, 61, 62, 113, 128

Constitution, commonwealth: drafted, 17; summarised, 17–20; amendment to, 20, 47–8, 86–7

Cook, Captain: on Aborigines, 28

Cook, Sir Joseph, 41; leader of Liberals, 48–9; at peace conference, 65

Country party, 80, 98; coalition with United Australia party, 80–1, 90, 92, 99; description of, 81–2; objects to Menzies, 109–10; in 2nd world war, 114; coalition with Liberals, 147; position of, 213

Cultural life, 88, 188–9

Currency, 26n, 93, 98n

Curtin, John: and peacetime defence, 103–4; leads Labour opposition,

Curtin, John—*Cont.*
108–9, 115, 120; character, 121–2; wartime government of, 122–31 *passim*; appeals to America, 122–3; argument with Churchill, 124–5; death, 132

DARWIN, 107, 219
Deakin, Alfred, 44, 47, 48; character, 40–1, 45; at Imperial Conference (1907), 41, 42; social reforms of, 45
Defence: naval, 41–4, 50, 59, 99–100, 101, 104; debate on in 1930s, 99–100, 103–4, 108, 110; against Japanese attack, 123; after 2nd world war, 155, 159–61, 202; reassessment of (1962–3), 202
Delhi Conference (1949), 142
Democratic Labor Party (DLP): origins of, 162; founded, 185; position of, 214–15
Development and Migration Commission, 84–5

ECONOMIC Depression, 92–3, 96; recovery from, 105–6
Education, 20–1, 106. *See also* Universities
Elections, federal, 18–19; (1901), 40; (1908), 41; (1909), 41; (1910), 41, 44; (1913), 44, 48; (1914), 44, 49; (1917), 60; (1919), 77; (1922), 80; (1925), 83; (1928), 90; (1929), 92; (1931), 94; (1934), 99; (1937), 103–4; (1940), 115; (1943), 128–9; (1946), 135–6; (1949), 142–6; (1951), 151; (1954), 157–8; (1955), 163–4; (1958), 189–90; (1961), 194–5; (1963), 210–11
European Common Market, 186, 196–8, 210
Evatt, Dr H. V., 169; as minister for External Affairs, 126, 130–1, 137–138, 143, 144; character, 152–3; as leader of Labour opposition, 152–164, 181–91 *passim*
External Affairs, department of, 68, 100

FADDEN, A. W., 121, 135, 158
Federation movement, 17
Financial Agreement (1927), 89–90
Fisher, Andrew: character, 44–5; seeks constitutional amendment, 47; wins 1914 election, 49; retires, 55
Free trade, 22
Free Trade party, 15, 16, 40

GALLIPOLI, 51–2, 59; significance of, 53–4, 64
General Agreement on Tariffs and Trade, 182
Gilmore, Mary, 88
Gipps, Governor: and Aborigines, 30, 31–2
Gold, 12, 21, 22, 74–5
Gordon, Adam Lindsay, 13
Grainger, Percy, 88
Griffin, Walter Burley, 87

HARPUR, Charles, 13
Harvester judgement, 46
Hasluck, P. M., 205; as minister for Territories, 171; and New Guinea, 176–7; comments on UN mission, 178; becomes minister for External Affairs, 212n.
Health services, 134, 156
Higgins, Henry Bournes, 46, 77
High Court, 126, 134; functions of, 19–20; and Arbitration Court, 46–7; and bank nationalisation, 141; and Communist party, 151
Hobart, Lord: on Aborigines, 26–7
Hodgson, Colonel, 142
Holt, H. E., 192, 212
Hunt, Arthur Attlee, 68

Hughes, W. M., 44, 47, 97; as attorney-general, 55; character, 56–57, 78; and conscription, 58–9, 62; leaves Labour party, 59–60; retains office, 60, 62–3; at peace conference, 65; post-war government of, 77–80; and Bruce-Page government, 90, 92

IMMIGRATION, 99; in colonial period, 12, 14, 16; after federation, 39–40; between the wars, 83–5, 89; after 2nd world war, 136–7, 163; changing character of, 207–8
Immigration restrictions: established, 38; justification of, 38–9; changes in, 165; assessment of, 206–7
Imperial Conferences, 79; (1902), 42; (1907), 41; (1909), 43; (1911), 43, 45; (1921), 78, 79; (1926), 86; (1930), 86, 94; (1932), 96; (1937), 96, 103
Imperial preference, 40. See also Ottawa trade agreement
India: in the Commonwealth, 143; relations with, 192–3, 203–4
Indonesia: independence movement of, 138, 142; territorial claims of, 154, 172, 174, 175; precautions against, 201–3. See also West New Guinea
Industrial arbitration, 45–7, 91–2, 139, 145
Irvine, Sir William, 48

JAPAN, 26, 34, 43, 44; in 1st world war, 50; attacks Manchuria, 97; policy towards in 1930s, 101–3, 110; Australian fears of, 115–16; brings war to Pacific, 122; peace treaty with, 138, 154–5; trade with, 186–209
Jones, Professor F. Wood: on aboriginal policy, 34–5
Joyce, Alfred, 14

KENDALL, Henry, 13

LABOUR party, 80, 83; founded, 14–15; organisation of, 15–16, 18; significance of, 16; and federation movement, 17; in first federal parliament, 22, 40, 41; and industrial arbitration, 45–6; split in (1916), 58–60; revival of, 82, 92–3; during Economic Depression, 94, 96; and appeasement policy, 101, 107; and defence in 1930s, 103–4; as wartime opposition, 115; and socialism, 132–3, 156–7, 216–17; and communism, 133–4, 145–6, 189–90; split in (1955), 161–2; and nuclear weapons, 199–200
Lambert, George, 88
Lang, J. T.: and Economic Depression, 93–4; downfall, 94–6; followers of, 94, 101, 104; government of in N.S.W., 133
Lawler, Ray, 189
Lawson, Henry, 13
League of Nations, 65, 97, 101, 103
Le Hunte, Sir George Ruthven, 68
Liberal party, 40; fusion of anti-Labour (1909), 48; joins National Labour, 60; gains office (1949), 146–7; organisation and character of, 147–8; position of, 213–4. See also United Australia party Nationalist party;
Literature, 12–14, 189
Loan Council, 89
Lyons, J. A.: in Scullin administration, 92; leaves Labour, 94; character, 97–8; government of, 98–109 passim; on appeasement, 101, 103, 108, 110

McCULLOCH, J. R.: on Aborigines, 29

INDEX

McEwen, John, 196-7, 212-13
MacGregor, Sir William, 66-7, 68, 70
McKay, H. V., 46
MacKellar, Dorothea, 88
Macquarie, Governor, 30
Mannix, Dr Daniel, 58, 62, 189-90
Melba, Nellie, 88
Melbourne, 21, 22, 105, 219
Melbourne *Age*, 22, 141
Meldrum, Max, 88
Menzies, R. G. (Sir Robert): and pre-war trade with Japan, 102-3; and appeasement policy, 107; resigns from Lyons ministry, 108-9; becomes prime minister (1939), 109-10; wartime government of, 111-119, 123; character, 114, 120, 121, 148-9; resignation, 120-1; organises Liberal party, 129; as wartime opposition leader, 135-46 *passim*; post-war government of, Chapters 10-12 *passim*; on colonial problems, 176-7; and Suez crisis, 182-5; and the Commonwealth, 184, 212; at United Nations, 192-193; on South Africa's leaving Commonwealth, 193-4; knighted, 210
Motor industry, 105
Murray, John Hubert Plunkett: character, 68-9; policy in Papua, 69-76 *passim*; influence of, 76
Murray, Sir Keith, 186
Music, 88, 188-9
Myall Creek massacre, 27

NATION, 188
Nationalism, Australian, 12-14, 85-86, 88
Nationalist party, 63, 83; formed, 60; in government, 77, 80; coalition with Country party, 80-1, 90, 92. *See also* United Australia party; Liberal party
Navy, Australian: origins of, 41-4; in

1st world war, 64; in 2nd world war, 113
Newcastle, 56, 105
Newcastle Morning Herald, 182-3
New Guinea. *See* Papua and New Guinea.
New South Wales, 11, 12, 15, 16, 21, 22, 85, 105, 115, 219; Aborigines in, 26-33 *passim*
New Zealand, 22, 42-4, 51, 87n, 117, 118, 129-30, 131, 155, 192
Niemeyer, Sir Otto, 93
Nolan, Sidney, 189
Northern Territory, 33, 34, 35, 107, 219-20

OBSERVER, 188 and n.
Oil production, 75, 209, 219n
Ottawa trade agreement, 96, 182

PACIFIC War Councils, 126-7
Page, Dr Earle, 89, 99, 109-10
Palmer, Vance and Nettie, 88
Papua and New Guinea, 142; seizure of German New Guinea, 50; mandate acquired over, 65, 69; Papua annexed, 66; administration of, Chapter 5 *passim*, 167-72, 176-17, 205-6; administrative union, 169-70; in Australian defence, 173; liaison with Dutch administration, 174-5
Parkhill, Archdale, 100
Paterson, A. B., 13
Peace Conference (1919), 65
Pearce, G. F., 100
Pearling industry, 26
Petrov case, 157-9, 163-4
Poetry, 13-14, 88, 189
Politics: state of, 217-18
Population: (1901), 21-2; (1914), 50; (1922), 83-4; (1938), 106; (1947), 137; (1955), 165; (1964), 219. *See also* Immigration
Port Kembla, 105

Port Phillip District, 11–12, 25–6; aboriginal protectorate in, 31–2
Premiers' Plan (1931), 93, 99
Protection, 22, 40
Protectionist party, 15, 16, 22, 40

QUEENSLAND, 11, 12, 21, 26n, 133, 219; Aborigines in, 32, 33

RAILWAYS, 21, 106
Referenda: (1911), 47–8; (1916), 58–9; (1917), 62; (1926), 83; (1946), 134–5; (1951), 151–2
Reid, G. H., 22
Roman Catholic Church: and education, 16, 20; and the Labour party, 16, 161–2, 189–90; and conscription, 58; in politics, 215–26. See also Sectarianism
Ryan, T. J., 82

SCULLIN, J. H.: character, 92; government of, 92, 97, 98; and Economic Depression, 92–3; defeated, 94; resignation, 122
Sectarianism, 162, 214–5. See also Roman Catholic Church
Snowy Mountains hydro-electric scheme, 144–5, 163
Social services, 45, 106, 109, 134, 156
Socialism: in colonial period, 14; and Labour party, 132–4
South Africa, 65, 78, 84, 192; Menzies on policies of, 193–4
South Australia, 12, 21, 219; Aborigines in, 33; industrialisation of, 105–6, 219
South East Asia Treaty Organisation, 160–1, 201
Spender, P. C. (Sir Percy): and Colombo Plan, 153–4; on West New Guinea, 154, 173; on New Guinea, 170–1
Stanley, Lord: on Aborigines, 31–2

States: at federation, 19, 20–1, 23; relations with commonwealth, 89–90, 91–2, 93, 95, 125–6, 218–19; during 1930s, 106–7
Statute of Westminster, 86–7
Stephens, James Brunton, 13
Street, Brigadier G. A., 108
Streeton, Arthur, 88
Strikes, 14, 62, 77, 83, 133–4, 145–6
Suez Canal crisis, 182–5
Sutherland, Joan, 189
Sydney, 11, 17, 21, 26, 105, 219; harbour bridge built, 95
Sydney Daily Telegraph, 183
Sydney Morning Herald, 31, 35, 39, 120, 141, 160, 195
Sydney Sun, 183
Syme, David, 22, 41

TASMANIA, 11, 22, 219; Aborigines in, 24–5, 27, 32
Taxation, 89, 107–8, 125–6, 192
Tench, Watkin: on Aborigines, 28–9
Theatre, 188–9
Theodore, E. G., 82–3, 92, 94
Townley, Athol, 202
Trade unions: in colonial period, 14; and Labour party, 14, 15; and conscription, 58, 61; in 1st world war, 61–2; federation of, 90–1; and industrial arbitration, 91; and communism, 145–6
Tudor, F. G., 59

UNITED Australia party: formed, 94, 98; coalition with Country party, 99; troubles within, 108–9; as wartime opposition, 114, 120, 121; replaced by Liberal party, 129. See also Nationalist party; Liberal party
United Nations: formation of, 130–131; and New Guinea, 169–70, 171–2, 178; Menzies at, 192–3

INDEX

United States of America, 44, 65, 78, 102; and commonwealth constitution, 17; isolationism of, 103; appointment of Australian minister to, 110; wartime relations with, 122–113, 126–7; and Japanese peace treaty, 138; and Suez crisis, 183, 184, 185; Australian dependence on, 198, 199, 201–3. *See also* American bases; ANZUS Pact

Universities, 20, 88, 106, 145, 179n; character and problems of, 186–8

VICTORIA, 11, 12, 16, 21, 22, 85, 98, 105, 219; Aborigines in, 31–2; Labour party split in, 162

WARD, E. J., 169

Wartime conditions and controls, 55–56, 77, 112–13, 129

Washington Conference, 78

Watson, J. C., 22, 38, 44

Watt, W. A., 80

West New Guinea, 172–8

Western Australia, 12, 21–2, 26, 85; Aborigines in, 26, 27, 30–4 *passim*

White, Major C. B. B., 51

White, Patrick, 189

White, T. W. (Sir Thomas), 108–9

White Australia policy: threats to, 42, 43, 83. *See* Immigration restrictions

Whitlam, E. G., 191

Wool, 12, 105, 135–6